HOW TO RESTORE YOUR
CHEVROLET
PICKUP

Tom Brownell

Motorbooks International
Publishers & Wholesalers ®

First published in 1991 by Motorbooks International Publishers & Wholesalers, P O Box 2, 729 Prospect Avenue, Osceola, WI 54020 USA

The information in this book is true and complete to the best of our knowledge. All recommendations are made without any guarantee on the part of the author or publisher, who also disclaim any liability incurred in connection with the use of this data or specific details

We recognize that some words, model names and designations, for example, mentioned herein are the property of the trademark holder. We use them for identification purposes only. This is not an official publication

Motorbooks International books are also available at discounts in bulk quantity for industrial or sales-promotional use. For details write to Special Sales Manager at the Publisher's address

Library of Congress Cataloging-in-Publication Data
Brownell, Tom.
    How to restore your Chevrolet pickup / Tom Brownell.
        p.   cm.
    Includes index.
    ISBN 0-87938-500-6
    1. Chevrolet trucks—Conservation and restoration.   I. Title.
TL230.5.C45B76 1991
629.28′73—dc20   90-24616

On the front cover: The Advance Design Chevrolet pickup from 1951 owned and restored by Mike Cavey of Kalamazoo, Michigan. Cavey invested 2,000 hours of work in restoring his truck. *Alan Delach*

Printed and bound in the United States of America

Contents

Acknowledgments

The following friends and Chevrolet truck authorities assisted in the writing of this book: David Bush, David Butler, Russell Emond, Ric Hall, Jim Hinckley, Bruce Horkey, Jessica Kibbey, Lawrence "Lars" Larson, Dick Matott, Ronald Olsen, Herb Parsons, Mark Sharp, Jon Bagley, Mike Cavey, Ralph Ricci, Alvin Shier, Karl Townsend and Bill Wales.

Introduction

Starting Out

So you've bought an old truck and are thinking of fixing it up, maybe even planning to restore it. If this is your first older vehicle, you're probably looking for tips and guidance. If you've restored other old cars or trucks before, you may be looking for advice or pitfalls when approaching a Chevrolet. Either way, this book is for you. It will show what needs to be done to bring the typical older Chevrolet truck back to first-class condition, and how to go about it.

As a Chevrolet light truck owner or admirer, you're probably not far from where Chevrolet truck collector Mike Cavey was when he bought a clean-looking pickup that had spent most of its life in Florida and had only recently been brought to Michigan. The truck had a fresh repaint and appeared to be a sound southern truck. It ran well and proved serviceable enough for Cavey to run for a couple of years in his business. Then he started to think about fixing it up. "I didn't plan a restoration, certainly not what I ended up doing," Cavey observes. But one thing led to another so that over a two-year period, with a time investment of 2,000 hours, Cavey turned his respectable 1951 pickup into the best restored truck in the world. That's a tall claim, but he's got the trophy hardware to back it up: Antique Automobile Club of America's (ACCA) Junior, Senior and Grand National awards, plus several Preservation recognitions.

You might not be aiming for Mike Cavey's level of perfection, but looking at what he did and how he did it will guide your fix-up or restoration to whatever stage you wish. Although Advance Design Chevrolet trucks like Cavey's 1951 are popular, your truck may be of the later 1955-1959 Task Force series, or a 1960s design, or an earlier 1941-1946 Art Deco model—the year doesn't make any difference. This book doesn't focus just on early 1950s Chevrolets. You will see models of various years in the restoration steps, but we'll let Mike Cavey's approach be our guide.

One might ask why Cavey chose a 1951 pickup to restore to the standards one would follow in building a show Corvette to compete for the Bloom-

ington Gold. The magic, to Cavey, was the fact that it was a pickup. What else represents a past era better than an old truck, and what truck is more universally recognizable than a Chevrolet? Look at the ads on TV that depict down-home scenes and you'll see what I mean. Invariably, the action centers around an old pickup that, almost always, is a Chevrolet—usually from the Advance Design series of the late 1940s to mid 1950s.

Through the years Chevrolet has consistently built memorable trucks. The styling treatment has been varied, but the Chevrolet parentage has always been there. In the early 1940s, a toothy chrome grille made a Chevrolet pickup instantly recognizable at any distance. In the later forties, the sedate styling of the Advance Design series made a conservative, value-first statement. By the mid-fifties Chevrolet trucks set out to promote a modern image with the stylish wraparound windshield, similarly contoured front and rear fenders and, of course, the showy Cameo.

Mike Cavey's 1951 Chevrolet pickup prior to restoration. This was a good, solid, original truck that Cavey had used for several years in his business. Plans didn't start out that way, but this truck ended up collecting enough trophy hardware to qualify for the title Best in the World.

The same 1951 Chevrolet Advance Design pickup after a 2,000 hour restoration. Without exaggeration, this truck is perfect in every respect. There isn't a single detail that has been overlooked.

An appealing feature of any older truck, but particularly a Chevrolet, is its simplicity. Fenders unbolt, the Stovebolt six-cylinder engines, used through 1962, are practically as easy to work on as a Briggs and Stratton lawnmower engine, and trucks continued the easy-to-rebuild straight-axle front end up to 1960. To a restorer, simplicity is always easier to deal with than complexity. Another strong plus for Chevrolet is the enormous parts availability. Just as parts vendors have made practically every part needed to build an entire vehicle available for Model A and T Fords, so too are nearly all needed parts being remanufactured for Chevrolet light trucks, particularly those in the Advance Design series.

Another bonus of owning a Chevrolet is the continued value associated with the name. Chevrolet trucks lead the pack in rising collector values. This means that if you buy and fix up or restore a Chevrolet truck, you are almost assured that you will recoup your investment. For any number of reasons, styling, design, availability of parts, nostalgia, collectors like Chevrolet trucks. Certain models, like the low-production and style-leading Cameo, are rising in value as quickly as the more popular Chevrolet cars.

If you have a hankering to add an older truck to your vehicle stable, you can't go wrong with a Chevrolet. If you own a vintage Chevrolet truck, then you've picked a winner. In either case, questions you're likely to be asking are where and how to begin the fixing-up process. First, though, some even more basic questions must be answered: What is your goal for your truck? What do you have available in the way of tools, equipment and shop space? What financial resources are you willing to invest in the project? And perhaps most important, what amount of time can you commit to restoring

Mike Cavey talks about his truck and its restoration. "This is something I enjoy," he says. Indeed, restoring a vintage Chevrolet truck can be a pleasurable and rewarding undertaking.

or rebuilding an old truck? We will take you through the process of answering these questions and get you started on your truck's restoration or rebuild—whichever approach you decide to take. A big part of a Chevrolet truck's appeal is that at one time or another, it's been in nearly every truck admirer's life. I first drove a Chevrolet truck while working at a dairy during summers while in college. The truck was a 1957 Chevrolet panel, painted white—the dairy's color—and I used it to haul ice from the ice plant, bottles from the warehouse and milk from our processing plant to stores. My memories of this truck have mostly to do with shifting without the clutch. Enough miles had tallied on the odometer that this truck was limber as a gymnast. Let off on the gas, plant both feet on the floor and the shift lever would go into most any gear you wanted. Obedient would be the best word to describe that truck. It didn't ooze hydraulic fluid out of its brakes, as did some of our other trucks. It started on the first twist of the switch, purred along the highway like a sewing machine and shifted like an automatic. What more could you want?

Chances are you've got memories of a vintage Chevy truck, too. This book's purpose is to help you turn those memories into a truck you can drive and enjoy.

1

History of Chevrolet Pickups

Chevrolet built its first trucks in 1918. Actually, to call this offering a truck stretches things a bit. More correctly, what Chevrolet sold as a truck consisted of a passenger-car chassis on which buyers could mount a variety of delivery or express bodies. For about a decade Chevrolet continued to offer car platforms for conversion to light trucks. The first pickup of sorts to wear the bow-tie emblem appeared in 1928. Actually, this "truck" was a roadster with a cargo box stuffed into the trunk. Chevrolet's first *real* roadster pickup, with a special open cab and standard pickup box, appeared in 1930, while the first closed-cab pickup debuted in 1931. These early Chevrolet light commercial models, like light trucks from most other manufacturers at the time, shared car body and mechanical parts extensively.

Early Chevrolet trucks are rare and present more than the usual challenges to those who find and decide to restore one. Replacement sheet metal for the early car-based commercials and first pickups is virtually nonexistent. When Winross Restorations, a specialty truck restoration shop in Palmyra, New York, restored a 1926 Series X one-ton, they had to fabricate the front fenders, hood sides, splash aprons, running boards and back fenders, and remake the entire wooden cab and express body. This extensive metal woodworking lies outside most hobbyists' skills and tool availability.

1935-1938: Car Styling

By the mid 1930s, Chevrolet pickups had established a reputation for dependability and were sold in larger numbers, but since the nation was now in economic depression, these trucks were far from plentiful. During this period Chevrolet trucks still shared car front-end sheet metal, but the trucks always wore the previous year's car styling and in some cases truck body metal was just different enough that similar-looking parts from a car won't fit. In 1936 Chevrolet sold two separate styles of trucks in the same year. Because of a change in cab design, the early 1936 models were

called high cab, and the later models were referred to as low cab. On the early models, carried over from 1935, the cab had a high crown—hence the high cab name. The new models, introduced mid-year, had a substantially lower cab roofline, which explains the low cab nickname. Chevrolet trucks continued to wear car grilles. The most substantial change during this period was the introduction, in 1937, of a completely reworked overhead valve (ohv) six-cylinder engine, now displacing 216.5 ci and fitted with four main bearings instead of three. This basic engine would remain the light truck powerplant until 1954.

1939-1940: Streamlined Design

A new tall, rugged-looking grille made the 1939 and 1940 light trucks look less like an extension of the car line. These trucks were also fitted with a

For 1937, Chevrolet trucks acquired a more streamlined-looking grille and a redesigned box. The six-cylinder engine also saw a major upgrade to four main bearings (from the former three) and a displacement boost to 216.5 ci. Mike Rand

7

In external appearance, Chevrolet's 1939 and 1940 light trucks are nearly the same except that the top grille bar is wider on the 1940 models. Inside the cab the differences are more noticeable. For 1940, a new dashboard featured the rectangular gauge cluster from the passenger car. Sealed-beam headlights were also used for the first time this year. The pickup pictured here is a 1940 model. Barry Weeks

Older pickups are the essence of simplicity. One appealing feature of Chevrolet pickups to collectors is the easy availability of parts. The Stovebolt six-cylinder engine, seen here, remained in production from 1929 to 1962. Parts for this engine can still be obtained through local auto parts stores.

new cab that now had a two-piece Veed windshield for improved visibility and a more streamlined look. Chevrolet trucks would use this cab with minor modifications until early 1947. At first glance, Chevrolet's 1939 and 1940 trucks appeared nearly identical, but there were a couple of ways to tell them apart. Assuming no modifications have been made, the easiest way was to look at the headlights. Headlights on the 1939 models used lenses and bulbs. In 1940, sealed beams became an industry lighting standard. The other tell-tale sign was the top grille bar. On a 1940 model, this bar was wider than on the 1939. On half-ton 1939 pickups, the bed was also slightly longer on 1940 models.

Although not available in as great a quantity as the 1941 and later models, Chevrolet's 1939 and 1940 pickups are popular with collectors. Attractions are the distinctive grille, more modern cab, hydraulic brakes and for 1940, the larger box and sealed-beam headlights. Parts availability is also an advantage. The basic mechanicals are the same as those on Chevrolet trucks through the next decade, and since the cab was also used on the next styling series, a wide assortment of patch and replacement sheet metal is available.

1941-1947: Juke Box Styling

The flashy, multi-toothed grille gives 1941-47 Chevrolet trucks a far less conservative look than the earlier models. On the 1941, 1946 and 1947 models, the grilles, bumpers, headlight rims and other decorative items were chrome plated. On trucks built during the short production run of 1942, a few assembled during wartime, and those built in 1945, the grille and other trim were painted. This so-called blackout look was unusual, and for that reason is now considered desirable.

Besides their styling appeal, these trucks also offer the benefit of a wide range of reproduction sheet metal as well as easily available mechanical parts. Owners of this model enjoyed the crank-out windshield (which provides refreshing ventilation for summer driving) as well as the truck's business-like, no-nonsense simplicity. These were the first Chevrolet light trucks not fitted with a car-style front bumper.

1947-1955: Advance Design Era

Chevrolet introduced its all new postwar Advance Design series trucks midway through the 1947 model year. In fact, both the earlier and newer style trucks were built simultaneously for a short two-month period as these trucks were being introduced. The overlapping production occurred because with the extreme demand for new trucks, General Motors didn't want any lag in production. The Advance Design series represented the first completely restyled postwar car or truck offering from any of the Big Three (GM, Ford and Chrysler). Also of significance, although Chevrolet's new trucks appeared nearly two years before GM's restyled postwar cars, the truck line clearly shows the major styling features of the corporation's coming car line.

To the public, Chevrolet's Advance Design models, particularly those built between 1947 and 1953, are coming to represent the classic old truck. Chevrolet's Advance Design series have become among the most sought after collector trucks. As witnessed with Model T and A Fords, a vehicle doesn't need to be rare to be desirable.

Several reasons account for the large and growing interest in the Advance Design series. The relatively plentiful supply plays a factor, as do the

GMC pickups shared sheet metal with Chevrolet, but used their own engines. This 1940 GMC is owned by Joe Persoon.

9

ease of repair and supply of parts. Nostalgia plays a big role as well; most of today's collectors grew up with these trucks—and to many, a 1947-1955 Chevrolet truck represents an instant flashback to the days of their youth.

Two significant mechanical changes occurred toward the end of this series. In 1954, Chevrolet installed its full-pressure lubrication, 235 ci six in its light-duty trucks. This year also saw a styling facelift that replaced the former split windshield with a single-piece curved glass and added a more massive grille. Trucks with this styling revision were sold in parts of two years, 1955 production being cut short by the introduction of a completely restyled Chevrolet truck line. The carryover models are referred to as First Series, while the restyled 1955 line is called the Second Series. Besides the fact that the short production run makes them rather rare and unusual, First Series 1955 models are also desirable because they used an open driveshaft in place of Chevrolet's familiar torque-tube driveshaft. The advantage of open drive is its compatibility with later, higher-geared (lower numerical ratio) rear axles.

The earlier years (1947-1953) in the Advance Design series were more difficult to distinguish from one another—though there were some tell-tale differences: 1947 and 1948 pickups had gas tanks under the front of the bed; in 1949 the tank was moved into the cab. The 1947-1950 light trucks were fitted with chromed front *and* rear bumpers, standard. Advance Design models from

Nicknamed the Art Deco series for the toothy chrome grille, Chevrolet's 1941–1946 trucks were far less conservative than previous models. Except for a limited production in early 1942 and the few civilian trucks built during the war years, this model used extensive chrome. This 1946 example is owned by Gerry Douglas.

Side-by-side examples of Chevrolet and GMC pickups of the 1941–1946 vintage. Note that the lower grille bars on the GMC, right, run horizontally.

Chevrolet called its highly popular 1947 to early 1955 trucks the Advance Design series. It takes a trained eye to recognize the telltale signs that indicate where a truck lies within this series. For example, ventipane windows appeared in 1951 so trucks without this feature were built prior to that date. This original 1953 Chevrolet pickup, owned by Sidney S. Cavitt, has only 33,000 miles on the odometer. Gary Henson

1947-1950 had left-hand cowl vents. Vent windows appeared in 1951. Most all chrome was discontinued in 1942, due to materials shortages caused by the Korean War. Push-button door handles also first appeared in 1952.

1955-1957 Task Force Era

Chevrolet's cars and light trucks received a total restyling and major chassis changes for 1955. The changes were so sweeping that even a corporation with GM's resources couldn't launch both Chevrolet's new car and truck lines simultaneously. Cars got the priority, delaying the new Task Force trucks until midyear. This new truck line represented the height of contemporary styling— complete with panoramic windshield, Frenched headlights, two-tone paint schemes, and prominent chrome on deluxe models. A new special pickup called the Cameo Carrier sported even more styling gimmicks, including a hidden spare tire, split rear bumper and a pacesetting flat-sided pickup bed. Actually, the Cameo camouflaged Chevrolet's narrow box to look like a wide, smooth-sided box by applying full-length fiberglass fenders that matched the contours of the cab.

Chevrolet broke tradition with its new Task Force trucks, just as it had done with its new 1955 cars, by introducing a totally new, 265 ci V-8 that had all kinds of hop-up potential. The early 265 had some design weaknesses; for example, it lacked an oil filter and had oil passage limitations, although both problems were corrected by the 1956 production year. In 1957, Chevrolet boosted the V-8 displacement to 283 ci. As many owners and past owners of Chevrolet trucks or cars with this engine know, the 283 ci V-8 was one of the toughest engines of all time.

There was almost no visible difference between the 1955 and 1956 light trucks. Both had 12 volt electrical systems, the egg-crate grille, and shared the same styling and mechanical options. The trained eye noticed a slightly different hood emblem on the 1956, and the side emblem was moved up above the fender crease. The 1957 models were easy to recognize by the trapezoid-shaped outline in the center of the grille.

Chevrolet's 1955-1957 trucks are favorites among collectors, with the Cameo being one of the most sought after models. Restorers of standard trucks benefit from easy availability of mechanical, interior and body parts. Cameo pickups can present some real parts hunting nightmares, however, since many of the trim parts are unique to this model.

1958-1959: Fleetsides

During 1958, an all-steel, wide-box pickup called the Fleetside replaced the Cameo. In keeping with the styling trends, Chevrolet trucks now carried quad headlights. A new grille extended across the front of the truck. Changes in the standard 1959 pickup models were most easily seen in a redesigned hood emblem and model designation spears moved forward on the front fenders.

Besides pickups, Advance Design light truck models also included the Carryall Suburban and Panel Delivery. Chevrolet also built a third variant of the panel body called the Canopy Express. This truck featured a full canopy top with open sides from which street vendors could display and sell their wares.

As an option, the Chevrolet Advance Design pickup could be ordered with rear quarter windows. This so-called five-window cab is popular among collectors. The technique for converting a standard three-window cab to a deluxe five-window is described in a later chapter. As in previous models, there is a close similarity between GMC and Chevrolet pickups of the Advance Design series. The major distinguishing difference of GMC trucks is the simpler grille design.

This extremely rare and unusual Chevrolet "pickup" is an Australian Ute, built on a 1950 passenger-car body and chassis. This car-pickup may have been the idea platform for the later El Camino. In this vintage it is, however, a uniquely Australian vehicle.

Chevrolet introduced a completely redesigned truck line midyear 1955. The new trucks featured panoramic windshields, taller cabs and more integrated hood and fender lines. Among the most handsome of this series is the Cameo with its wide-side pickup box. A 1957 model is pictured here.

Chevrolet's pickups from the late 1950s don't seem to overly excite collectors, but the 1959 El Camino with its gull-wing fins and star-ship front-end styling can easily draw a crowd and has attracted collector interest for two reasons. Cars, including this car-truck, representing the pinnacle of 1950s styling excesses are much in vogue today. The other reason for the first series El Camino's popularity is the availability of hot engines. Although Chevrolet installed its dependable six as the base engine, the range of optional V-8s listed for the El Camino included everything in the Chevrolet catalog. Chevrolet even shipped a few 1959 El Caminos with the high-performance fuel-injected 283 ci V-8. Transmission offerings also ran the gamut from standard three-speed, to Powerglide, to Turboglide, to the close-ratio four-speed of Corvette fame. Collectors interested in a hot truck shouldn't overlook an early El Camino. *Hot Rod* magazine ran a new 1959 El Camino with a tri-carburetor 348 up to 90 mph in a standing-start quarter mile and turned a respectable 0–60 mph time of 8.7 seconds. Early El Caminos are still fairly plentiful and the muscle engine examples are desirable. As with most Chevrolet models, mechanical parts for late 1950s Chevy trucks are plentiful. Body parts are also plentiful in that the cab is shared with the 1955–1957 models.

1960–1966: Modern Trucks

The 1960–1966 model run represented the first truly modern light trucks. Although Chevrolet trucks of these years consistently broke sales record, their styling—which mixed aircraft-appearing pods and intakes with a basically boxy and conservative design—has yet to excite collectors. However, the use of modern engines, comfortable suspension and plentiful supply is bringing these trucks into the collector limelight.

Three facelifts occurred during this series' six-year styling run, the most popular of which seemed to be the slant windshield cab of 1964 and later. Some collectors have been puzzled by later-style hoods on earlier 1960 and 1961 trucks. There's an easy explanation for this: Chevrolet listed only the 1962 and later hoods as replacement parts.

From 1961 to 1963 the El Camino disappeared from production. The official reason was lack of a suitable two-door station wagon as the body platform. Actual reasons included sluggish sales of the 1960 El Camino, and Ford's downsizing its Ranchero to the Falcon platform. A second El Camino series, based on the mid-sized Chevelle, began in 1964. These trucks are popular among collectors, due in part to the variety of engine offerings, but also to the increasingly deluxe trim and interiors.

Not to be overlooked among Chevrolet's early 1960s pickups are the novel Corvair trucks. Two models, called Loadside and Rampside, were offered. Of the pair, the Rampside with its swing-

Chevrolet gave its trucks a mild facelift for 1958 that included quad headlights and a redesigned grille. Also in this year, a wide Fleetside box replaced the Cameo. Although the fiberglass rear fenders on the Cameo pickup gave the appearance of a wide box, in reality these dressy pickups still used the old narrow pickup box. Sales of the Cameo had never been brisk, but the Fleetside quickly became Chevrolet's most popular pickup model.

Among the more exciting features of the 1955 and later Chevrolet trucks is the availability of the optional V–8. The 1955 and 1956 models featured a Ferrari-inspired egg-crate grille. This example is a 1955 model. GMC trucks in this Task Force series are marked by a mammoth, two-bar grille design. Through the 1950s and into the 1960s, GMC continued to use engines from GM divisions other than Chevrolet.

In 1959 Chevrolet introduced the El Camino to compete with Ford's Ranchero. Riding on a car chassis and using car sheet metal, one of the El Camino's main attractions was the wide range of engine choices, which included Chevrolet's hot fuel-injected V–8. Among the transmission options were a close-ratio four-speed. So although the El Camino could be fitted out as a working truck, it could also be optioned as a blistering hot sports hauler.

down side-loading ramp is the more desirable. Both have a stepped box floor (necessitated by the rear engine) that proved awkward for carrying long, flat loads. Today Corvair pickups are quite rare, yet they sell at reasonable prices. Besides their unusual engineering and design, benefits of these trucks include good riding qualities and excellent maneuverability.

1967-1972: Custom Sport Trucks

Probably the second most popular Chevrolet trucks, after the Advance Design series of 1947-

In 1960 Chevrolet unveiled a completely restyled truck line that picked up the futuristic look of GM's car lines. Undoubtedly the most notable feature of these trucks is the jet-intake pods in the hood. More significant than the styling, these trucks rode on independent front suspension which, for the first time, gave truck owners and operators the comfort of a car-like ride.

Among the most popular collector trucks are those from Chevrolet's 1967-1972 series. Shown here is a 1969 Camper Special with the extended 8½ ft. box. Known as the Longhorn, this model is a rare and desirable truck. Through the 1967-1972 series, the GMC line continued to be distinguished by a simpler grille than its Chevrolet counterparts. Aside from the grille and emblems, GMC and Chevrolet trucks were now nearly identical.

1955, are the 1967-1972 models. The styling of these trucks, with its blending of angular lines and rounded contours, seems to have a timeless look. To many collectors, this design series represents Chevrolet's first success in bringing the front-end styling, the cab and the lines of the Fleetside box into an integrated whole. Earlier Chevrolet trucks, including the snazzy Cameo Carrier, still belonged to the two-box school of pickup truck styling.

Although the eight-cylinder models are a bit heavy on fuel consumption, there are plenty of reasons to recommend Chevrolet light trucks in this styling series to would-be collectors. Well-preserved examples are still available, and reproduction, good used and factory original parts are quite plentiful. Comfortable touring and travel vehicles, these trucks are ruggedly built and are rapidly appreciating in value—particularly the deluxe Cheyenne models.

If you enjoy the go-anywhere ability of four-wheel-drive, a Blazer from this series warrants consideration, though easily restorable examples are becoming few and far between.

1973-1989: Working Trucks

Chevrolet trucks in the more recent styling period of 1973-1989 are still too new to be looked at seriously by collectors. But if you own one of these trucks and would like to keep it for many years to come, then you'll find plenty of tips and techniques in the pages that follow that will help you preserve, recondition and possibly even restore your vehicle.

1990-On: Super Sports

The 454 SS and its successors promise to be instant collector trucks. While most of these special trucks may never see hard work, they will need the storage, care and other preservation tips described in this book.

Chevrolet's limited production 454 SS has become an instant classic. Distinctive in its color scheme (black exterior, red interior), markings and potent big-block V-8 engine, the 454 SS is the first of a new breed of muscle trucks.

2

Rebuilding Versus Restoring

There are two ways to approach the repairs and cosmetic upgrading needed by most older trucks. One is to leave the truck as intact as possible while making whatever repairs are needed to various mechanical components (the engine, brakes, front end, steering and so on), then doing bodywork and refinishing, replacing the flooring in the bed and redoing the interior. We'll call this approach *rebuilding*. The other approach is to disassemble the vehicle to the last nut or bolt and then overhaul all mechanical assemblies, strip off all paint, root out all traces of rust and, in effect, reduce the vehicle to a collection of parts that can then be reworked to better than factory condition. This approach we will call *restoration*. The goal of restoration is to bring your truck as close as possible to what it was like when it rolled off the assembly line, but with the quality finish and workmanship that could be expected on a Rolls-Royce or other craftsman-built vehicle.

The decision whether to rebuild or restore should be based on thoughtful consideration of the pluses and minuses to each approach. To help you make that decision, the merits of both approaches will be examined in five categories: your goal for the vehicle; its intended use; the amount of money you are able (and willing) to put into the vehicle; the amount of time you have to spend on the rebuilding

With rebuilding, the truck is kept basically intact and worked on one assembly at a time. The rebuilding approach is being taken here with an Advance Design Chevrolet pickup. The owner has removed the bed in order to prime and paint the cab. The paint has been removed from the door by sanding, rather than sandblasting which would require that the door be removed from the truck. Steve Weisgerber

15

or restoration process; and your patience or endurance. Weighing both approaches by these criteria should help you decide which direction to take.

Rebuilding Approach

Although your truck will be inoperable for short periods during the rebuilding process (while the engine is being overhauled, for example), this piecemeal approach allows you to drive the truck during most of the upgrade. Another benefit of rebuilding is being able to spread the cost of most upgrades over as long a period as necessary, while still using the truck. Rebuilding also takes less shop space than restoration because the truck is never completely apart. If this is your first experience reworking a vintage vehicle, you're not as likely to lose interest in the project if you take it one component at a time rather than scattering the parts all over your garage and then having to muster the

Those taking the rebuilding approach generally start with a sound, original truck. The floors on this Texas truck are not rusted through. Since this truck has not been exposed to a high-moisture climate or road salt, the only rust on the chassis and body is on the metal's surface. Although it could be a candidate for a frame-up restoration, the truck can be brought to very presentable condition by the rebuilding approach. Steve Weisgerber

endurance to stick with the project for two or three years while every part is cleaned, rebuilt, painted and reassembled into the finished truck.

If you're fortunate enough to find (or own) a vehicle that has escaped the ravages of time and hard use, you'll impress far more people by doing just those necessary cosmetic and mechanical repairs than if you take it all apart and strip and paint every inch of metal so that it shines like a newborn. Any truck can be restored, but only an exceptionally well cared for truck can be preserved in its original condition.

A goal of rebuilding, especially if you are starting with a truck that's in fairly good condition, is to bring your truck back to what it looked like when it was two or three years old. It won't be so perfectly manicured that you'll have to shoo the neighbor kids away, and you won't be afraid to leave it in a parking lot. However, people will still stop and tell you how good your truck looks, and many will probably tell you that it reminds them of one they owned. That's what rebuilding accomplishes. It doesn't build a monument; it rekindles the past. For many collectors, that's the kind of old truck they want.

The steps to rebuilding a typical older truck include removing the fenders and pounding out the dents, repairing rust (typically found in the cab cowl and rear corners), most likely overhauling the engine, definitely reworking the brakes, replacing the wiring, upgrading the interior and repainting the exterior. Of course, numerous other jobs may also be called for—from replanking the box to replacing the window glass.

The one major drawback to the rebuilding approach is the likelihood that there will always be something you wish you had done more thoroughly. For example, you're likely to repair only visible body damage and overlook deteriorated cab supports and rusted inner body panels. Repairing hidden damage is just as important in rebuilding as it is with restoration, but since the truck isn't taken apart, not all problems are likely to get noticed during the appropriate phase of work. Later, when you're hooking up an exhaust system, you may glance at the cab supports and suddenly realize that the body is supported by Swiss cheese. Welding new metal into the support brackets at that stage can be a lot harder, especially if the nearby exterior surfaces have just been freshly painted.

Restoration Approach

Unless you ship your truck off to a professional restorer, you can plan on a ground-up restoration taking from one to three years—maybe considerably longer. Mike Cavey logged more than 2,000 hours restoring what had been a quite well-preserved, original 1951 Chevrolet pickup. A few basic calculations tell you that 2,000 hours is fifty forty-hour weeks—or the equivalent of a full-time job for a year. Cavey managed to complete his truck in just about two years, doing all work in his spare time. To make this goal possible, a friend helped out on a regular basis, his son reworked the engine and he has a very understanding wife.

During restoration, the truck will be spread all over your shop or garage. Some parts may even sneak their way into your living area. I have a speedometer for my truck sleeping in a desk drawer. A friend of mine went so far as to store the headlights from his 1930s vintage truck behind the living room sofa (he was afraid they'd get banged up in the garage). In these circumstances, there's always the danger that you'll misplace some of the parts (you'll need to develop a workable inventory system). I couldn't find the throttle linkage to my truck until after I brought home a replacement from a scrap yard. Of course, there's always the risk of getting discouraged by all those piles of parts.

The benefit of restoring is that every part of the vehicle needing attention gets it. When the restoration is finished, the truck should be better than new. At that point you will face the restorer's dilemma. Can you drive and enjoy your truck, and endure the inevitable scratches, chipped paint and oil film on the formerly immaculate engine compartment, and grime on the undercarriage? Or must the truck now be an object to be looked at and not touched or driven?

Determining Standards

If your plans are to restore your truck so that it can compete in the show circuit, you will do everything possible to make sure every detail, up to and including the placement of the seam on the door weatherstripping, matches exactly with original standards. If, however, you are restoring or rebuilding your truck so that it can be driven and enjoyed on the highway, you will be more inclined to consider modifications that will increase your driving comfort and bring the truck up to modern highway standards. A complaint of most older-truck owners is the low-speed rear axles installed in the days when a pickup may have seen the open highway only once or twice a week taking its owner to town. A pickup of 1930s or 1940s vintage is likely to feel uncomfortable at speeds much over 50 mph. During this same period, the buyer didn't have the pick of several rear-axle ratios, so finding a higher geared (lower numerical ratio) rear end for your truck may not be possible.

What's the alternative? The simplest, and in many ways most desirable, solution is to install an overdrive transmission. But Chevrolet didn't offer overdrive as an accessory until the mid 1950s. True, the torque-tube driveline Chevrolet used in its half-ton trucks through 1954 prohibited overdrive as fitted by other manufacturers—notably Studebaker and Willys. But today, installing overdrive in torque-tube Chevrolet trucks is a regular occurrence at OverDrive Inc., a business specializing in retrofitting overdrive transmission to any vehicle, including light trucks.

Converting the electrical system to 12 volts is another popular upgrade among collectors who plan to drive their trucks. If you change to a 12 volt electrical system, you'll have plenty of capacity for power-hungry accessories such as air conditioning and a modern radio and sound system. The higher voltage will also spin the starter faster, making the engine start more easily. You can modernize in these ways and still have a truck that looks stock.

Restoring an older truck to original standards requires extensive research. If your truck has been repainted, and chances are it has, you'll want to determine its original color. If there's another color you prefer, you'll need to find out whether it was offered for your year and model truck, and if not, what were the other color options. You will also need to research original engine-color schemes as

Rebuilding Versus Restoring

	Rebuilding	**Restoring**
Goal	To make a reliable-running truck that looks as it might have when originally in use.	To bring the truck to showroom or better-than-new condition.
Approach Advantages/ disadvantages	Start with a well-preserved truck. Spread costs over as long a period as necessary. Truck will be driveable through most of rebuild period. Takes less shop space than total disassembly. Less likely to lose interest.	Start with any-condition truck. Lack of funds at any critical stage will delay completion of the project. Truck will be inoperative through most of restoration period. Requires space equivalent to two-car garage. For average hobbyist, a frame-up restoration will take one to three years.
Results	It's likely there will be some things you overlooked and wish you had done more thoroughly.	Every part needing attention will get it. When finished, the truck will be better than new.

well as whether the engine that's in your truck now is the one installed at the factory. If pinstripes were used on the wheels and cab, you'll need to find out the location, size and color options for the stripes. Sometimes pinstripes will show up during the paint-removing process. If not, you will need to determine the stripe's location from a truck with its original finish or a correctly striped show truck. When restoring a truck for show competition there'll be myriad details, including the proper-style cap on the tire air valves, the correct spark plugs with painted or plated bases, original-style markings on the door and windshield glass, the right coating for the bed wood and all sorts of similar facts that will require research to establish authenticity.

It's misleading to think that entering the show circuit is the only reason for restoring a truck as close to original condition as possible. Maintaining originality can also be personally satisfying by giving you the sense that you've preserved a reminder of a bygone era, and is the best assurance for maximizing your truck's value. Anyone can rework an older truck with new parts and coat it with any color their heart desires; it takes stamina to track down original parts and to stick to the original colors and overall appearance.

Gathering Information

Before you scatter your truck all over the garage, you should acquire a set of shop manuals; a Chevrolet parts manual for your year and model truck is also highly desirable. These manuals are available from the literature dealers listed in the appendices, and also can often be found at swap meets. While you're at it, order catalogs from several parts suppliers specializing in vintage Chevrolet trucks. A supplier listing, with addresses, can also be found in the appendices. You will use the shop manual to take the truck apart, as well as put it together. By following the disassembly steps in the manual, you'll find that things come apart easier—and you're less likely to break hard-to-replace items. Besides the Chevrolet service manual, it's also advisable to have a copy of the *Motor's* or *Chilton's* manual covering your year and model truck. To gain full understanding of how a component operates, and to learn the assembly or disassembly sequence, it is often helpful to be able to read the instruction from more than one vantage

As parts are reworked, they will be installed back on the truck. Here the rear fenders have been repositioned, waiting for the box. Steve Weisgerber

point. The parts manual and parts supplier catalogs will help you identify parts needing replacement and will suggest sources and prices for these parts.

To get a sense of what your truck looked like when new, you should scout out and purchase sales literature for your year truck. These brochures will show original engineering and styling features, upholstery style, engines and interior and exterior colors. The sales brochures will help you spot changes that have been made to your truck over the years, and will guide you toward its authentic preservation. Sales literature for Advance Design and later Chevrolet trucks is quite widely available and reasonably priced. Earlier literature is harder to find and correspondingly more expensive. In addition to the sales literature, you should also purchase one or more of the Chevrolet light truck reference books listed in the appendices.

For Advance Design and Task Force series trucks of 1947–1959, reprints of the original factory assembly manuals are also available. These books, which consist largely of illustrations showing detailed views of chassis and body assemblies, are invaluable guides to restorers who want to make sure that their trucks are as close to original as possible.

Estimating Costs: Parts

Whether you decide to restore or rebuild your truck you should prepare an estimate of expenses you expect to incur. Included in this estimate will be costs for parts, labor, transportation and supplies. You can estimate parts costs by going through a catalog from a major Chevrolet parts supplier like Jim Carter's Vintage Chevrolet Parts, based in Independence, Missouri (see appendices for address). List all the items you think may be needed and the price of each item. Then add up the total amount. In actuality, you will probably shop around for parts, finding some at swap meets, others at auto supply stores and some at salvage yards, rather than place a shopping order from a single vendor's catalog. It's unlikely, however, that your parts bill is likely to be less than the estimate because unanticipated replacement or repairs are inevitable. In fact, it will almost certainly exceed your estimate—the question is by how much. I suggest a twenty percent fudge factor.

Labor charges you will pay others to do your truck's body, mechanical or trim work can grow very large, very fast. For this reason, most collectors try to do as much work on their trucks as they can. The problem many first-time rebuilders and restorers encounter in trying to redo their trucks themselves is the lack of proper tools and the skills to use them. Bodywork is an example. You can't do much in the way of metal repair without a welder and even if you invest a few hundred dollars in a

suitable capacity welder, the tool isn't much use until you know how to use it.

Labor Costs

In estimating labor costs, make a list of the jobs you want to do yourself, then indicate whether your current tool assortment will be adequate for each job, or if additional tools and skills are needed. For example, most of the mechanical repair on a vintage Chevrolet truck can be done with a ½ in. drive socket set, assorted wrenches, pliers, screwdrivers, a file, hammer, chisel, hacksaw, hydraulic jack, jack stands and a few specialty tools like a gear puller. But for an engine overhaul and bodywork you will need a larger stock of specialized tools and equipment.

Steps in Restoring a 1946 Chevrolet

by Ralph Ricci

The following is a quick run-through of the steps I've taken to restore my 1946 Chevy pickup.

First, I removed the cab, box, front fenders, running boards, engine and drivetrain and had the frame sandblasted and painted. This I hired done by a local man with a portable unit. His charge was $125, which I think was quite reasonable.

Next, I replaced all brake lines. For this truck, replacements are available from any auto parts store.

After removing all metal from the inside of the cab, I used a household-type drill and a 5 in. sanding attachment with a #80 sanding disc to sand all surfaces to the bare metal. The cab was then primed and sent to an auto bodyshop for the finish coat. I have found that most paint supply houses can custom mix the correct color paint.

The dash and other nonremovable parts were also finished at a bodyshop.

The other exterior surfaces were sanded and primed with a marine waterproof primer (black).

I sent the windshield crank to Washington state for repair.

I replaced and painted all clutch-head screws. These special screws were purchased from Roberts Motor Parts.

After the cab had been finish painted at the bodyshop, I replaced the headliner (this job takes two people and clutch-head screws).

I glued old-style carpet underliner padding to the insides of the door panels, roof and rear of the seat to quiet the noise. (Do this *before* installing the headliner.)

I replaced the window channels with parts purchased from Pro Auto Parts, in Windsor, Connecticut.

A local glass shop cut and replaced the windshield glass and one door glass.

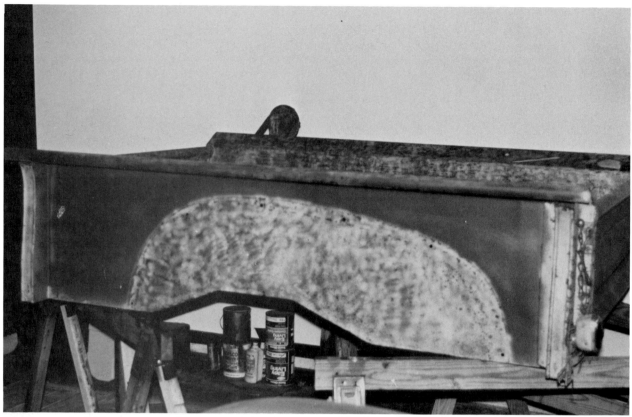

Whether a rebuilding or restoration approach is taken, the pickup box will typically be restored as a separate unit. In many cases, rust and dent damage will require taking apart the box to replace or repair the sheet metal.

The floor will also be replaced. The work on this box is being limited to removing the old paint and refinishing.
Steve Weisgerber

The results of restoration can be a stunning show truck such as this 1951 Advance Design series pickup owned by Mike Cavey. Over 2,000 hours went into completely reworking every part of what had been a well-preserved, original truck. The benefit of restoration is that when you're finished, every part of the truck is like new—or better. Mike Cavey

The question here is, how large a tool investment are you willing to make to do as much of the work on your truck as possible? If you find working with your hands to be a therapeutic pastime (and many do), then you'll find the tool investment to be a great savings over the cost of having others do the work. Besides, once you've made the initial investment, the tools are yours—probably for a lifetime. If you plan to do as much of the work on your truck as possible, include the tool and training costs in the labor expenses category.

There will always be some work you will need to hire out and for this you should get estimates. In many cases, shops will be reluctant to quote a price for mechanical or repair work on an older vehicle, not wanting to be held to the quote when unforeseen problems develop. You can explain that for now, you're just looking for a ball-park figure which will probably be on the high side. In the labor cost category you will include specialty work such as chrome plating, and jobs better left to experts such as instrument gauge repair and windshield replacement.

There are other ways, besides doing the work yourself, to shave labor costs. One is to share work with friends. The times I've been able to do this have been among my most enjoyable restoration experiences. As an example, a friend and I both needed to rebuild the steering and front end on our collector vehicles. So we took the front ends on both our vehicles apart, determined the parts we needed, pooled our orders and got a small discount for placing the larger order, then set up an assembly-line operation for cleaning, refinishing and rebuilding both front-end and steering assemblies. This approach was much more efficient than if we had overhauled each vehicle separately, but more importantly, we learned from each other and had a great time in the process.

Another cost-saving alternative, sometimes available, is to have major mechanical or bodywork done by students in a vocational-technical program. Admittedly, there are some risks here. Parts can be lost and the quality of the instruction will determine the outcome of the finished product. I teach at a technical college that trains students in engine rebuilding, bodywork, machining and similar trades, and have consigned my truck to these programs for all of its bodywork and painting, plus some engine and other mechanical work. The process is not very speedy and problems do arise, but any lower quality work, such as a heavy orange-peel texture that appeared in the paint near the bottom of the driver's door, has always been made right. The big plus to having a vo-tech program assist in a vehicle's rebuild or restoration is the nominal labor charges. A hoped-for offshoot is giving the students an appreciation of older vehicles.

Supply Costs

Your expense estimate must also include a listing of supplies. This category covers everything from sandpaper and painting supplies, to masking tape, miscellaneous nuts, bolts and fasteners, weatherstripping glue, plastic sheathing to protect parts from dust, sand for sandblasting, reference literature including sales brochures and service and parts manuals—in short, all the odds and ends that you will need to complete your truck's restoration or rebuilding project. There's really no way you can accurately project supply expenses in advance. You should allow $400 for paint and at least half that amount for the manuals and other books that you will use in rebuilding or restoring your truck. Add in another $400 to $600 as a ball-park figure for the supplies you are not able to itemize.

Transportation Costs

The last category in your cost estimate is for transportation expenses. These may include hauling the cab to a chemical stripping facility, traveling to scrap yards and swap meets to hunt for parts, UPS or freight charges for parts you may order from parts vendors, as well as traveling to look at original, restored or in-process trucks. You

may think of these travel expenses as part of the enjoyment of your hobby, but they are also part of the cost of restoring or rebuilding your vehicle, so you might as well project some figures and tally them in. Whether or not you will be using your

Although restoration eventually results in the truck's being taken completely apart, this is not the first step. Before approaching the truck with a wrench, it is necessary to document its original condition. However, once disassembly begins, the truck will be stripped to the bare chassis. Believe it or not, the owner of this truck did the entire restoration in his driveway. Here's an example of an important detail that should be noted prior to paint stripping or sandblasting. The location of the stripes on the wheels of a 1948 ½ ton Suburban will guide the painter in replacing the stripes after this wheel is refinished. Note that the outer stripe aligns with the center of the valve stem. The two inner stripes lie just outside the lip of the hubcap. Width measurements of the stripes should also be taken and recorded. Lloyd Dennis

Taking inventory of your truck's parts needs can include deciding which accessories you would like to add. A popular accessory for 1967–1972 Chevrolet and GMC trucks is a tachometer which can be installed in the instrument panel's center gauge window. This 1969 C-20 Longhorn pickup lacked the tachometer; the decision was made to add this accessory during the refurbishing process.

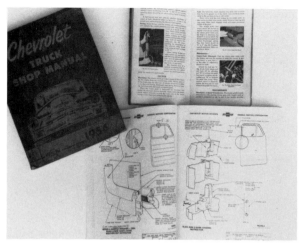

You can draw up a rough estimate of the cost of parts to rebuild or restore your truck from a vintage Chevrolet truck part supplier's catalog. The actual parts bill is likely to exceed this estimate because of unanticipated replacement or repairs. Besides this guide, you should purchase a Chevrolet shop manual for your truck. General service manuals like Chilton *or* Motor *are also very helpful. If you are planning a frame-up restoration you will find* factory assembly manuals *to be extremely beneficial. These manuals are available in reprinted form for Advance Design and Task Force series trucks.*

truck in any business capacity, be sure to keep a log of travel and related expenses to use in calculating an accurate appreciation figure should you decide to sell your truck sometime in the future.

When you add up all the expense estimates, you may want to take a deep breath before you hit the total key on your calculator. Even rebuilding an older truck can be a more costly undertaking than you would think—and restoring is likely to run considerably more. But don't let that sour you on sprucing up your old truck. You'll find that some of the costs can be trimmed and overall the expenses will be spread over the duration of the project. If restoration seems outside your budget, you might consider the rebuilding approach.

Shopping for Parts

Whether your approach is rebuilding or restoration, you'll spend a sizeable part of your time hunting parts. The quicker you develop reliable parts sources, and tap into a good parts network, the smoother your parts hunting will be and the less likely you are to be taken on price and inferior quality. In a hobby where over ninety percent of the businesses are reputable and are as concerned about their reputations as you or I, there are, unfortunately, still a few shysters and often their

If you are taking the restoration approach, here's a view of what a portion of your shop or garage will look like while your truck's chassis is being rebuilt. Disassembly for restoration literally takes the truck apart to the last nut and bolt.

catalogs are the ones that newcomers find first. The supplier listing in the appendices is compiled from recommendations by many Chevrolet truck restorers. But even here it pays to shop around. A good policy is to order catalogs from several suppliers, then compare prices and place small orders at first to test the service. When you are satisfied that you've found a supplier whose service and quality you can trust, then you've got a green light to go ahead with your larger orders.

In shopping for parts, don't overlook the local auto parts stores. NAPA auto parts stores, a nationwide network of independently owned stores served by a massive warehousing system, probably have the most complete listings of parts for older vehicles. Not only are the items usually less expensive through a NAPA outlet than a restoration supplier, but there are no separate handling and shipping fees. Usually your local store can get the part within twenty-four hours after placing your order, if the part is not already on the store's shelves. If your area doesn't have a NAPA store, check parts availability at other large auto parts outlets.

Whether you're rebuilding or restoring, you'll also want to explore that most enjoyable parts source—the scrap yard. Unfortunately, old-fashioned yards filled with vintage vehicles are fast disappearing. Serious collectors shroud these haunts with the secrecy of a gold prospector—but once they've picked their parts, most will share their discovery with you. The question is who to ask. That's where joining a club for old-truck collectors comes in. Members usually will share their finds and help one another in that all-important parts search.

With the exception of some body and trim parts that have all but disappeared from circulation, Chevrolet truck parts are quite easy to find. One reason for this, besides the fact that during nearly the entire collector period Chevrolet trucks were the nation's best-seller, is the interchangeability of engine parts, as well as body parts in certain years, with the Chevrolet car line. Most body parts also interchange between Chevrolet and GMC. You'll find needed interchange information in Hollander manuals that are the mechanic's bible of parts substitution. Although copies can sometimes be found in general repair shops, the easiest access to this valuable interchange information is to buy your own reprinted copy (see appendix for information). A set of Hollander manuals is quite expensive, making these books a good investment for a club—or you might suggest to the community librarian that some of these manuals be purchased for the library's automotive section.

Suggestion: When replacing an original part with a reproduction item, don't throw away the original until you have the reproduction and are sure it is exactly like the original. If it isn't, make it match. When you are rebuilding a truck to enter in national competition this can mean pounding jig marks into reproduction sheet-metal parts.

Working at Your Own Pace

Working on your truck can be great therapy from the pressures of everyday life if you follow a few common-sense guidelines. The first, of course, is don't let the truck become the driving compulsion of your life. If this happens, then daily life will become an escape from your truck, not the other way around. The simplest way to turn working on your truck from a relaxing pastime to a compulsion is to set deadlines on your work. Repair or restoration of an older vehicle never agrees with deadlines. Sometimes jobs will go smoother than expected, but not often. More commonly, the unexpected will throw your work off pace. The most common schedule saboteurs are missing or incorrect parts, but setbacks can also arise that seem providentially placed to test your patience. I've had my share; one of the more memorable was finding water in seven of the eight cylinders of my 1969 Longhorn's Chevrolet engine. The truck came

---

Chevrolet Pickup Clubs

It's not uncommon to have questions about your truck that the reference information you have collected does not seem to answer clearly. Often these questions can be answered by contacting a club devoted to vintage trucks and asking assistance from the club's technical advisor for your year Chevrolet. Here is an example of such a question, and the advisor's answer, reprinted from the Light Commercial Vehicle Association's newsletter *Plugs 'n Points*.

Question: I own a 1953 Chevrolet half ton truck for which I have been trying to locate seat belts. Since I want to keep the original seat, do you know where I can locate, preferably new, lap belts?

The side hood ornaments on my truck are Chevrolet/Thriftmaster with the number 1430 below. It is clear from the serial number 3–1314 that the truck is a '53. Was the hood replaced from another truck? What nameplates should be on the hood? Is the plate Chevrolet/Thriftmaster legitimate?

Answer: GM didn't start using seat belts until 1957. The 1430 designation is for a ¾ ton cowl and chassis. Your number, 3–1314, is for a Canadian half ton pickup delivery. The Thriftmaster nameplate was used pre–1950, I believe. These markings show that the hood has been replaced. The Chevrolet/Thriftmaster nameplate is legitimate, but for an earlier truck. The nameplate on your 1953 Canadian half ton should read "Chevrolet" with the number 1300 underneath.

out of the bodyshop and refused to crank over, let alone start. The truck had been inside for the winter and while the body was receiving a fresh new look, the engine was quietly self-destructing. Heartbreaks like this often seem to strike in the final steps, often the night you're putting on the last touches in preparation for tomorrow's show.

Scheduling the Work

The second guideline to making the time you spend working on your truck enjoyable is to take the jobs in manageable chunks. While it's smart to keep an eye out for parts and information you may need for later jobs, even a frame-up restoration should be handled one job at a time. If the current stage of work is sandblasting, then give your attention to that step and deal with concerns about metal repair later. If while working on larger projects, such as rebuilding the drivetrain, metal repair or refinishing, you sense frustration or impatience setting in, it's a good idea to break away and concentrate on a smaller, more manageable job that you can complete in one or two evenings or

When disassembling a truck, it is critical that you develop a system for storing and cataloging the many small parts and hardware items. The boxes in this photo are storing myriad small parts from a 1958 Cameo.
Trent Stephan

a weekend. That way, you'll have the satisfaction of seeing something through to completion and you'll return to the larger project with renewed confidence in achieving your goal.

As mentioned earlier, it also helps to work with a partner or friend. Besides getting more than twice as much accomplished, when one partner becomes discouraged the other will provide the encouragement to move ahead. Mike Cavey said that he would never have been able to restore his Grand National award-winning 1951 Chevrolet pickup without the help of his friend, Brad Rose. Not only does Rose possess skills and equipment that Cavey does not, but Cavey says he stuck more faithfully to his project knowing that someone else would be at the shop waiting for him to show up. Cavey also says that he couldn't have driven himself to achieve his truck's level of perfection—"best in the world." Details like putting in those extra hours to ensure a perfect fit on the front-end metal and hood took a buddy's saying, "Let's give that one more try."

Another way to avoid old-truck burnout is to alternate between smaller jobs and larger projects. If you live in a northern climate, winters may be a dead time as far as working in your shop is concerned. But you can keep your truck progressing by rebuilding smaller assemblies like the starter, generator or carburetor in your basement. You can also take time to send instruments out for rebuilding, or have the chrome plating done. That way, you'll feel like your truck is progressing, even if you aren't standing, toes numb, on bone-chilling concrete, gripping an icy wrench.

Choosing the Rebuilding Approach

Disassembly for Repair

If you have decided to make your truck presentable and driveable by the rebuild approach, you will limit disassembly to just those parts or sheet metal that need reworking. For example, a must-do job on any older vehicle is inspecting and overhauling the brakes. If you're working through a brake system for the first time, it's good advice to take apart only one side at a time. That way, if you get stuck putting a front or rear brake back together—and the instructions in the service manual are not clear—you can always pull off the drum on the opposite side of the truck and use its brakes for a reassembly guide (providing, of course, that someone hasn't cobbled up the brakes in a previous repair). When doing sheet-metal repair, installing patch panels in the cab for example, it is sometimes advisable to do some further disassembly to make the job easier. With the patch panels, you might also want to remove the doors. *Always* remove the gas tank before doing any welding in its vicinity. You'll need to remove the pickup box to get to the back of the cab and to replace its cross braces and wooden floor. The engine will be removed from the truck for rebuilding, and the list goes on.

The basic guideline here is to take apart only one or two assemblies at a time. While the engine is out of the truck for rebuilding, it makes sense to overhaul the brakes and replace the wiring. Overall, though, you will keep the truck as intact as possible so that you can continue to use and enjoy it while doing the upgrades. Whenever you do any disassembly, be sure to save all nuts and bolts (have empty coffee cans or plastic buckets handy to hold the hardware) and place all parts where they won't get bumped, damaged or misplaced. As much as possible, have replacement parts on hand *before* starting the repair. This way your truck won't be laid up while a supplier back orders out-of-stock parts.

Choosing the Restoration Approach

Establishing a Timetable

Before you begin a frame-up restoration you should establish a plan that includes your projected and fall-back time schedules and budgets. Your schedule should include a fall-back timetable to keep discouragement in check during those unforeseeable, but seemingly inevitable setbacks. Virtually everyone who works on an old truck experiences setbacks—some amusing, some downright devilish. One of the most troublesome setbacks in my rebuilding experiences was an improperly ground crankshaft that caused the rods to bind so tightly the engine wouldn't turn when reassembled. To free the engine it had to be disassembled again, and I had to find an engine craftsman who could fit the rod bearings to the crank—not a normally advisable procedure but one that an old-time engine man is able to do successfully. The alternative would have been to have the crank reground (decreasing the bearing size still more), then buy another set of larger oversize bearings.

Mike Cavey tells of having one of his truck's freshly painted rear fenders tumble off its sawhorse onto the shop floor, requiring him to strip off the new paint and refinish the fender all over again. Another friend had placed the just refinished tailgate to his truck in the sun in front of his shop to dry. Kids playing baseball in a nearby field hit a fly ball that landed—you guess it—smack in the middle of the tailgate. In addition to repainting, this restorer had a baseball-size dent to work out of the tailgate.

You can consider yourself lucky if a setback of some sort doesn't come along in the restoration or rebuilding process. When it happens, instead of getting down on yourself and crying "Why me!" it's a lot healthier and less stressful to say to yourself, "These things come with the territory," and move on. For setbacks, cost overruns and work that wasn't expected, your restoration budget should

include a contingency—I'd advise thirty percent. If the extra isn't needed, you'll be money ahead when you're finished. But if you don't allow for unanticipated extras, you may fall short of resources to finish your truck—just when the end is in sight.

Researching Your Truck

Most first-time restorers begin by taking their vehicle apart. This is totally the wrong approach. It's true that the vehicle will have to be disassembled, but this is *not* the first step. You should begin by researching your truck as thoroughly as possible. We'll discuss the research step in more detail later because it is also the starting point if you decide to take the rebuilding approach. Part of what's involved in the research (which really means learning all you can about your truck) is documenting your vehicle as completely as possible. Documenting begins with writing down as much information as you can find on the truck itself. This includes data codes, the original color scheme (usually visible underneath the hood, on the back of the cab behind the seat and other places that aren't likely to be repainted), engine and chassis numbers, and details such as mileage, accessories, tire sizes and the like.

Preparation Steps Checklist

Decide whether rebuilding or restoring is the best approach for you.
Establish standards:
    Will the truck be modified or stock?
    If modified, what components will it have?
Document the truck with notes and photos on:
    Weatherstripping location
    Original colors
    Pinstripe location (if any)
    Original and nonoriginal accessories
    Repair work needed (if any)
Purchase parts and service manuals, locate sales
   brochures and resource books.
Begin research:
    Decode truck's data plate
    Determine original color
    Learn correct coating for bolts and fasteners
    Find out if engine is correct/original
    Determine if drivetrain is original
Estimate costs:
    Estimate parts costs
    Determine tool investment
    Estimate cost of professional services
    Project supply costs
    Factor-in travel expenses
Set up supply network:
    Order reproduction parts supplier catalogs
    Gather scrap yard references
Decide where to begin:
    Restoration begins with complete disassembly
    Rebuilding places mechanical/safety concerns
    first

Documenting is also done by taking clear color photos of the truck from every conceivable angle. A quality camera, preferably a 35 mm, should be used for the photos. If you're not a shutterbug and don't have a 35 mm camera with an adjustable lens, ask a friend whose hobby is photography to take the photos for you. Offering to buy the film and treating the photographer to a dinner out should be a good trade for a half-hour-long photo session.

Be sure the photos are taken from every angle, front and back, top and bottom. Note such details as the location of the weatherstrip around the doors and the location of the seam if the weatherstripping is original, the location and width of striping on the wheels or body, the presence or absence of welting between the fenders and body—everything you can think of. From your research you will also make a list of everything about the truck that you find to be nonoriginal. Examples might include incorrect taillights (from a hardware or auto supply store), signal lights on trucks not originally fitted with them, an incorrect engine, replacement sheet metal, missing hubcaps and so forth.

Listing Needed Replacement Parts

Also, before taking the truck apart you should list all the items you know you'll be needing to replace—either because they're missing, worn out, damaged beyond repair, incorrect for your truck or are desirable accessories not currently found on your truck. Missing items may include such items as the floor mat or the correct taillight. Chances are you'll find plenty of parts that are worn out or damaged beyond repair. One likely example is the exhaust system. Another is the radiator. One or more of the fenders, or the box, may fit this category as well. An item that's incorrect for your truck could include the engine. In trucks that have seen plenty of work, it's not unusual for the truck to be running on its second or third engine.

Depending on the year and model, you may find a number of desirable accessories to put on the list. In the mid fifties, Chevrolet even offered an

One of the advantages of a frame-up restoration is that the chassis can be completely cleaned, overhauled and put in A–1 condition. This means that you won't have to take your truck apart again later to fix something you overlooked. The disadvantage of a frame-up restoration is that the truck won't be driveable until all the parts are *rebuilt, refinished and reassembled. As a result, you may have to forego driving your truck for a couple of years while the restoration is in process—with the possible consequence that during this period you may lose sight of the eventual goal.*

electric shaver that plugged into the cigar lighter receptacle as a convenience item. If you are more concerned about comfort than authenticity, you may also want to make an upgrade category in which you can list such parts necessary to convert to a 12 volt electrical system, a modern radio and an air conditioning unit. Make the list as complete as you can without taking the truck apart. Then you can begin to lay out the restoration timetable and draw up a budget estimate. An example of such a list follows.

Parts Needed for 1969 Chevrolet C-20 Long-horn Pickup:

Outer grille molding to replace dented original

Tachometer and tachometer wiring harness, desirable accessory

Rechromed instrument panel to replace worn chrome

Floor mat replacement for original mat

Door weatherstripping to replace original rubber

Window weather seal to replace original

Modern radio; desirable upgrade

Disassembly for Restoration

Now you can begin to take your truck apart. If you are taking the restoration route, you will remove the bed, cab and front clip (fenders, hood,

The owner of this truck has removed the front clip to clean and paint the cab firewall and forward chassis assemblies. This piecemeal approach means that the truck is laid up for shorter periods. The disadvantage is that projects like cleaning the frame are less efficient when done on smaller areas than if the entire chassis is stripped and refinished as a unit.

When disassembling a truck for repair, only those parts and assemblies needing work are removed from the truck. This owner is doing bodywork and an engine overhaul simultaneously, but he has left the basic truck intact. Normally only one overhaul or repair task would be tackled at a time.

Details such as the color scheme for the engine and accessories will require careful research. This owner has gone so far as to purchase a reproduction of the original Delco battery. The engine compartment looks the way it did when it left the factory.

Swap meets are an excellent source of hard-to-find parts. This vendor specializes in sheet-metal parts for vintage Chevrolet trucks. Perhaps you can spot the rare Cameo pickup box fenders near the center of the photo.

Scrap yards are another parts source. Here, a Chevrolet truck collector's young son has spotted a desirable five-window Advance Design series cab.

and grille assembly), as well as running boards (on trucks so-equipped) to expose the chassis.

As you remove the truck's sheet metal, be sure to save all bolts and avoid breaking bolts as much as possible during disassembly. Ways to keep rusty bolts from seizing on the nut and breaking are to soak the bolt and nut well with penetrating oil for several days before attempting to turn them loose. Then, if the nut still refuses to turn, apply heat with a welding torch. It's important to save the old bolts because new hardware does not match the thickness of the original bolt head and nuts. Even though you are careful, some of the bolts will break and others will be disfigured by rust. To replace these, you will need to remove additional bolts from a parts truck or carcass in a scrap yard. When you have removed all body parts, inspect them closely for hidden damage. Look underneath the cab to check the condition of the cab supports. Also check for rust on the inside bottoms of the doors and similar spots that are easier to see now that the body assemblies can be moved around. All sheet-metal parts should be stored inside to prevent further deterioration, and where they won't be bumped into or damaged.

Suggestion: If you are disassembling an early 1947-1953 Advance Design grille, number the bars with tiny notches on the backside so that you can put the bars back in the right locations.

With the chassis laid bare, you can remove the engine and drivetrain. You will keep these assemblies intact for now. This done, you can strip off the front end, steering and suspension—leaving just the bare frame. More specific instructions for removing these assemblies are given in the chapters that deal with overhauling the engine, front end and other major components.

Once you have the truck stripped to the bare frame, you're at the starting point of the restoration process. Just as the frame was the platform on which the truck came into being as it moved along the assembly line many years ago, the cleaned, derusted and repainted frame is now the centerpiece around which the restored truck will come together. Of course, various assemblies such as the engine will be rebuilt separately. But the truck won't begin to take form until you have refinished the frame.

Although shop manuals provide fairly detailed disassembly and rebuilding instructions for your truck's mechanical components, working on a twenty- to fifty-year-old vehicle is different than overhauling the same vehicle when new. The rebuilding instructions in this book will take those differences into account and will guide you through difficulties you may experience and provide tips for making old parts work like new.

One tip that is important to a successful restoration is not to throw anything away until the truck is finished and you are absolutely sure that the old, original part is of no more use—even as a pattern. For example, that old, ratty cardboard headliner may look useless when you pull it off the truck, but it may serve as a helpful guide when installing the replacement headliner several months later. To store small parts, you should collect old coffee cans, or cut the tops off plastic milk bottles. These containers can hold nuts, bolts and other miscellaneous small items. You can label the contents of the coffee cans on strips of masking tape applied to the outside. The milk cartons can be labeled with a

Along with this photo, Chevrolet truck collector Alvin Shier penned the note, "We here in the West don't pussyfoot around. When we do something, we get serious right away." Shier didn't really attack the roof of his truck's cab with an axe, but sometimes a job will seem frustrat- *ing enough to contemplate violent measures. The best advice when this happens is don't. Instead, put down the tools and come back to the job the next day when you're refreshed. Alvin Shier*

When possible, work with a friend. This will help break the work into manageable chunks and the friend will provide encouragement when you need it, and vice versa.

permanent marker. As you're disassembling your truck, make it a practice to label everything. Then place all the items in well-organized storage. Otherwise, when you start reassembly, you'll waste lots of time looking for misplaced items.

Looking Ahead

The chapters that follow describe the major restoration and rebuilding steps that are typically followed in refurbishing an older truck. Each is presented as a do-it-yourself process that is easily within the capability of anyone with an inclination to learn and has the do-it-yourself spirit. Where special tools are required, these are mentioned with the jobs. If a substantial tool investment is required (as is the case with sandblasting), alternative sources to getting the job done are suggested.

One last bit of advice. Don't wait until your truck is finished to show it off to your family and friends. A repainted chassis deserves display as much as, if not more than, the finished truck. After all, when the body and box are back in place, who will see that hygienic undercarriage on which you lavished so much time and attention? Some restorers have even been known to haul their truck's chassis to shows. Spectators will be amused, and some will later remember the time when your truck rolled in as just a black framework. Above all, if you find yourself getting too serious, remember, you're working on that old truck because it's *fun*.

3

Shop and Tools

Three differences separate the average hobbyist restorer from the restoration professional. Typically these differences lie in the nature of the shop facility where the work is to be done, the completeness of the tool set used to do the work, and the level of the skills in performing various mechanical and body repair techniques as well as familiarity with special tools such as welding outfits and spray painting equipment. Although hobbyists are resourceful in solving their shop space needs (it's not uncommon to hear of vehicles having been restored out-of-doors, though this approach isn't recommended), before starting a restoration or the repair jobs needed to bring an older truck back to prime, you should take a close look at your work space and compare what's available to the recommendations given.

Needless to say, you don't expect to purchase every tool that might be useful in restoring an older truck—after all, resourcefulness is part of the game too. But some jobs (such as spray painting) do require the necessary tools. In this chapter you

will learn what tools should be considered the basic tool set for rebuilding or restoring an older vehicle, as well as recommendations for specialized tools that you should either consider purchasing, plan to rent, or work out an arrangement where they can be borrowed.

In the process of restoring or extensively repairing (rebuilding) an older truck you will develop and discover skills through trial and error,

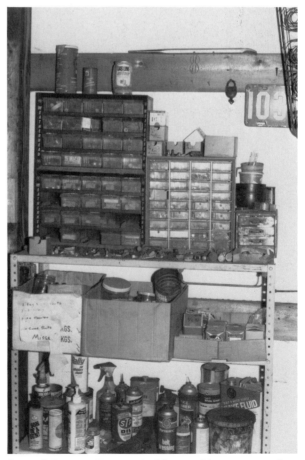

Organizing small parts in bins and boxes saves time when you are looking for the right size bolt or fitting.

Shop space for a frame-up restoration will need to be ample enough to allow room to work on the frame plus store the rest of the truck. A spacious shop like this one gives plenty of room for the disassembled truck, plus new and spare parts. Shop space can be maximized with wall cabinets and tool racks. Mike Cavey

31

practice, reading, and getting help and guidance from more experienced friends. Finding those who can guide you through this new territory will be one of the most important steps you can take to help ensure that your old truck will end up the beauty of your dreams rather than a half-completed project that has consumed your energies and finances with nothing in return. Experts who will help you in your restoration can be found at the parts counters of auto parts stores, general repair shops, adult auto mechanic courses and through involvement in a local old-car or truck club.

As you're sure to discover along the way, many difficult or seemingly impossible jobs are made easy by knowing the right approach. You'll discover some of these tips in this book; you will learn others from the experts you have found to help you when the going gets tough. If enthusiasm overshadows your mechanical and body repair experience, you may find it beneficial to enroll in adult auto mechanics, welding, or bodywork classes at a nearby skill center, vocational high school or a vo-tech college. Often the instructor will let you work on whatever part of your truck relates to the skills being taught (in a welding class you might practice by installing patch panels, for example). Where this is the case, for the small outlay of a tuition fee, you

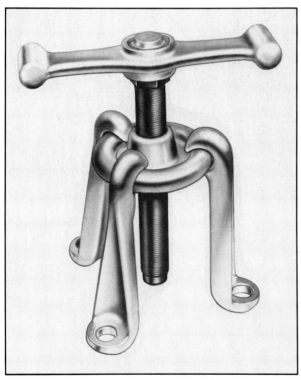

Pullers are high on the priority list of specialty tools. You'll need a puller to remove the steering wheel, crankshaft pulley and many other applications. The puller shown here is specially designed for removing rear brake drums on trucks with tapered rear axles.

receive not only valuable instruction, but also the use of expensive tools and warm, dry, well-lighted shop space as well.

One of the basic skills for working on any older vehicle is knowing how to light and handle a gas welding outfit. This chapter explains the basics of gas welding, an essential skill for heating, cutting and joining metal. As you take your truck apart there will be many times when a gas wrench, as mechanics often call a gas welding outfit, seems to be an indispensable tool. Welding as a repair process is discussed in more detail in chapter 10.

Shop Needs

The space needed to store and work on an old truck grows as the truck is taken apart. For a while you can economize on space by storing dismantled parts in the bed, but sooner or later that comes off too. Then there are the spares and replacements, which sometimes include a parts truck or two, that need to be housed—or at least parked. And you'll really kick yourself if you toss out rusted or damaged original parts from your truck, only to find that you need them to check a fit or paint scheme after they're gone. The best policy is to save *everything* until the restoration is finished and all this, plus room to work on the truck amounts to more shop space than many hobbyists have available. What's to be done? The first step is to realize that shop space is likely to be a problem. If you have a two-car garage, you can get by but the daily driver(s) may be parked outside for a long while. If you have less than a two-car garage, you might consider putting up temporary storage for the course of the restoration. There are other options to explore as well.

For my restoration and storage needs I lease a nearby barn which was once the carriage building to the town's former mansion, now a fraternity house. The barn provides space to store my collector vehicles and is adequate, if not an altogether suitable facility, in which to do mechanical work. The building is not heated, so I have to schedule projects for warm weather.

Another alternative that works for several collectors I know is to work with others who have the facilities you don't. Members of the Light Commercial Vehicle Association's Virginia Blue Ridge chapter take turns bringing their trucks into the "club house"—a member's three-car-plus garage—for specific restoration projects. Another collector I know does restoration projects in a friend's shop, with the understanding that he will assist on the friend's projects. There are undoubtedly hundreds of stories of how resourceful restorers have solved their garaging problems. The challenge is for you to solve yours.

Besides the physical space in which to park the truck, store the parts you remove and others you acquire along the way, and work on the parts you have dismantled, a restoration shop also needs some special facilities. In order to remove the engine, you will either need a strong overhead support beam from which to suspend a come-along or chain fall, or you will need to rent a "cherry picker" engine hoist. For spray painting, you should install a high-volume fan in a window or vent hole to exhaust paint fumes and dust. If you plan to do your own finish painting, you will need to rig a spray booth (this can be done by putting up walls of sheet plastic and installing a ventilation system). For welding, some portion of the floor should be concrete or other noncombustible material. Parts storage will take less space and be more organized if you set up shelving. Paints and chemicals should be stored in locked cabinets to prevent access by children. You will need a sturdy work bench, storage places for tools, 220 volt service for an arc welder and air compressor, good lighting and a heat source if you live in a seasonal climate and plan to work in cool weather.

If you are in the position to construct a shop for restoration purposes, then you should consider helpful extras like running water with a sink for cleaning up after work, a floor drain for washing your vehicles and a set of permanent ramps or pit for servicing your truck and doing repairs. You'll also find it helpful to run galvanized pipe for air compressor lines with outlets in various locations in the shop. Running pipe for the main compressor lines has at least three advantages over uncoiling a length of air compressor hose each time you use air tools. First, you avoid the nuisance of having to uncoil and coil the hose; second, you won't lose air supply through restrictive hose connections; and third, the pipe will assist with moisture condensation, helping prevent water from passing into sandblasting or spray painting equipment and air tools.

Those who plan to do their own sandblasting are advised to construct a three-sided pen outside the building to catch the dust and conserve the sand. If you set up a degreasing bath of the type described in the stripping and derusting chapter, then you should also construct an enclosed area (either inside or outside the shop) for the alkaline bath. It is crucial that you take every measure to prevent children (your own or those in the neighborhood) from gaining access to harmful chemicals that you may be using in the restoration process. You will also need to plan and work out an environmentally sound means for disposing of an alkaline degreasing solution and other chemicals that if simply dumped would leach into the soil and contaminate ground water.

Basic Tools

Having a vehicle professionally restored can be expensive. The only way I know that you can avoid a professional shop's $30-$50 per hour fee is to restore or repair the vehicle yourself. More than likely, the repair or restoration will take you a little longer than if you hired out the work, and along the way you may even get a little frustrated. But when the job is done the feeling of accomplishment will be rewarding and the money saved will be substantial.

The only drawback to doing your own restoration and repair work is the investment required to purchase needed tools. Approaching restoration with an inadequate tool set is bound to produce frustration as well as damaged or incorrectly repaired parts. It isn't necessary to own every tool in the professional's shop, but the home handyman's tool set won't be adequate either. The tool set described below will get you through most restoration and rebuild jobs. Remember, money spent on tools can be considered a lifetime investment and you can shortcut some of the tool costs either by renting from a rent-all store, or by teaming with friends or club members to buy more expensive tools on a cooperative basis.

Socket Wrenches

The single most used tool for mechanical repair is the ⅜ in. drive ratchet and sockets. The ⅜ in. drive ratchet is big enough to tackle most jobs on a light truck, yet is still small enough to get into tight spots. The socket set should contain ten sockets ranging from ⅜ to ¹⁵⁄₁₆ in. increments of ¹⁄₁₆ in. Sockets generally come in either twelve-point or

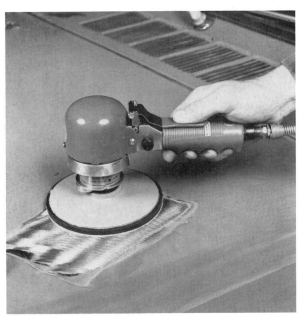

Assuming you purchase or already own an air compressor, you'll find a variety of air tools useful in overhauling or restoring an old truck. This tool is a dual action (D/A) sander which is used to remove paint from dent or rust areas and to prepare an old finish for repainting. The Eastwood Company

six-point. Unless you have a specific need for twelve-point sockets, I most definitely recommend six-point. Six-point sockets have more surface area to grab the nut or bolt, making it easier to remove the nut or bolt without slipping or damaging it. For this reason, they are far more effective with rusted bolt heads and nuts than twelve-point sockets. It is also a good idea to have a swivel coupling and a range of extension bars.

Adding to this basic set, a ¼ in. drive ratchet and socket set is handy for really small jobs while a ½ in. drive socket set is needed for larger jobs. On a light truck you can get by without the ¼ in. drive set, but you'll need the ½ in. drive bar and sockets to loosen larger, rust-frozen nuts and bolts.

Combination Wrenches

On combination wrenches one end is open and the other end is boxed—hence the name. This style of wrench is handy for hard-to-reach locations where if you can't turn the bolt or nut with the box

A welding torch is virtually essential for restoration or repair work on an older vehicle. As an alternative to a full-sized welding outfit, you can purchase a portable gas welder like the Toteweld by Arco.

end, you can usually get a bite with the open end. A set of combination wrenches should range from ⅜ to 1 in. in increments of 1⁄16 in.

Chisels and Punches

Chisels will be used to remove rivets and corroded nut and bolt heads that are too rusted or have rounded over so as not to hold a wrench. A set of four chisels ranging in widths from ⅜ to ¾ in. should cover all jobs. The punch set should include starting and drift punches that are used to drive out rivets and roll pins, an aligning punch for lining up holes and a center punch used to mark a spot for identification or centering a drill. A brass drift is also a valuable tool and is used for tapping into place bearings or other parts that are easily damaged.

Pliers

A variety of pliers are needed for various jobs requiring holding, pinching, removing, cutting and squeezing. Pliers that should be found in the basic tool set include standard slip-joint pliers, 9 in. channel locks, needle-nose pliers and diagonal cutters.

Hammers

Two ball-peen hammers are needed: a 12 oz. for light jobs, and a 24 or 32 oz. for big jobs. A plastic-tipped or brass hammer is absolutely critical for any job when it is possible to scratch or damage the part with a steel ball-peen hammer.

Screwdrivers and Miscellaneous Hand Tools

The basic tool set should also contain a variety of screwdrivers, ranging in shank length and blade size and with Phillips as well as slot heads. Other miscellaneous hand tools include a hacksaw and selection of flat and round files. If you're building your tool inventory from scratch, you can buy tool sets containing most of these items at relatively low cost from Sears.

Jack Stands and Jack

To support the truck chassis during restoration and repair, professional-grade jack stands are a necessity. Avoid light-duty jack stands sold in discount marts. The heavier duty stands have a ratchet release for the load-head and thicker gauge steel legs and braces. *Never* support the truck on a stack of blocks. Jack stands are relatively inexpensive and should be selected as though your life depended on the quality of their design and construction—since that is literally the case.

Although a regular platform-style hydraulic jack will be adequate for raising the truck off the floor, you will find that a repair-shop style floor jack on rollers is a much more convenient tool to use. It also has the advantage of letting you wheel the truck around on the shop floor, sometimes enabling you to park the truck in an otherwise inaccessible space.

Specialty Tools

In the process of your truck's restoration or repair, you will probably invest in several specialty tools needed to perform specific jobs or to make those jobs easier. Specific tools for specialized jobs are identified in the various chapters. The specialty tools listed here should be considered musts for a ground-up restoration.

Brake Tools

Nearly all older vehicles need a thorough brake overhaul. Brake tools needed for this job include a tubing bender and flaring tool for creating replacement brake lines with the right length and shape to match the originals, as well as a tubing cutter and brake spring spreaders.

Pullers and Engine Overhaul Tools

Pullers will be needed to remove the steering wheel, the crankshaft pulley (if you decide to rebuild the engine) and taking apart other mechanical assemblies.

Engine overhaul will also necessitate its own tool list including valve spring and piston ring compressors. A gasket scraper and wire brush are handy items for parts cleanup. Important to most work and critical to engine work are measuring tools. For basic measurements I suggest a linear caliper. It is not as exact as a micrometer, but it can be quite accurate to three decimal places and is more affordable in price.

Torque Wrench

One of the most important specialty tools is a torque wrench. This tool, which attaches to ½ in. drive sockets, is used to tighten nuts and bolts to proper torque specifications. A torque wrench should be used on everything from head bolts to lug nuts and will prevent stripped threads from overtightening, or damage that results from parts coming loose due to undertightening.

Gas Welder and Air Compressor

Although they require a larger investment than any of the tools mentioned, a welding torch and air compressor are virtually essential for any serious restoration or repair work on an older vehicle. If you have to stagger the purchase of these two items, buy the torch first. You will use it during disassembly. The air compressor can be used for sandblasting and painting, and is an excellent power source for a variety of air tools.

When you buy a gas welding outfit you typically purchase the gauges, hoses and torch, and rent the tanks. The oxygen and fuel gas tanks come in a variety of sizes and are best transported around the shop on a cart (also purchased). As an alternative to a full-sized welding outfit, you can purchase portable gas welding outfits like the Toteweld by Arco. This small-scale gas welding outfit has the same capability as the bigger setups, but has a more limited capacity. When selecting a gas welding outfit, it is essential to pick one using oxygen cylinders (the cheap, pelletized-oxygen units have neither the capacity nor the durability for the heat applications you will encounter while disassembling your truck). For the fuel gas, you can use either acetylene or MAPP (short for stablized methylacetylene-propradiene). Propane does not produce enough heat.

In selecting an air compressor, you need to consider the horsepower rating of the motor and the size of the air storage tank. Hobby-sized portable air compressors with motor ratings of 3 or 4 hp will be adequate if also coupled with a 30 gallon (minimum) air tank. For sandblasting and extensive use of air tools, you are better off to consider a stationary air compressor with a 5 hp or stronger motor and a 40 gallon or larger air tank.

Spray Painting Gun and Air Tools

Even if you decide to have a professional apply the finish coat, you will save a great deal of money (and transportation hassle) if you apply the primer coat. For any automotive painting, an external-air-source spray painting gun is essential. Further, the quality of the gun determines (to a large extent) the quality of the paint application. Along

Another useful specialty tool is the hydraulic press. This tool could be used to replace the king pin bushings in the wheel spindles.

with the spray gun you will need a professional-grade painting mask, moisture filter at the compressor outlet and quick-connect couplings on the gun and air hose. A more in-depth discussion of spray painting equipment is provided in chapter 11.

Air tools save time with both mechanical and body work. Among the more popular air tools are impact and socket wrenches, die-grinder, drill, cut-off tool and sanders. These tools need a large volume of air to operate efficiently, hence the concern for large air storage and recovery capability.

Sandblaster

As you will learn in the next chapter on cleaning and derusting, there are two types of sandblasters: siphon and pressurized. If you purchase an air compressor, you will most likely want to add a sandblaster to your tool inventory. Siphon sandblasters are quite inexpensive and work well for smaller jobs. You will find that owning a sandblaster also boosts your popularity with fellow old-truck restorers.

Since the restoration of a vintage vehicle calls for body and mechanical repair work that is quite different than that done on newer trucks, you will find a number of other specialty tools helpful for work such as buffing bright trim, cutting and shaping body repair panels and many other jobs. A wide assortment of specialty tools for restoration work is available from The Eastwood Company in Malvern, Pennsylvania (see appendices for address). Ordering Eastwood's catalog will familiarize you with tools that apply for specific applications. When specialty tools are needed, or advised, for various repair or restoration procedures, they will be listed in the chapter.

Tool Storage

If you are going to build up a good set of tools, you will want to take care of them. The three basic choices for tool storage are: a tool box, a roller cabinet or a combination of both. The tool box must have easily working drawers, a functional lock and enough room so that the tools don't lie on top of each other. After that, it is really personal preference. The basic tool set should fit into a tool box. As you add to your collection, however, you may find a roller cabinet is better suited to your tool storage needs. Beware of low-quality roller cabinets often seen in discount marts that are undersized, flimsily built and have such small rollers that they do not move around easily. Quality roller cabinets and accompanying tool boxes that are designed to sit on the top of the cabinet are available from Sears as well as professional tool suppliers like Snap-on.

Tool Quality Versus Price

Tools can be categorized in three ways: bad, good and excellent. Bad tools are the cheapest, both in cost and quality. Examples are the "Made in Taiwan" tools found in discount marts. These tools aren't worth bringing home. I bought one of the cheap screwdriver sets once and chipped the blade on the first screw I attempted to turn.

An example of good tools is the Sears Craftsman line. These tools come with a lifetime guarantee, have a high standard of quality and sell at a reasonable price. An added attraction of Craftsman tools is that they are offered at low sale prices periodically during the year. Another benefit is that most Sears stores will replace broken tools on-the-spot with no questions asked.

In the excellent tool category are Snap-on, Mac or other professional brands. These are the highest quality tools made—and the most expensive. They not only have a look of quality, but feel different in your hand: like a well broken-in baseball glove. These tools also come with a lifetime guarantee and in most cases will outperform any other make of tool, including Craftsman. One measure of tool performance is the tool's fit on a rusted bolt. A Snap-on dealer once had me try one of his wrenches on a rusted bolt that my Craftsman wrench would simply slip off. The Snap-on wrench not only took a firm grip, but turned the bolt loose.

The quality-to-price ratio of Craftsman tools is hard to beat, though. If you are working within a budget, Craftsman tools are the best way to go. But if you truly enjoy mechanical work, expect to work on vehicles for years to come, and can afford them, then Snap-on, Mac or other professional tools are what you want. Their quality look will increase your pride in your work and you will find that once you have developed the feel of working with high-quality tools, picking up a lesser quality tool will give you the feeling that you're just holding a chunk of steel in your hand.

4

Cleaning, Sandblasting and Derusting

As you take your truck apart you will encounter years of caked grease and grime on mechanical parts and most likely rust on the body metal. Removing grease coatings from mechanical parts not only makes rebuilding assemblies like the engine and front end easier, but thorough cleaning is also important if your truck is to have that fresh from the showroom look. Welding doesn't work well on rusted panels and paint won't adhere over rust, so stripping off paint and thoroughly derusting body metal are the preparation steps to bodywork and refinishing.

Cleaning and derusting are the biggest challenges facing any old-truck rebuilder or restorer. Your thoroughness will determine the outcome of all subsequent rust repair and refinishing steps, as well as the truck's overall appearance when you're done. Actually, cleaning and derusting consist of

three different processes that can either be done separately, or in some cases in combination. These processes are: degreasing, paint removal, and derusting.

There are various methods for cleaning and derusting your truck that you can use to prepare your truck for the next steps of mechanical and metal repair. If you are taking the restoration approach, cleaning and derusting is the first major step after complete disassembly. If you are taking the repair approach, you will clean various mechanical components as you overhaul them. Derusting may occur at isolated stages as you repair and refinish your truck's sheet metal. As you will

Small parts can be cleaned quickly and easily in an alkaline solution consisting of household lye (used for opening clogged drains) and water. Raising the water temperature increases the speed with which the alkaline solution will clean the metal, so it's best to clean the parts on a warm day and to fill the parts-cleaning container with hot water. Another alternative is to place the cleaning solution in a metal container and apply heat via a propane stove.

The degreasing spray at a coin-op car wash works well to clean mechanical parts. After degreasing, rinse the parts with a clear water spray. Where water could collect internally, as with these carburetors, be sure to dump out the water to prevent corrosion and other problems. Car washes should also provide proper water filters in their drains to protect the environment from hazardous chemicals.

discover, cleaning and derusting can be a time-consuming process that is done more efficiently all at once rather than piecemeal. This means that if you are taking the repair approach, you may find it expedient to clean or derust as much of your truck as possible without taking the truck apart.

Degreasing

The typical chassis on an older truck is coated with grease and road debris an inch or more thick in places. It may also be covered with a scale of rust. There are several methods for cleaning heavy grease from engine and chassis components. The easiest is to take the chassis (or the truck if you are using the rebuilding approach) to a shop that does steam cleaning—if such a place exists in your community. If a steam cleaning service isn't available, you may still have the option of renting a steam generator from a tool rent-all shop and

cleaning the chassis yourself. Steam jennies, as they're called, are about the size of a large, portable air compressor and consist essentially of a pump and boiler that produce a high volume of steam, which is then blasted against the grease-coated chassis parts at great pressure. To help in the cleaning action, detergent is often mixed with the water being converted into steam.

Using a steam jenny requires no special training except the caution to wear protective clothing to avoid scalding yourself with the steam. The steam nozzle is simply worked back and forth against the grease-coated chassis parts until all the grease and debris have been washed away. Using a steam jenny, you can clean an entire chassis, including the engine, transmission and rear axle, in a few hours.

If a steam jenny isn't available from a local tool rent-all, you may find a power washer to be nearly as effective. This tool can be connected to a hot-water faucet and also mixes detergent with high-pressure water spray for fast, effective cleaning. A power washer is a tool you may wish to own. It can also be rented from most any tool rent-all.

Another alternative is to haul your truck's mechanical parts to a nearby car wash and use the engine cleaner cycle to degrease the parts. You will

The caustic solution cleans off grease and paint, but does not remove rust. With small parts, rust can be removed using chemicals like mild phosphoric acid. When working with alkaline degreasing or acid derusting chemicals, safety precautions need to be observed. Be sure to wear goggles or other eye coverings and protective clothing, including rubber gloves. If any chemical splashes into the eyes or onto the skin, wash the contacted area immediately with clean water.

After a few minutes in the alkaline bath, most parts will be ready for rinsing and preparation for refinishing.

38

find this approach to be more effective if you scrape off heavy grease buildup first with a putty knife. The car wash method works essentially like a power washer. The difference is that you bring the parts to the wash location, as opposed to the other way around.

If you are working with a small budget and time is of less concern than expense, you can clean the chassis the old-fashioned way with a putty knife, scrub brush and solvent. This approach can be time consuming, but the only cost may be a few scrub brushes and several gallons of solvent. When degreasing engine and chassis parts by hand, you'll save yourself a lot of time by first scraping off the buildup, using a good grease-cutting solvent like Gunk, and working in warm temperatures. If the grease coating is fairly thin and you work the solvent into the grease residue with a scrub brush, when you hose off the solvent the metal will wash clean enough for sandblasting. If the metal doesn't need derusting, you should inspect the degreased area closely for any traces of grease buildup, then remove whatever grease remains, and wash off the degreaser with a painting preparation solvent. At this point the metal should be ready for refinishing.

To prevent the bare metal from rusting, the parts should be treated with a mild phosphoric acid solution—available at automotive paint supply stores and specialty suppliers under trade names like Panel Prep. This acid treatment will also help ensure that the primer coat bonds well with the metal.

Because gasoline is flammable it shouldn't be used as a degreasing solvent. Instead, use a less flammable fuel like kerosene or a commercial parts-cleaning solvent. To protect your skin, rubber gloves and long clothing should be worn when working with any solvent. It is also important to protect your eyes by wearing safety glasses or a face shield.

Alkaline Degreaser Bath

An effective degreasing bath for cleaning smaller parts can be made by setting up an alkaline solution in a large metal pail, old oil drum or even a container as large as a livestock watering tank. The alkaline degreasing solution consists simply of household lye (sold in grocery stores either as lye or Drano) and water in a mixture of approximately 24 oz. of lye per gallon of water. A metal container is advised because heat can then be applied to raise the temperature of the degreasing bath.

In setting up an alkaline bath for my parts degreasing needs, I have used a 55 gallon oil drum in which I have poured about 40 gallons of water and 96–120 oz. of lye. To heat the alkaline solution, I placed the oil drum on concrete blocks and built a small wood fire underneath. As an alternative to a wood fire, a propane heater can be used. When heated to near boiling, the lye solution will remove even heavily caked-on grease coats in just a few minutes. The alkaline solution works equally well removing paint. I found that the 55 gallon oil drum would hold wheels, front-end assemblies, transmission housings and engine blocks, as well as

Sandblasting is the fastest method for stripping large assemblies like the chassis. Note the industrial-capacity portable air compressor in the background. Sandblasting requires a great volume of air. With the equipment shown here, the entire chassis can be stripped clean in little more than an hour. Working with a small, hobby-sized compressor, this same job would take the better part of a day—or longer. Mike Cavey

39

The running gear has been left in place for sandblasting because in this frame-up restoration everything will be taken apart, cleaned and rebuilt later. Otherwise there would be danger of sand contaminating and destroying bearings and other moving parts. Mike Cavey

A simple barrier like this V-shaped enclosure prevents sand dust from blowing out of the sandblasting area. A barrier like this also helps conserve sand since the sand residue can be swept up, strained and reused at least once. Mike Cavey

other smaller parts. Caution: Do not immerse mechanical assemblies in the alkaline solution unless they are taken apart or will be disassembled and rebuilt later.

Numerous other cautions apply to the alkaline bath degreasing method. Always wear rubber gloves and a full covering of clothing. Tie lengths of wire to the parts before dipping them into the bath so that you won't have to fish the parts out of the solution. Small parts can be immersed in a wire mesh container. Always wear face protection to prevent the alkaline solution from splashing into your eyes. It is extremely important to make sure that children and animals cannot reach the alkaline bath. Options are to set up the alkaline solution inside your shop and make sure the container is covered and access doors are locked when the alkaline bath is not in use, or to build a secure enclosure around the bath if it is outside. You will also need to haul the solution to a sealed landfill after the degreasing business is finished. Although the alkaline degreasing method is effective, if you question your ability to follow these safety demands you should use another approach.

Sandblasting

Following degreasing, most parts will need to be cleaned of what remains of the old finish and whatever rust lies on the surface or has penetrated more deeply into the metal. As with degreasing, paint and rust can be removed by several methods. The most common and inexpensive paint- and rust-removal method is sandblasting. Other methods use chemicals. Attempting to remove paint and rust by a sanding, grinding or wire-brushing is not very effective since these mechanical methods can abrade the metal and leave seeds of rust in visible or microscopic pits that will fester and bleed through after the metal is repainted.

In many communities you will find commercial sandblasting outfits listed in the Yellow Pages. These businesses will strip paint and rust from chassis parts, wheels, bumpers and sheet metal for generally reasonable prices. The main disadvantage to commercial sandblasting is your lack of control over the sandblasting process. While a commercial sandblaster isn't likely to damage a bumper or frame, high-pressure sandblasting can easily warp sheet metal. If you will be resorting to sandblasting to strip and derust body parts, you

either need to make sure the commercial sandblaster agrees to be very careful with these parts to avoid warpage (and then expect to have to do some straightening) or sandblast the metal yourself, taking great care not to stress the metal.

If you live in a suburban development, sandblasting at home may be against zoning regulations and is sure to upset your neighbors (the process is both noisy and dirty), but if you live in a more rural setting the equipment investment to do your own sandblasting is reasonable enough that you may well decide to set up your own sandblasting operation. To do so, you will need an air compressor, preferably 4 hp or larger with a minimum of a 30 gallon air storage capacity. These heavier-duty home-shop air compressors are available from Sears, as well as farm and specialty tool suppliers. An air compressor should be considered a basic shop item as it is also used to power air tools (impact wrenches, sanders, grinders, drills, buffers) and spray painting equipment, as well as a sandblasting outfit.

Most portable air compressors need two modifications before being used to power a sandblaster. The first is to install a moisture separator between

After sandblasting and disassembly, the truck is just a collection of parts. Those items not needing metal work should be primed and painted promptly to prevent rerusting. As with alkaline stripping, sandblasted *metal should be treated with mild phosphoric acid to retard rusting and help ensure strong paint adhesion.*
Mike Cavey

the outlet connection on the compressor and the air hose. Typically, the air hose is connected directly to the air tank, allowing moisture that builds up inside the tank—particularly when operating the compressor on humid days—to pass into the sandblaster through the air hose. Any moisture passing through the air hose will almost instantly clog the sandblaster. A moisture separator does what the name says—it removes moisture from the air stream, allowing only dry air to travel down the air hose. These are inexpensive devices that can be purchased from the company selling the air compressor. The other modification required for many hobby-sized air compressors is to replace the restrictive ¼ in. air hose with ⁵⁄₁₆ in. (minimum) inside-diameter air hose, no longer than 50 ft. Sections of hose should not be spliced together due to the air restriction at the connection. These modifications are also recommended when running air tools and for spray painting.

Siphon and Pressure-Feed Units

Sandblasting units are of two types: siphon and pressure feed. Both are available from restoration tool suppliers like Tip Sandblasting, The Eastwood Company and others (see appendices for details). The siphon-style sandblaster is cheaper, but also less effective than the pressure unit. Basically, a siphon sandblaster sucks sand into the air stream that is blown through the nozzle by the air compressor. A siphon sandblast is not as strong as a pressurized blast and uses more air—an important factor considering the limited capacity of smaller, home-shop-sized air compressors. This does not mean you should rule out a siphon sandblaster. If you will primarily be sandblasting small parts (either your truck is largely rust-free or you plan to have the larger parts commercially sandblasted or chemically derusted), the siphon blaster will work fine. I own a siphon unit and have used it to clean my truck's door trim panels, license plate brackets and other smaller parts. It handles jobs of this size very easily. However, on anything larger (a wheel, for example), the siphon sandblaster has proven to be more trouble than it's worth.

A pressure-style sandblaster does as its name implies: it pressurizes a sealed container and uses that pressure to blow sand out through the nozzle. The result is a more powerful blast and more efficient use of compressed air.

Sandblasting Basics

There isn't much art to sandblasting. Basically, you point the nozzle at the part and blast off the

Once every square inch of metal is cleaned of paint and rust, metal repair can begin. Note that small patch work has been performed on the lower front and side edges of the cowl. Mike Cavey

paint and rust. Sandblasting isn't very effective against grease, which is the reason that heavy grease buildup has to be removed first. You will find that blasting at an angle seems to wash off the paint and rust and is not so likely to stress and warp the metal. However, on large, relatively flat panels like the hood, it is best to sandblast only on reinforced areas and strip the paint from the rest of the panel with paint remover or a D/A (dual action) sander. Other than that, basic sandblasting precautions are to wear full-length clothing, protective gloves (welding gloves work well), a sandblasting hood and a dust mask. Some tie their shirt sleeves and pants cuffs when sandblasting in an attempt to prevent dust from blowing inside their clothing, but not much is gained as the dust sifts in anyway.

Coarse sandblasting sand is available from most auto parts stores, but regular sand from a building supplier, beach or sand pit works nearly as well and is less expensive—often free. The main advantage of sandblasting sand is the sand's extra-coarse grit which enables it to be reused, sometimes several times. If you shovel your own sand from a beach or sand pit, be sure the sand has dried thoroughly before sandblasting. Nothing produces

greater frustration than trying to sandblast with moist sand. The nozzle will clog as soon as you start, and each attempt to unclog the blockage will soon be followed by reclogging. If the sand is damp when you are ready to start blasting, spread a tarp on a sunny area of your driveway and cover it with a thin layer of sand. When the sand turns white it is dry and ready to be used. If you decide to blast with sand you've gathered yourself (from a beach or sand pit), you will need to strain the sand through a window screen or similar fine mesh before using. If you don't strain the sand, larger pebbles and debris will clog the sandblaster's nozzle.

Problems

The biggest problem a restorer encounters when trying to sandblast at home is an insufficient air supply. As mentioned earlier, the minimum-sized compressor should have a 3 to 4 hp motor and at least 30 gallons of air storage capacity. But even this size air compressor will require frequent resting periods to restore the air supply. Periodically you should give the unit a rest to let the compressor cool down. If you find the air compressor you own to be inadequate for the amount of sandblasting you are doing, one solution is to bor-

The inside of the cab will be completely stripped and derusted as well. All glass, instruments, wiring, hard- *ware and interior coverings must be removed before sandblasting.* Mike Cavey

43

row a friend's portable compressor (or rent a portable unit from a tool rent-all) and power the sandblaster from both compressors. (You will need to connect the air lines from the two compressors with a Y-fitting.) Borrowing a friend's compressor might be an occasion for you to work together sandblasting parts for both of your vehicles. Sandblasting with two people will be a faster operation, since one can keep the blaster full while the other handles the parts. The other answer to a limited compressed air supply is to rent a commercial-sized air compressor and use this rig while you are doing larger sandblasting jobs like stripping the frame.

Another of the problems with sandblasting is the volume of dust it produces. One way to avoid this, and to economize on sand, is to build a two- or three-sided pen in which the sandblasting will be done. The pen walls need be no higher than 3-4 ft.

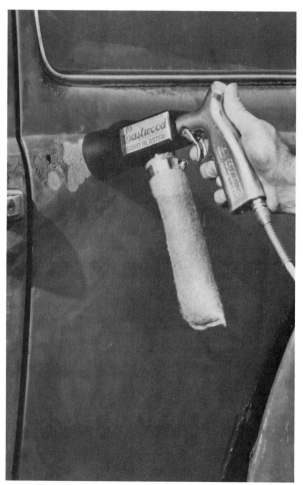

When the truck isn't being completely disassembled, a spot sandblaster is ideal for cleaning rusted areas to bare metal. The rubber nozzle contains the sandblast so that the tool can be used near window glass and trim. The spot sandblaster is easily powered by a hobby-sized air compressor. The Eastwood Company

and 8-10 ft. long. You will place parts to be sandblasted in the center of the pen and blast toward the walls. This way most of the sand and much of the dust will settle inside the pen. The sand can be scooped up and reused at least once. The fine dust can be swept up and disposed of on the garden, lawn or other spot where it can work into the soil.

Sandblasting is an effective way to rid metal parts of rust because the tiny sand grains penetrate into pits and scour out all traces of corrosion, however microscopic. However, sandblasting is not very effective for cleaning hidden areas like the insides of doors, rocker panels and boxed frames. If rust is left unchecked in these areas, you're likely to find corrosion blistering through the metal in a few years. Ways to remove or neutralize rust on hidden surfaces are described in the chemical cleaning methods that follow.

Treating Sandblasted Parts

The bare metal that is exposed by sandblasting needs to be treated to prevent rusting, which will occur rapidly if any moisture is present. For short-term rust protection, and to ensure good paint adhesion, wash freshly sandblasted parts with metal prep—a dilute phosphoric acid solution available from auto parts stores as a painting preparation product under a variety of names including Metal Prep, Metal Etch and others. Tell the counter clerk that you are looking for a dilute acid product to etch bare metal in preparation for painting. You can apply the acid solution with an old paintbrush or rag. Douse the part liberally (while keeping it off your clothes) and let the solution run into seams and crevices. When the chemical dries, the treated metal will be a dull gray color. If you need to store the parts temporarily before painting, place them in as dry a location as possible. If longer storage is planned, prime the metal with a nonlacquer-based primer. If you use a lacquer-based primer or leave the parts bare and they are stored in a high-moisture environment, you will quickly see your efforts dissolve in a fresh coating of rust.

One further caution: Be careful not to sandblast mechanical parts such as front-end or rear-end assemblies unless these units will be completely disassembled and rebuilt. *Never* sandblast the engine or transmission. Sandblasting will leave the bearings of mechanical assemblies packed full of grit, which will quickly grind these delicate parts to scrap.

Chemical Paint Stripping

Alternatives to sandblasting use chemicals to clean off paint and rust. We'll discuss paint stripping first, since older paint coatings should be removed before applying a new finish. A number of commercial chemical paint-stripping products are available from auto supply stores as well as specialty restoration supply shops. Most are brushed or sprayed on, allowed to work and the paint is then scraped off with a putty knife. The problem with these products is that the paint doesn't scrape clean. More often, the stripper will lift one layer at a time. This means tedious scraping to remove each layer. Often, you'll end up sanding off a paint coating that no amount of stripper seems to loosen.

For removing most factory enamel or urethane finishes, you will have more success using a stripping product called Wet/Dry, distributed by T.N. Cowan Enterprises out of Alvarado, Texas (see appendices for address). What makes this paint stripping product unique is that it penetrates into the paint and dries. Rather than scraping a wet, gooey paint layer, with Wet/Dry the paint actually flakes off. Not only does it work quickly, it also eliminates the need to work with caustic chemicals. But before you conclude that this product is the answer, you should know that Wet/Dry does not work well with lacquer or finishes that contain a mixture of paints. It is most successful with factory enamels.

Commercial Metal Cleaning

Because paint stripping can be a time-consuming task, many restorers prefer to sandblast metal parts (eliminating both paint and rust at the same time) or use a commercial chemical stripping method that not only removes paint and rust, but will also dissolve Bondo and any other nonmetal coatings. This stripping and derusting process, which combines caustic chemicals with electrolysis, is done by commercial establishments that often call themselves "metal laundries." Many belong to the RediStrip franchise chain. The locations of chemical metal-stripping firms can be found in the Yellow Pages of telephone directories for larger cities, and in listings that appear in old-car hobby magazines like *Hemmings Motor News* and *Old Cars News and Marketplace*.

With commercial metal cleaning, the parts to be cleaned are placed in large tanks containing caustic chemicals (many establishments have tanks large enough to submerse the entire truck cab or box). A combination of chemical action and electrolysis dissolves paint and eats away rust in anywhere from a few minutes to a few hours, depending on the condition of the parts. The advantages of commercial metal cleaning are that all the metal is cleaned, even hidden inside surfaces, the process does not abrade or eat away good metal, the only work you have to do is transport the parts to the derusting establishment, and the caustic chemical bath will dissolve any body filler, leaving the parts ready for metal repair and

If the truck is basically rust-free, the old finish can be removed with paint stripper. Paint stripping products can be purchased locally through auto parts stores that sell refinishing supplies, and from specialty mail-order *restoration services. The Advance Design pickup shown here is being stripped to bare metal by a chemical paint-removing process.*

finishing. Many firms will apply a protective phosphoric coating to the parts after cleaning to retard rerusting and improve paint adhesion.

Despite the benefits of commercial metal cleaning, this method is not without disadvantages. The service can be quite expensive—several hundred dollars for an item the size of the truck cab—and there have been reports of the caustic chemicals leaching out of body seams after painting. If chemicals are trapped in seams where the body panels are joined, they will eventually work to the surface of the metal where they will bubble away the paint. If this should happen, the only way to stop the paint from lifting would be to try to bake the chemical out of the seam with heat—a process that has no assurance of success.

Derusting

Besides commercial metal cleaning, there are two chemical derusting processes you can do at home. One uses a mild acid to eat away the rust; the other converts the rust into a stable, protective coating. Acid derusting works best with smaller parts that can be dipped in a plastic container holding a mild solution of phosphoric acid. While other acids can also be used to derust ferrous metal parts, phosphoric acid is preferred because it is inexpensive, less dangerous than other more caustic acids like sulfuric or hydrochloric, works in a relatively short time frame and leaves a protective coating that actually improves the paint bond with the metal. Dilute phosphoric acid is available

from local automotive paint supply stores and restoration suppliers like The Eastwood Company under product names such as Twin Etch and Oxi-Solv. Instructions on the container give mixing proportions with water—typically 1:1. A lidded plastic pail makes the best container for the acid derusting solution since the chemical quickly develops a rotten-egg smell.

Rusted metal should be completely immersed if possible and checked at frequent intervals (every hour or so for a fresh acid bath; older acid works more slowly). Acid derusting will eat away the

Smaller metal parts and assemblies can be derusted at home using mild phosphoric acid solutions or a phosphoric acid gel. The caution here is to keep the acid away from your eyes and skin (rubber gloves are advised) and to avoid derusting chassis parts like the wheels and brake drums by this method. Acid derusting can produce hydrogen embrittlement, which could cause a stressed part to crack or break.

Metal laundries, as the commercial rust- and paint-removing services call themselves, are equipped with huge tanks that can hold an entire chassis, cab or pickup box. Rust is removed in these tanks by a process called reverse electrolysis. The advantage of commercial stripping and rust removal is that this process does not eat into the metal. Also, rust and paint are removed from hidden inside surfaces as well as visible external surfaces. The cleaned and derusted parts are often given a phosphoric acid coating to retard rerusting. Note the large metal basket used for immersing smaller parts. Before taking parts to the commercial metal laundry, call for a cost estimate. This service can be expensive.

46

metal as well as the rust and if the parts are left in too long, they can be destroyed. It's best to try a few scrap parts first, to get used to the speed of the chemical action. Be careful not to dip nonferrous metal parts (brass or aluminum) in the acid derusting bath because they will dissolve quickly.

Acid derusting will not work on painted or grease-coated surfaces, so it is necessary to first make sure that the parts are stripped to bare metal. For larger metal parts such as fenders that won't fit in an acid derusting bath, acid gels can be used to clean surface rust or even areas of heavier rusting. These gels are available in two forms: common Naval Jelly, which can be purchased at virtually any hardware store, and Jenolite, a somewhat more concentrated acid gel available from T.N. Cowan Enterprises. Like any acid derusting treatment, the gel will not work over paint or grease. Terry Cowan recommends sanding painted metal with surface rust with a D/A (dual action) sander before applying Jenolite. Another approach is to remove the paint with a paint stripper, then apply the acid gel. As the gel dries, it leaves a dark gray coating. If any traces of corrosion remain, a second acid treatment can be applied (the acid gel is wiped onto the metal with a paintbrush). When all rust has been removed, the metal can be primed right over the acid coating.

Although mild acids or acid gels provide an effective derusting, there are two drawbacks to this approach. One is the fact that acid removes rust by eating into the metal. This means that some good metal is lost, along with the rust. If the metal is thin, due to severe rusting, it's possible that in the process of getting rid of the rust, the acid treatment may also destroy what good metal remains. The other problem with acid derusting is that the acid can cause something called hydrogen embrittlement which weakens the metal and can cause parts that are stressed to crack and break. For this reason, suspension parts, wheel, brake drum or other components on which the car's mechanical safety depends should not be derusted using the acid method.

Rust Neutralizing

Another derusting process called rust neutralizing doesn't remove rust, but converts it to an inert coating that seals the metal against further rusting. Rust converter products, such as Zintex from T.N. Cowan, have a watery consistency and can be sprayed, brushed or poured onto the metal. The rust conversion treatment works particularly well on inner door surfaces, much of which can't be reached by sandblasting, or chassis parts that you don't want to sandblast and shouldn't derust with acid.

As with the acid derusting processes, it is necessary that the surface be clean of grease and

paint. If possible, loosen any rust scale with a wire brush. If you are treating the inside surfaces of the doors with rust converter, it helps to have the doors off the vehicle and placed horizontally (outside skin down). Then you can simply pour on enough rust converter to cover the inside surface through the opening in the inner door panel. You can spread the neutralizer evenly over the inside surface of the outer door skin by picking up the door (it's good to have help with this) and tipping it up and down and from side to side. This will also let the neutralizer penetrate into seams. When you feel that the outer skin is completely coated, flip

The acid bath removes rust by eating into the metal. Avoid dipping soft metals into the bath as they will be quickly consumed. Wire brushing to break up heavier rust scale speeds up the derusting process.

Rust converters like the product shown here can be sprayed into areas that you can't reach with conventional rust-removal methods. This treatment actually alters the rust molecules through a chemical conversion process into a nondestructive black oxide similar to gun bluing or black oxide plating.

the door over to coat the inner panel. Some of the liquid will spill out through the panel opening, so it's a good idea to spread out newspapers on the shop floor in the area where you are doing this.

As the rust converter works, the rusty surface will turn from red-orange to black. The black color indicates that the rust (iron oxide) has been converted to iron phosphate, an inert coating on the surface of the metal that will block further rusting. After the black coating appears, the instructions call for washing the metal, then sealing the surface with a coat of paint. To prime the inner door surfaces, you can use the same method used for spreading on the neutralizer. Let the primer coat dry, and repeat with a finish coat.

Rust converter penetrates into pits and seams and is ideal where rust removal is impossible or impractical. This process can also be used in combination with other rust-removing methods. In reality, no one rust-removing process is ideally suited for all conditions. More likely, you will use a combination of degreasing and paint- and rust-removal methods to bring your truck to the point where it is ready for metal work, refinishing and mechanical rebuilding.

Completion of the cleaning and derusting steps marks the turning point in the restoration or repair sequence. Up to this stage, you have been undoing. From this point on (with the exception of mechanical assemblies) you will be redoing. With sheet metal, the next steps will be to remove dents, repair rust damage and tears, and perform the refinishing process. Time spent in cleaning and derusting may not be visible in the overall restoration or repair sequence, but these steps are extremely important to the appearance of the finished product. Of course, cleaned parts are also much easier and more pleasurable to work with. Now the dirty work is behind and you can progress toward your goal—a truck you can step out in with pride.

5

Gas Welding Techniques

One of the most useful tools for restoring or over-hauling an old truck is a gas welding outfit. Mechanics often refer to their welding torch as a gas wrench, and for good reason. Rust-frozen exhaust manifold studs, king pins and chassis bolts are virtually impossible to remove without heat. If you do manage to turn the bolt, more than likely it will break off—and in the case of a manifold stud this means drilling out the bolt and retapping the hole, a time-consuming and frustrating task. In the

The first step to gas welding is lighting the torch. To do this, just the fuel gas valve is turned on and lit with a torch igniter. Do not use a butane cigarette lighter to ignite a gas welding torch. The lighter could explode causing serious injury or death. Once the fuel gas flame has been lit, the oxygen valve at the torch handle is opened and adjusted until the correct shape and heat intensity flame is achieved.

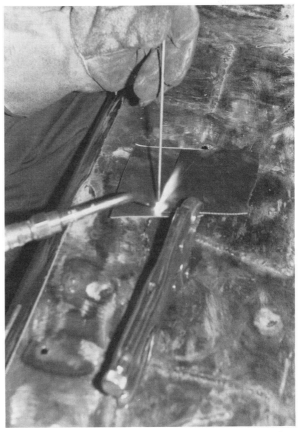

Here is an overlap joint, one of the methods for welding in patch panels, being practiced by a welder. Unless you are an experienced welder, you should practice with small pieces of metal scrap as shown here before setting out to weld patch panels into your truck. Note that the two pieces of metal are tightly clamped together with vise grips. A filler rod is being used to fuse the metal at one end of the overlap joint.

case of rust-frozen king pins, the only way to remove the pins without heat may be to disassemble the axle as much as possible and take it to a machine shop where the pins can be forced out with a hydraulic press. Using a gas welding torch to heat the axle ends is a much easier and quicker approach. Of course, a gas welding outfit can be used for repairing metal as well. Once you purchase a gas welding outfit, you will wonder how you worked on older vehicles (and newer ones, too, for that matter) without it.

As mentioned earlier, you purchase the set of gauges, hoses, and welding and cutting torches, plus various-size torch tips. The tanks (one for oxygen and the other for the fuel gas) are typically rented. This equipment, plus a cart to move the tanks outfit around in your shop, is available in welding shops, auto supply stores and tool retailers like Sears.

Most gas welding outfits use acetylene as the fuel gas. When burned in pure oxygen (from the oxygen tank), acetylene yields temperatures in the

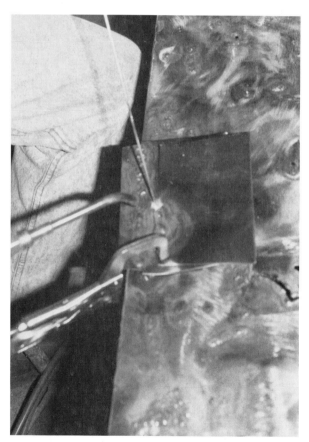

Notice that the patch is being joined with welds spaced about 1 in. apart. When gas welding thin-gauge body metal it is important not to overheat the panel to which the patch is being joined. One way to reduce heat build-up is to work across the panel with a series of tack beads. In a larger panel these would be made in an alternating pattern first on one end of the seam and then the other.

1,800 degrees Fahrenheit range required to heat metal to a cherry-red state. MAPP is an alternative fuel gas that has a couple of advantages for the hobbyist. First, it rates superior to acetylene in safety and ease of handling. Second, since it is distributed in liquid form, a MAPP canister provides more fuel pound for pound than an equivalent tank of acetylene. Finally, MAPP has nearly the same heat value as acetylene, making it effective for both welding and cutting.

Safety

When gas welding, it is essential that you carefully follow several safety rules. If you enroll in a welding class at a skill center or technical college, these will be taught at the outset of the class. If you learn to use a gas welding outfit from a book and practice, or are taught by a friend, you may overlook important safety steps. The principal safety rules to follow are:

• Never weld near flammable vapors or a gas tank.

• Never place the tanks in a position so they might fall over—a tank with a broken valve is lethal.

• Never run over the welding hoses with the welding cart or damage the hoses in any other way. Keep the hoses coiled up when not in use.

• Never oil the regulators, hoses, torches or fittings. The combination of oil and oxygen can produce a deadly explosion.

• Never use the oxygen jet to blow away dust, and never allow the oxygen jet to strike oily or greasy surfaces.

• Always wear welding goggles when looking at the flame.

• Always wear welding gloves and protective clothing.

• Do not carry a butane lighter in a pants or shirt pocket when welding. A spark from the welding operation could explode the lighter, with deadly consequences.

Gas Welding Techniques

Although welding takes some skill and practice, little skill is needed to use a gas welding torch to heat rust-frozen parts. Since you are not going to cut the metal, you do not need to use a cutting torch. Rather, you will use a welding torch with a medium to large tip. If you have purchased, but have not had instruction in how to use a gas welding outfit, then learning how to set the dials on the tanks and light the torch should be your first step. Instruction in welding (both gas and arc) is available at low cost from technical colleges and adult education programs sponsored by skill centers or vocational high schools. The classes are typically in the evenings and last for ten to sixteen weeks. Enrolling in a welding class will thoroughly acquaint you with safety principles as well as instruct you in the theory of welding technology, and provide sufficient practice to make you a moderately skilled welder. These steps for using a gas welding torch to heat rust-frozen bolts are not intended to replace formal instruction. Instead, they are intended as a quick reminder or review.

Step One

Before heating a rust-frozen bolt or other component to be removed from a vehicle, make sure that you will not be directing the torch in the direction of any flammable material (the gas tank, gas line, undercoating and so on). Before lighting the welding torch, you need to open the regulator valves on both the oxygen and fuel tanks. Make sure that both valves on the torch handle are closed before opening the regulator valves. Now you will open (turn counterclockwise) the valve on the oxygen cylinder (always painted green). Turn the valve slowly until the regulator pressure gauge reaches its maximum reading. Then turn the valve open all the way. Only the fuel tank valve is opened next. Open this valve just a quarter turn, so the fuel cylinder can be shut off quickly in an emergency.

Now adjust the oxygen pressure at the torch by opening the torch valve on the oxygen line (also green) and adjusting the oxygen regulator so that the low-pressure gauge (which registers the flow of oxygen to the torch) reads between 8 and 20 pounds per square inch (psi). When this setting is achieved, close the torch valve on the oxygen line.

Adjust the fuel pressure by repeating these steps with the torch valve on the fuel line. Set the fuel regulator so that the pressure reading is between 8 and 9 psi. (This is the pressure setting for a medium to large tip; a small to medium tip would require a pressure setting of 4 to 5 psi.)

Step Two

Before lighting the torch, it is important to purge the lines. This is done by briefly opening both torch valves. As soon as you hear the hiss of gas escaping from the torch, close the valves. Now you will light the torch. As the first step, open the fuel valve slightly (approximately one-half turn). As soon as the valve is opened, strike a spark at the tip with a torch lighter. Do not use matches and *never*

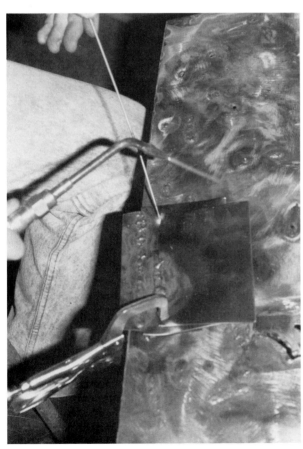

Now that the welder has placed tack welds along the end of the seam, he will come back filling in the gaps. Here, too, the gaps will be filled in an alternating pattern, first at one end of the seam and then the other.

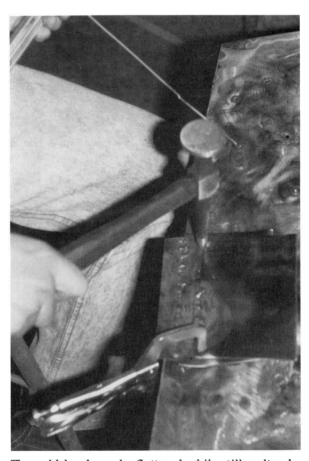

The weld bead can be flattened while still molten by striking it with a hammer. A variation of this technique called hammer welding is used by experienced body men to join metal with seams so smooth that little or no filler is needed.

use a cigarette lighter to ignite a welding torch. If you have opened the fuel valve too far, the flame will ignite, then blow out. If the setting is correct, a sooty, yellowish flame will lick out of the torch tip.

Open the oxygen valve at the torch slowly and gently. As you do so, the flame will change in shape and color. If you open the oxygen valve too far or too fast, the flame will blow out with a pop. If this happens, don't be alarmed. Just close the oxygen valve and relight the flame.

Step Three

Once the flame is burning in the oxygen supplied through the torch (rather than in the air), the oxygen and fuel gas need to be mixed for maximum heat. This is done by adjusting both valves until the correct proportions of fuel and oxygen are emerging from the tip. To achieve this setting, put on your welder's goggles and slowly open the oxygen valve. You will see the flame separate into three distinct parts: a small, light-colored cone at the tip, surrounded by a darker colored cone, and the flame's

Here the welder lays down a continuous bead of filler metal. This technique is used when heat warpage is not a problem, as in repairing cracks on thicker-gauge metal.

outer halo. A flame with a larger outer cone has too much fuel and too little oxygen. Continue to open the oxygen valve until the outer cone disappears and the inner cone has a smooth, round shape. When you have adjusted the flame to this description, you may need to increase the flow of both fuel and oxygen (in equal proportions) to achieve a hotter flame. As you increase the flame's strength, you will probably also need to readjust the oxygen and fuel settings to bring the flame back to the correct-shape cone.

Step Four

When heating metal to loosen rust-frozen bolts or king pins, always apply the heat to the area around the bolt or pin—never to the bolt or pin itself. Heat enables you to loosen a rust-frozen bolt by expanding the metal into which the bolt is threaded, thereby breaking the rust's grip. If possible, play the flame all the way around the bolt, keeping the torch moving, until the entire area begins to glow a cherry red. If you are heating a casting, like an exhaust manifold, and fail to keep the torch moving, heat will build in one spot and may crack the part.

When the metal begins to show that reddish glow, you can turn off the torch, grip the bolt with a socket or combination wrench and turn it loose. The bolt should turn fairly easily. If it doesn't, apply more heat—making sure to direct the torch toward the surrounding metal.

After removing the bolt, do *not* touch it with your bare hands and don't let the bolt drop or lie on a wooden floor. The bolt will have reached a temperature of several hundred degrees from the heat transferred through the adjoining metal and will take quite awhile to cool.

Step Five

When you are finished using the welding torch, always close the valves on both the oxygen and fuel tanks, then purge the lines by opening both valves at the torch. You will hear a momentary hiss as the gas in the lines escapes. Now close the valves at the torch, roll up the hose and hang it on the tanks so that it will not drape on the floor. Then roll the welding cart to a space in the shop where it will be out of the way.

A gas welding outfit is one of the handiest tools in an old-truck restorer's or rebuilder's shop. Not only does it make disassembling parts far easier, but it also prevents parts from being damaged beyond reuse during the disassembly process. Later, we'll see how the gas wrench can also be used in the repair and rebuilding process.

6

Front-End Overhaul

From 1918 until 1960, Chevrolet light trucks used essentially the same design for the front suspension—namely, a solid axle attached to the front of the frame by two semi-elliptical leaf springs. This simple design is very rugged and gives a moderately comfortable ride. But like any mechanical system, a straight-axle front end is also subject to wear and on most older trucks, both the suspension and steering linkage are worn enough to require a complete rebuild. The steps that follow describe the basic steps in overhauling any pre 1960 Chevrolet light truck front end. The intent is to give you an overview of the rebuilding sequence, and to point out some of the difficulties you are likely to encounter in working on parts that may be nearly as old, or older, than you are. Certain specifics may differ on

A straight-axle front end gets its name from the beam axle that connects both wheels and supports the springs. Chevrolet trucks used this style front axle from 1918 to 1959. Front-end overhaul procedures are more or less *the same during this forty-one-year period. The restored chassis of a 1951 Advance Design pickup is pictured here.* Mike Cavey

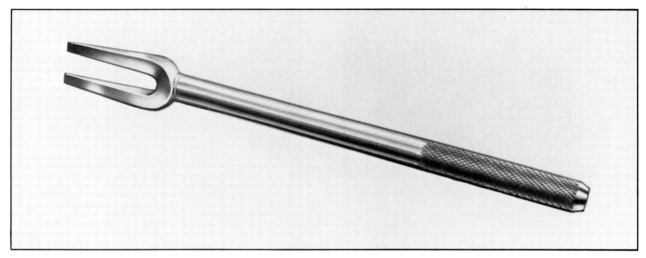

This tool, called a tie-rod separator, is used to pry apart the steering linkage. The Eastwood Company

your truck, so you may need to refer to a service manual for your year and model.

A straight-axle front end gets its name from the beam axle that connects both wheels and supports the springs that form the suspension system and hold the axle in place. Each end of the axle forms a yoke through which short, rugged steel shafts—called king pins—hold the spindle arms to the axle. These king pins allow the spindle arms to rotate on the axle yoke and in so doing allow steering movement for the front wheels. Attached to the spindle arms is a steering linkage consisting of a tie rod and drag link. This linkage connects both spindle arms so that when the steering wheel is turned in one direction, the front wheels track together in the same direction.

Rugged and durable though it is, this front suspension and steering system has several wear points which show up in sloppy steering that may become loose enough for the front wheels to chatter and shimmy after hitting a bump. Sloppy steering has a number of causes: worn king pins or bushings, worn tie-rod ends, loose wheel bearings, excessive wear or incorrect adjustment in the steering box, or a combination of these conditions. Along with loose steering, other front-end problems include a slouching front stance (the truck tips to one side or seems to settle lower than normal in the front) and rapid tire wear. A slouching front end traces to sagging or broken springs or worn spring shackles. Rapid tire wear can be caused by a bent axle or incorrect tie-rod adjustment that pitches the tires toward each other (called toe-in) or away from each other (called toe-out).

Tools

Rebuilding a straight-axle front end is within a handyman mechanic's skills, but requires a rather complete tool set, plus a few specialty items and shop manual. At a minimum, the tool set should consist of: a ½ in. socket set, hefty ball-peen hammer, assorted chisels, pliers, screwdrivers, punch set, bushing drivers, bushing reamer (optional), gas torch (optional, but recommended), puller, tie-rod separator (optional, but recommended), bench vise and shop manual. The shop manual will give an overview of the various repair sequences and is needed for toe-in and other settings.

Assessing Wear

A front-end overhaul should begin by checking its overall condition and diagnosing its problems. To do this, you will perform three simple tests. For the first test, grip the steering wheel and turn it back and forth slightly. As you do so, look for movement of the front wheels. If the steering wheel has a noticeable amount of free movement (called play) through which the front wheels are stationary, the tie-rod ends and steering linkage may be worn, the steering box may need adjusting or have internal wear or damage, or these conditions may exist in combination.

The second test requires that you park the truck on a level surface—which in most cases can be the garage floor. Here you will check for sagging or broken front springs and worn shackle bushings. This is done both visually and by measurement. For the visual check, sight along the springs. Are the springs curved in an arc, or are they essentially flat? Most front springs had some arc when new. Now closely inspect the individual leaves for breaks. Misalignment is another clue of a broken leaf. Often broken leaves can't be spotted until the spring is disassembled, but if one spring is flatter than the other (has more sag), you'll probably decide to remove and overhaul both springs. If you are taking the repair approach and the springs seem to have more or less normal arc and don't show any broken leaves, you probably should let well enough alone.

On a frame-up restoration, you will remove and disassemble both front springs, have leaves re-arced, then paint, lubricate and reassemble the spring assemblies. While inspecting the front suspension, also look for worn shackles (these are the brackets that attach the ends of the springs to the frame). Wear can usually be detected by elongated sockets at the spring eyes. As a sure test for spring sag and worn shackles, measure the distance from the floor (for this measurement to have meaning, it is crucial that the floor be level) to each frame horn. The difference in the two measurements is the amount of spring sag and possible shackle wear.

The third test checks for looseness anywhere in the front-end assembly. To do this, you will need to jack the front end off the ground and place jack stands under either end of the front axle. Now lower the truck onto the jack stands, making sure the stands are supporting the truck's weight, and block the back wheels to keep the truck from rolling. You can begin checking for looseness by inspecting the U-bolts that hold the springs to the axle. Sometimes a U-bolt is broken or loose. A broken U-bolt can actually cause the front axle to move as the truck is going down the road. Also inspect the bolts holding the steering box to the

frame. If the steering box is loose you can expect to feel play in the steering.

Next check the wheel bearings and king pins for play by gripping the tire with one hand on the top and the other on the bottom. Now attempt to rock the tire by jerking one hand toward you while pushing the other away. More than the smallest amount of free movement (about $3/16$ in. is tolerable) indicates that either the wheel bearings or king pins, or both, need service.

To make a final check for looseness in the steering assembly, grab hold of the ends of the tie rod (the long rod that connects the two wheels) and pull forcefully up and down to check for play. If the tie-rod end moves up and down, there is wear in the sockets and the socket ends will need to be serviced or replaced. If you twist the tie rod you

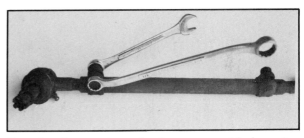

Tie rod and connecting rod ends are removed by loosening the clamp bolts and spreading the clamp. If the threads are rusted, it may be necessary to heat the metal surrounding the tie rod end.

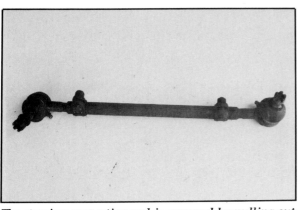

The steering connecting rod is removed by pulling out the cotter keys, loosening the nuts, then prying or driving the connecting rod studs out of the pitman and steering arms. Since the studs may be rusted in place, you may need to heat the ends of the pitman and steering arms with a torch before the studs will pop free.

Tie-rod ends on 1960 and later light-duty Chevrolet trucks are threaded into the tie rod and are replaceable. In most cases, these threaded tie-rod ends will be available through a local auto supply store.

may feel some rotating movement; this is normal. Make the same checks for looseness on the ends of the steering connecting rod.

After making these checks, you should write down all of the areas where you have noticed looseness. Front-end assemblies on older trucks typically show extensive wear due to infrequent lubrication and hard use over rough, unpaved roads. If your goal is restoration, you will probably decide to completely overhaul the front end. If your goal is to make the truck serviceable, you now know the areas that need attention. The next section describes how to bring a straight-axle front end back to safe operating standards.

Front End Disassembly

For restoration, you will completely disassemble and rebuild your truck's front-end suspension and steering system. This is the approach that will be described here. If you are upgrading your truck by repairs, you can begin your overhaul at whatever point is necessary, depending on your truck's problems, and follow the sequence from there.

Typically this is the point in a frame-up restoration where the body and other sheet metal have been removed from the chassis. The engine and drivetrain have also been pulled, leaving just the frame and front-axle assembly. To remove the axle and its attached suspension and steering components, you will start by disconnecting the shock absorber arm on lever-style shocks, or the nut from the lower rod on double-acting shocks. If the truck is equipped with a stabilizer bar, remove this next. Now you can disconnect the brake flex hoses (on trucks with hydraulic brakes) from the front wheel cylinders. In most cases these hoses will have dried out and cracked and will need to be replaced later during brake overhaul. If the hoses are in this condition, the simplest way to get them out of the way is just to cut them. On an earlier truck with a mechanical brake system, you will disconnect the front brake rods or cables instead of the hoses.

Now the steering connecting rod also needs to be removed. (This is the short rod on the left side that attaches to the pitman arm from the steering box; it is also commonly referred to as a drag link.) The steering connecting rod attaches to the pitman arm at the steering box and to the left steering arm by a tapered bolt, nut and cotter key. This rod is removed by pulling out the cotter keys, loosening the nuts, then prying or driving the connecting rod studs out of the pitman and steering arms. Since the studs are tapered and will have become tightly wedged into the holes in the pitman and steering arms, you'll find that attempting to separate the parts with a hammer isn't effective and will probably ruin the connecting rod for reuse.

A better approach is to use a special tool called a tie-rod separator which should pry out the studs with a minimum of effort. Another alternative is to force the stud out of the pitman and steering arm with the puller. Although the tie-rod separator and puller are effective on newer vehicles, on an older truck the connecting rod studs have probably been wedged in the sockets for a long time and the two are likely to be rust-frozen together. In this case you will need to heat the ends of the pitman and steering arms with an acetylene or MAPP gas torch. With some heat on the metal surrounding the connecting rod studs, the tapered studs should drive out of the pitman and steering arms easily. Since the ends of the steering connecting rod are not repairable, the entire rod will need to be replaced if the studs in the ends are worn or if the threads on the ends of the stud have been ruined during disassembly. Fortunately, replacement steering connecting rods are readily available from vintage Chevy truck parts suppliers.

The final step in removing the front-end assembly from the frame is to detach springs by taking apart the spring shackles. If the shackle bolts are rusted, they can be heated or cut with a torch. You will be replacing the spring shackles, so any damage to these parts is of no consequence. With the spring shackles apart, the front-axle assembly can be removed away from the frame to an area of the shop where it can be worked on further.

Front Axle Disassembly

In the next series of steps you will break down the front-end assembly into its individual components. When this is done, you can clean and degrease the parts, sandblast items as needed, then begin the rebuilding or refinishing process.

Spring Removal

You will start the disassembly steps by removing the springs. This is done by loosening the U-bolts that hold the springs to the axle. Typically the nuts to these bolts will be rust-frozen. Squirt plenty of penetrating oil on the nuts before attempting to loosen them. If you have access to a torch, heating the nuts will ensure they come off easily. Whenever possible, avoid damaging or destroying original nuts and bolts because modern replacements rarely match the originals in bolt-head size and appearance. When the U-bolts have been removed, you can further disassemble the springs by loosening the center bolt. Also, you need to remove the bushings from the spring eyes. This is best done with a bushing driver.

Keep the spring sets separate by tying together the leaves from each spring, or placing each set of leaves in a separate box. Label the springs left or right side as appropriate. Later, when the front-axle system is completely disassembled, you will clean and sandblast the spring leaves and have them re-arced. For now, you just want to make sure they don't get misplaced or mixed up with other parts.

Tie Rod Removal

Now you can remove the tie rod (the long rod running parallel to and just behind the front axle). On trucks through 1959, the tie rod attaches to a steering knuckle arm at either end through an adjustable end assembly. In 1960 and later light-duty Chevrolet trucks, the tie-rod ends are threaded into the tie rod and are replaceable.

To loosen the tie rod, remove the cotter keys that fit through the end plug in the tie-rod sockets. If the truck has been kept well lubricated, the end plug should be able to be loosened quite easily. A

The easiest place to disassemble the front suspension is out from under the truck. Air wrenches make fast work of removing nuts and bolts. A hefty hammer may be needed to drive out spring shackles and kingpins. Chrystal Edgerly

large-bladed screwdriver can be used to turn the plug. Lacking this, you can insert a chisel in the slot on the plug and turn the chisel with a crescent wrench. If the plug doesn't move, spray penetrating oil around the outline of the plug, let the oil soak in and try again. If the plug still won't budge, you will have to heat the metal around the plug with a torch. Once the plug turns freely, you will need to work the steering knuckle arm out from the tie-rod socket. When you have repeated this procedure at the other tie-rod end, the rod can be pulled free. Be sure to label and save all parts.

Brake Removal

To get at the wheel spindles (which attach to the yokes at the axle ends), you first have to take off the brake drums, disassemble the brakes and remove the backing plates. The brake drums should slide off rather easily after you loosen the spindle nut and remove the outer wheel bearing. Sometimes, however, the brake shoe contact area has worn so thin that there is a lip on the edge of the drum and this lip catches against the linings. If this is the case, you will have to loosen the brakes (back off the shoes) before the drum will pull loose. Be sure to use a wrench to turn the spindle nut, not a pliers. The serrated jaws on a set of pliers will cut into the nut, making it difficult to fit on a wrench when you or someone else decides to use the right tool. Also, be sure to separate right- and left-side bearings and other parts.

Once the brake drum is removed, you should pull the inner wheel bearing out of the drum. This is best done by using a special bearing puller. You can also remove the bearing by prying the bearing seal out of its groove and driving the bearing out of the race by gently tapping on the bearing cage with a punch. Another easier method for removing the inner wheel bearing is to replace the nut and washer on the spindle, then slip the brake drum over the nut and let the hub rest on the spindle. Now pull the drum toward you with a swift, sharp tug striking the inner bearing against the spindle nut. This will pop the bearing free without damage to the cage nearly every time.

Before removing the brake shoes and related parts, take photos of the brake assembly. These photos may be useful in reassembling the brakes later. Now you can remove the springs and clips holding the brake shoes in place. Be sure to save all parts. The service manual for your truck should explain the sequence for removing the brake shoes, but in most cases you should be able to work through this mechanical puzzle fairly easily. With the brake shoes out of the way, you will see the bolts holding the backing plates to the wheel spindles. Remove the cotter keys from the bolts at the nut end and loosen the nuts. The backing plates will then slide off the spindles. Set aside the bolts and nuts for plating. At this point you are ready to drive out the king pins and remove the wheel spindles from the axle.

King Pin Removal

The king pins fit through holes in the spindle and axle yoke. They are held in place by wedge-shaped locking pins that are driven through a small hole near the end of the axle and kept from working loose by a nut that is usually found on the back side of the axle. To remove these locking pins, loosen the nut and drive the pins out of their holes with a punch. You may also find dust seals at the top and bottom of both king pins. These are metal disks that have been wedged into the holes in the spindle yoke. It is not uncommon for these seals to be missing, either because they were not installed on an earlier overhaul, or because they have worked loose and fallen out. The dust seals are made of soft metal and can be removed easily by forcing a small, sharp chisel into the seal and prying it out of the hole. With the seals removed, you can attack the king pins.

Sometimes king pins will slide out of the axle as easily as pushing a knife through butter, but more often the pins are rusted to the axle and move about as willingly as a boulder being pushed by a toy truck. Before attempting to drive out the king pins, spray penetrating oil into the openings at the bottom and top of the spindle yoke, the locking pin hole and into the openings between the axle and spindle. It's difficult to get the oil directly into the hole in the axle end where the king pin is likely to be rust-frozen, but efforts should be made. After letting the oil penetrate, place the end of the axle on a cement block, anvil or other stationary object that will not absorb the force directed against the king pin, and attempt to drive the pin out of the axle using a hefty 24 oz. hammer and a punch that is slightly smaller in diameter than the pins. If the pin moves after several sharp blows, apply more oil.

If fortune is smiling, by alternating hammer blows on the pin with squirting oil into the openings, you will soon have the king pins out and the axle assembly completely apart. More likely, however, the king pins won't move in the least. If this happens, you have two alternatives. Assuming the front axle is out of the truck (as has been described in the preceding steps, but may not be the case if you are using a repair approach), you can take the axle to a machine shop and have the pins pressed out on a hydraulic press.

The other alternative (which you will have to use if the axle is still in the truck) is to heat the axle ends with a torch until the metal glows red. Note that a propane torch won't apply enough heat; you will have to use an oxy-acetylene or MAPP gas welding torch. Once the metal around the pins has been heated, you should be able to drive them out using strong, sharp blows as described earlier. You won't be reusing the king pins from your truck, so you can throw them out, along with their related hardware.

Cleaning, Derusting and Inspecting Parts

Now the axle assembly should be completely apart. Either at this point or after you have cleaned the spindles you will need to remove the king pin bushings from the spindle yokes. This is best done with a bushing driver. An alkaline degreasing bath (described in the previous chapter) will make short order of the accumulated grease and dirt commonly found on the front axle and its associated parts. Rust, which is likely to be found on the axle and brake drums, can be removed by sandblasting. Front-end parts should not be derusted using acid because of the danger of embrittling the metal.

After the axle has been cleaned, you should check it for trueness. Since many trucks have experienced rough use, it is not unusual to find that the front axle has been bent or twisted. You can check for twisting by laying the axle on its side on the shop floor and looking to see if both axle ends touch the floor (this assumes that the floor is smooth and level). You can check for bends by sighting along the axle. If evidence of twisting or bending exists, you need to take the axle to a machine shop and have it straightened.

The tie rod should also be checked for straightness. If this long rod is bent or kinked, you may want to consider finding another that is straight and true. The other option is to straighten the rod that you have. This should be done "cold." Heating the rod to straighten it will cause the metal to lose its temper and allow it to bend more easily in the future. While inspecting the tie rod, also check the condition of the steering arm balls which fit into the sockets on the ends of the tie rod.

Few trucks are maintained as conscientiously as cars and if lubrication has been neglected, the steering arm balls have probably worn into an egg shape. Out-of-round steering balls will cause the truck to steer hard and can also be a factor producing play in the steering. You have the choice of replacing the steering arms or having new balls welded onto the arms. These steering balls are available from vintage Chevrolet truck parts suppliers.

You should have the work of cutting off the old steering arm balls and welding on the new balls done at a machine shop. Strong welds here are critical. If a weld should fail and a steering ball break off on the road, the truck would go out of control.

If you haven't taken the springs apart, this needs to be done next. Removing the center bolt is all that's necessary to separate the leaves. The leaves can then be cleaned and derusted (either by sandblasting or wire brushing). Before reassem-

bling, the springs should be re-arced. This is done by a spring shop. After re-arcing, the leaves should be primed and painted.

Before assembling the springs, either place strips of Teflon or a liberal coating of grease between the leaves. This is done to enable the leaves to slide freely against one another, and greatly improves the ride. After replacing and tightening the center bolt and installing new bushings in the eyes at the ends of each main leaf, the springs are ready to be installed on the axle.

Front End Assembly

All front-end parts should be primed and painted in preparation for reassembly. While refinishing is going on, you can send the nuts and bolts out for zinc plating; any commercial plating shop should be able to provide this service. You should also draw up a parts list and begin gathering the items you will need to reassemble the front end. These will include a king pin set, new steering connecting rod (if the ball studs on the old rod show wear or if the studs have battered ends), tie-rod-end assembly kits, replacement steering balls (if the old balls are worn out-of-round), new or relined brake shoes, brake return springs, wheel

The king pin kit consists of bushings which are installed in the spindle yoke, the steel rod which is the king pin itself, a thrust bearing, shims, and a locking pin.

cylinders, spring shackles and wheel bearings (these should be replaced if the old bearings show signs of wear or spackling—chips in the rollers—or if the inner wheel bearings have broken apart in the process of removing them from the brake drums). You will also need new inner wheel-bearing seals.

Although you can get all these items from vintage Chevrolet parts suppliers (see appendices for listings), you may also be able to purchase some of the items at a nearby NAPA auto parts store. Buying parts locally has the advantage of saving shipping costs and delays, and if the items aren't right you can easily return them. Also, due to NAPA's enormous warehouse inventory, parts listed but not in stock can usually be shipped to a local store within one or two days.

Once the chassis and other front-end parts have been refinished, you will start reassembling the front end in the reverse order from that in which you took it apart. This means that the new king pins will be installed first.

Reinstalling King Pins

There are basically three things to remember when installing king pins: first, make sure the grease holes in the bushings are in line with the grease fittings; second, place the thrust bearing in the correct location (between the axle and lower spindle yoke); and third, shim the space between the axle end and spindle yokes so that there is no more than 0.005 in. gap and no free movement. If

Often the king pins are rusted to the axle bores and need some persuasion to be driven out. Chrystal Edgerly

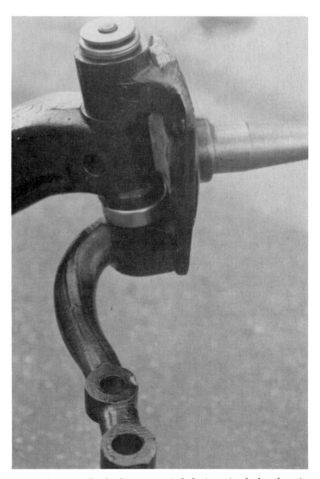

After driving the locking pin tightly into its hole, the pin is secured by placing a nut and lock washer on the pin's threaded end.

The king pin is held in place by a locking pin that fits into a hole in the axle yoke.

you follow these guidelines, you will have accomplished the first step in ensuring that your truck steers easily and runs down the road straight and true.

The procedure of replacing the king pins begins by installing new bushings in the spindle yokes. This is best done with a bushing driver, available from a specialty supplier like The Eastwood Company, and an arbor or hydraulic press. Most hobbyists don't have a press, and if that's your case you may choose to have these bushings installed at a machine shop.

If you'd rather install the bushings yourself, you can press the bushings in place using a bench vise. When using a vise to press the bushings, you first need to start the bushings in the holes in the spindle yoke. To start the bushings, round the edges of the bushings slightly with a file, lubricate the hole in the spindle yoke, then tap the bushing into the hole with a plastic hammer. You should place a large washer over the end of the bushing you are tapping to make sure that no damage is done to the bushing's soft metal. Be sure that the hole in the bushing lines up with the grease-fitting hole in the spindle yoke. Once the bushing is started, you can place the spindle yoke in the bench vise (insert a block of wood between the bushing and vice jaw to prevent the jaw from cutting into the soft metal of the bushing) and slowly press the bushing into its hole by tightening the vise.

When all four bushings have been installed (remember to make sure they are all correctly aligned with the grease-fitting holes), the new bushings need to be reamed to the diameter of the king pins. You can do this yourself if you have a reamer of the correct diameter (this tool can be purchased from an auto parts store or specialty tool supplier), or you can have them reamed at a machine shop. The cost of having a machine shop do this work will be approximately the same as the expense of the tool. So whether you do the work yourself or hire it done may depend on whether or not you want to add a bushing reamer to your tool inventory. If you decide to buy the reamer, note that you will need a tool that is long enough to ream both bushings at once. This is necessary to establish proper alignment for the king pins.

Now you can begin to assemble the king pins by fitting a spindle yoke over one end of the axle. Place a thrust bearing (or washers on three-quarter-ton and larger trucks) between the axle and the lower yoke. Note that a thrust washer is supplied only with king-pin bolt kits for ½ ton trucks. Make sure that the closed side of the thrust bearing is at the top. Now check the clearance between the upper face of the axle end and the upper yoke. This clearance should not exceed 0.005 in. If greater clearance exists, insert shims in this space until the required clearance is met. As you install the shims, check the gap with a feeler gauge. Too loose a fit will cause sloppy steering, but too tight a fit will make for hard steering. As you fit the shims, make sure the holes in the spindle ends line up with the hole in the end of the axle.

With the shims in place you can fit the king pin into the hole. Make sure that the notch for the locking pin faces toward the locking-pin hole in the axle. With the king pin in place, drive the locking pin through its hole in the axle until the pin is wedged tightly against the king pin. Now install a lock washer and nut on the locking pin's threaded end and tighten. To seal the king pin against dust and moisture, place a soft metal plug, rounded side up, in the hole above the king pin on one end of the spindle yoke and wedge the plug into place by giving it a sharp tap on the crest of the bulge with a

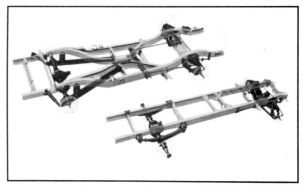

At this stage the front end has been rebuilt, including brakes, and reassembled in the chassis. The next steps are to add the steering column and mechanical assemblies—the engine and transmission.

ball-peen hammer. Do the same with the other spindle end. Now repeat this procedure with the other spindle, and the task of installing the king pins will be completed.

Reinstalling the Tie Rod

If the tie-rod ends have been replaced, the new ends need to be threaded into the tie rod. Be sure the threads are cleaned and well lubricated, as it is important that the rod be able to turn easily in order to set the front wheel toe-in. Before threading on the ends, slide the clamps that lock the ends in place onto the tie rods. Do not turn the ends fully into the tie rod, but leave about one third of the threads showing. Position the ends so that roughly the same number of threads are showing in front of each. Now you need to replace the end assemblies, consisting of a spring seat, spring, two ball seats and an end plug. Assemble these parts in the sequence shown, with the steering-arm ball sandwiched between the two ball seats. When all the parts are assembled, tighten the end plug until the spring is fully compressed, then back off to the first cotter-pin hole. Insert and lock the cotter pin by bending back the ends. If the grease fitting has been

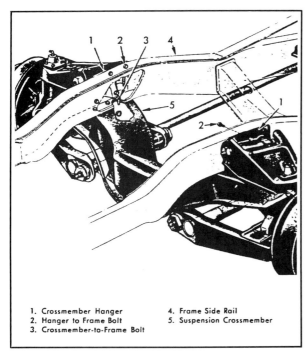

1. Crossmember Hanger
2. Hanger to Frame Bolt
3. Crossmember-to-Frame Bolt
4. Frame Side Rail
5. Suspension Crossmember

In 1960 Chevrolet introduced an all-new independent front suspension that featured torsion bars. This suspension was very well designed and for the first time gave trucks a car-like ride. Even though the independent front suspension really has nothing in common with the former straight-axle front end, rebuilding procedures for this more refined suspension system are no more complicated than the earlier style and can be done by a handyman mechanic using the tool set described at the front of this chapter. Chevrolet Division, General Motors

removed, it needs to be replaced so that you can lubricate the end assembly. Now repeat the same procedure at the other tie-rod end.

Final Assembly

If a stabilizer bar is included in the front-end assembly, reinstall this component. Now you are ready to mount the front springs. This is done by centering the springs over the axle and clamping them in place with U-bolts. If the frame is ready (cleaned, primed and painted) you can attach the front-axle assembly by replacing the spring shackles. If the steering box is also in place, you will also hook up the steering connecting rod. Remember that if the ends of this rod are worn (if they show excessive free movement) or damaged, then this part needs to be replaced. The shock arms also need to be connected to their mounts on the frame. The remaining steps—replacing the backing plates and brake assemblies and adjusting the tie rod for correct front wheel toe-in—are covered in later chapters.

With the front end reinstalled in the chassis, the next steps are to replace the drivetrain. Often the transmission and differential do not need to be overhauled. Procedures to follow for rebuilding these assemblies, if you suspect or know of mechanical problems, are described in the shop manual for your series truck.

Chevrolet's K Series four-wheel-drive trucks used another style front end that mounted the springs to the drive axle. Chevrolet used the ball-and-socket type steering seen here on its 4x4 trucks through 1969. Jon Bagley

Independent Front Suspension Overhaul

In 1960, Chevrolet made one of the biggest advances in light-truck development by replacing the beam front axle with independent front suspension (IFS). Chevrolet cars had acquired IFS in the 1930s. Beam axles had been retained in trucks due to their simpler, more rugged design. However, a beam axle gives a much inferior ride to IFS—hence the expression "rides like a truck." In designing an independent front suspension system for their division's and GMC's trucks, Chevrolet engineers faced the challenge of how to build a suspension that would take hard use without coming out of alignment and causing premature front tire wear. The resulting torsion bar design proved so rugged that Chevrolet also used it on its heavy-duty trucks through 1962.

There are almost no similarities between a beam-axle front end and Chevrolet's torsion-bar independent front suspension of 1960–1962. A beam-axle suspension has essentially no adjustments except toe-in. With independent front suspension, adjustments are also made for caster (the angle of the steering axis from vertical) and camber (the inclination of the wheels from vertical). Both of these adjustments need to be made at a front-end shop, although toe-in can be set at home. Chevrolet's independent-front-end design abandoned king pins for a more advanced ball-joint system, and replaced the ball and socket tie-rod ends with sealed units. When the sealed tie-rod ends wear out they are simply replaced.

Wear points on the torsion bar suspension, besides the tie-rod ends, include the ball joints and bushings in the control arms. In addition, the torsion bars that function as springs can become fatigued, causing the front end to sag. If the independent front suspension shows wear (as evidenced by uneven tire wear and steering wander) it should be rebuilt. If the truck has front-end sag (which may be noticeable visually or can be checked by measuring the height from a level surface like a shop floor to the frame horns), the torsion bars should be replaced. Instructions for overhauling the torsion bar IFS are shown in Chevrolet's 1960 truck shop manual (the 1961 manual is a supplement). Rebuilding an IFS front end is really no more complicated than a beam-axle system and can be done by a handyman mechanic using a tool set as described in this chapter.

In 1963, Chevrolet re-engineered its truck front ends, reverting to the former I-beam system on its heavier-duty trucks and replacing torsion bars with coil springs on its light duty C–10 through

Here's a style of independent front suspension that you won't see unless someone has modified your truck. This is an increasingly popular modification of a truck that originally had a straight-axle front end to a car A-arm and coil-spring independent front end. The result is a smoother ride and improved steering, but authenticity is lost in the process. Barry Weeks

C–30 models. Four-wheel-drive K series trucks never adopted IFS. The coil spring IFS is similar in design to the torsion bar system, but costs less to build. Like the torsion bar system, the coil spring design has adjustments for caster and camber. The rebuilding process is much the same except that a spring compressor is needed to remove the coil springs and control arms. Apart from the need to purchase or rent a spring compressor, overhauling a coil-spring suspension system is also within the handyman mechanic's skills. After rebuilding, the IFS suspension needs to be adjusted and aligned at a front-end shop.

Both IFS suspension designs are extremely rugged. Trucks that have seen only highway use and have been lubricated at regular intervals will easily travel in excess of 100,000 miles without requiring suspension system rebuilds. This means that if you are restoring a relatively low mileage 1960 or later Chevrolet truck, the suspension may require only cleaning, painting and lubrication to serve your truck safely and reliably for many more miles.

7

Steering Overhaul and Adjustment

From 1941 onward, Chevrolet trucks used a ball-bearing steering gear developed by GM's Saginaw division. This steering system, called recirculating ball, is superior to the standard worm-and-sector steering box design used earlier because the moving balls provide a rolling, rather than a sliding contact between the worm gear on the steering shaft and sector shaft, which turns the wheels. The result is easier steering action and less wear between the parts.

While the Saginaw recirculating-ball steering box is a rugged unit, wear does occur and the steering mechanism can get out of adjustment. When loose steering is noticed, it is important to determine whether the cause is in the front end (loose king pins and tie-rod ends) or in the steering box, or a combination. Play in the steering box can be detected by having an assistant hold the pitman

arm at the bottom of the steering box while you turn the steering wheel. If free movement is noticed while the pitman arm is held rigid, you may be able to take up the slack by adjustments, or the steering box may need to be rebuilt or replaced by a tighter unit.

In some cases, the steering box may be free of play, but excessively high effort may be required to turn the wheels. Causes here may be a low or dry lubricant level in the steering box, improper steering adjustment, or overtightened tie-rod ends (on pre 1960 trucks with adjustable-type tie-rod sockets). Another cause of hard steering is under-inflated tires.

Correcting Loose Steering

After making sure the steering play is not caused by wear in other front-end parts, the steering gear should be adjusted to make its action as responsive as possible. Specific instructions for adjusting the steering on your year and model

In 1941, GM introduced a vastly superior steering box developed by its Saginaw division. The chief feature of this design is an endless row of ball bearings that circulate around the worm shaft to ease steering effort and minimize wear between the steering worm and sector.
Mark Tomandl

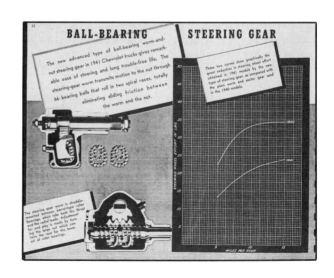

Chevrolet truck are given in the service manual. The steps presented here are offered as an overview of the general procedure for adjusting a Chevrolet recirculating-ball steering box, and are not intended to replace the instructions in the service manual.

Adjusting steering play begins by disconnecting the steering connecting rod from the pitman arm. It is important to note the relative position of the two parts before disconnecting them so as to put them back in the same position. The rest of the procedure will be done at the steering box.

Two adjustments will be made. One corrects for slop that has developed between the worm gear and the roller bearings that support the worm gear and its attached steering shaft. The second adjustment reestablishes proper alignment between the sector and ball nut. (The sector is the shaft and crescent-shaped gear that turn the pitman arm and steering linkage. The ball nut is a block-shaped gear that moves with the steering worm via the recirculating-ball bearings and in so doing turns the sector gear.) When both of these adjustments are set correctly, the steering should have the correct pull (between 2 and 2½ lb.) and no play should be felt in the steering box. Of course it is possible for these adjustments to be set correctly and the steering still be excessively hard, and for play still to exist. With a truck that has seen hard service and little maintenance, other causes of steering box problems include worn sector bushings and/or steering shaft bearings, a worn sector gear and ball nut, worn roller balls or a bent sector shaft.

Adjusting Bearing Tension

To adjust bearing tension, loosen the lock nut at the end of the sector shaft (on the side of the steering box toward the engine) and turn the adjustor screw—the screw has a slot head and is turned with a screwdriver—a few turns counterclockwise. This unmeshes the contact between the sector gear and ball nut and in so doing removes the tension or load from the worm bearings. Now turn the steering wheel slowly and gently in one direction to the stop, then back one turn. Be careful not to turn the steering wheel hard against the stop or damage to the ball guides can occur. Since the first adjustment you will be making affects steering effort, you need to determine how much pull is required to turn the steering wheel. Although there are professional tools (usually found only in a service garage) to test the pull needed to turn the steering wheel, you can also check the pull with a fishing scale—the small hand-scale fishermen use to weigh their catch. To do this, attach the fishing scale to the steering wheel rim above the cross spoke and pull directly down on the spoke. The force required to turn the wheel should be between 1 and 1½ lb.

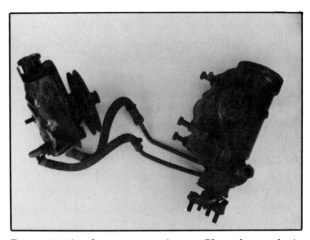

Power steering became an option on Chevrolet trucks in the 1960s. Upgrading from manual to power steering is really very simple requiring basically two steps: replacing the manual steering box with a power unit and mounting the power steering pump on the engine.

To set the worm bearings to the correct tension (bearing tightness against the races on the steering worm) loosen the lock nut at the bottom of the steering box and turn the worm bearing thrust screw until no movement can be felt between the worm gear and its bearings. This movement can be detected by pushing or pulling on the steering wheel. To make sure you have not overtightened these bearings, test the pull on the steering wheel. It should be within the limits mentioned. If, when the worm bearing tension is set correctly, the steering box feels lumpy as you turn the steering wheel, then the bearings are probably worn and will need to be replaced. This is a more complex job that requires removing the steering column from the truck and disassembling the steering box. After making this bearing adjustment, check to make sure that the bolts holding the steering box to the frame are tight. Now you will adjust the mesh between the sector gear and ball nut. The first step in this procedure is to move the steering wheel to its centered position. To do this, you will gently turn the wheel all the way in one direction to the stop, then in the other direction to stop, counting the turns between stops. When the steering wheel has reached the second stop, turn back half the number of turns. This is the center position. In the event that the steering wheel is not mounted so that spokes are not in a horizontal position at the center position, mark the wheel at the center of the rim with masking tape.

With the steering wheel in centered position, turn the adjustor screw on the engine side of the steering box (at the end of the sector shaft). This adjustor should be turned clockwise until all looseness (lash) has been taken out of the mesh between the gear teeth. To tell when the lash has

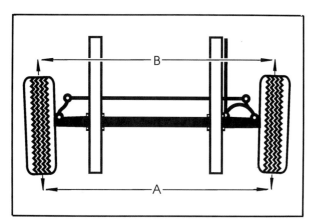

A vehicle has better directional stability if the wheels point toward each other slightly in the front. This shorter distance between the wheels in the front than at the back is called toe-in. Mark Tomandl

been removed, measure the amount of force needed to turn the steering wheel. A pull of 2 to 2½ lb. is correct. When that amount of pull is reached, tighten the adjusting screw lock nut and again check the steering pull. If it has changed, loosen the lock nut and reset the adjusting screw.

After adjusting the steering box, reattach the steering connecting rod to the pitman arm and check for play in the steering. This is best done by jacking the front end off the ground, having a helper hold a front wheel while you turn the steering wheel, and noticing any free movement in the steering wheel that is not felt at the front wheel. If the tie-rod ends and king pins are tight, the steering box either needs to be rebuilt or replaced. Instructions for removing and rebuilding a Saginaw recirculating-ball-bearing steering box are found in the service manual for your year and model Chevrolet truck. Rebuilt steering boxes are available for many years of Chevrolet light trucks and unless you are an experienced mechanic or desire to rebuild a recirculating-ball steering box as a challenge, you will find installing a rebuilt box to be a much simpler (and typically more satisfactory) approach.

If adjusting the steering box appears to have eliminated excess play, make sure that the box is filled with lubricant before operating the truck on the highway. Chevrolet owners manuals call for filling the steering box with chassis lube. The lube is pumped into the steering box through the opening on the upper side of the box which is sealed with a pipe plug. Do not install a grease fitting in this hole. Grease should not be put into the steering box under pressure. When these trucks were in regular use, mechanics often added a small amount of 90 weight gear oil to the grease in the steering box to help lubricate the upper bearing and to reduce

steering effort in cold weather. Although the manuals do not call for this, you may want to fill the box nearly full with chassis lube and top it off with 90 weight gear oil.

Alignment

For directional stability, it is desirable that the front wheels point toward each other slightly in the front. The degree to which the front wheels are angled inward is called toe-in. If the wheels point outward, the condition is called toe-out and results in rapid tire wear. At least two methods, not requiring special tools, can be used to set the front wheels of your truck to the correct toe.

The first of these shade-tree mechanic techniques for setting toe-in begins by jacking up the truck so that the front wheels are slightly off the shop floor. Now, spin the wheels and spray a thin line of paint (use a light-colored aerosol spray) along the center of the tire. When the paint has dried, spin the wheel and scribe a line in the center of the tire using a nail, Phillips screwdriver or similar pointed tool. Lower the truck so that the front tires rest on the floor. Now measure to the midpoint of the tires and mark an X across the line at the same height on the front of both tires. Also do this on the back of both front tires.

Using a carpenter's tape, measure the distance between the Xs at the front and back of the tires. The measurement from X to X across the back should be slightly greater than across the front. Typically, the correct toe-in has the measurement at the back of the tires between ¹⁄₁₆ and ⅛ in. greater than the measurement at the front. Toe-in is adjusted by loosening the tie-rod ends and turning the tie rod. Note: The wheels need to be raised in order to make this adjustment.

The second do-it-yourself toe-in check is made using a gauge comprised of two sticks of wood clamped together (1 in. stock works well for this). As an alternative to making this gauge The Eastwood Company sells an inexpensive, yet precision toe-in gauge. With the front tires resting on the shop floor, loosen the clamps and extend the sticks (or the metal rods of the toe-in tool) until they touch the outermost tread about halfway up the back of the tires. Tighten the clamps so that the gauge is set to this length. (Using the toe-in tool, this measurement is made to the outer edge of the tire.) Now move the gauge to the front of the tires and check the amount of toe-in. As in the previous procedure, the correct toe-in is a difference of ¹⁄₁₆ to ⅛ in. greater distance at the back of the tires than at the front. After the toe-in has been set, torque the bolts on the tie-rod end clamps to 100–120 lb-ft. Be sure to install cotter pins to ensure that the bolts don't work loose.

8

Engine and Mechanical Rebuild

Restoring an old truck is more than making it look nice; you also want it to run like a well-oiled watch. Given the mileage many older trucks have traveled and the hard work they've seen, engine overhaul is likely to be in order (and will almost certainly be done if restoration is the goal). The transmission and differential may also require rebuilding or replacement with tighter units. Smaller mechanical assemblies—the carburetor, generator and alternator—are likely candidates for overhaul as well. The question with these mechanical repairs is whether you feel capable of doing the work yourself. If you're adventuresome enough to tackle rebuilding your truck's steering and front end, overhauling a carburetor or the generator and starter will easily be within your skills.

This Chevrolet 235 ci six is fitted with the famous old Fenton cast-iron headers and an Offenhauser dual-intake manifold, plus a Wayne cover set (rocker and pushrod) in finned and polished aluminum. A new Mallory dual-point distributor with centrifugal advance really puts these engines through their paces. Note the special alternator bracket, available from Patrick's.

GMC sixes like this Jimmy 270 ci are agreeable to performance modifications. The engine is fitted with the famous Howard five-carb log manifold and chromed Fenton cast-iron headers. The head is a Sissel-worked 270/H (big port) with competition port work and stainless valves. Dual-valve springs and tubular pushrods help the solid lifters follow the full-race profile of the Howard F-5 grind camshaft. Pistons are McGurk style, for a 9:1 compression ratio.

Rebuilding an engine requires extreme attention to detail and knowledge of how to assess the condition of the internal parts, as well as a basic understanding of how to put everything back together. This isn't to say that overhauling an engine is beyond the skills of a hobbyist restorer; it can be done, but you're likely to need a little expert help—or at least advice—along the way. To get you started, this chapter presents an overview of how to check the engine's condition and gives guidelines on having needed machining done. Step-by-step instructions for rebuilding and assembling an engine are found in the Chevrolet shop manual for your truck.

In the process of rebuilding an engine, it is possible to make small but significant modifications that will enable the engine to deliver more power and improve both the truck's performance and fuel economy. Although solidly dependable, the Chevrolet Stovebolt six is not generally thought of as a performance engine. Yet these engines respond well to even mild hop-up techniques like installing a split manifold. Owners of small-block Chevrolet V–8s will find any variety of hop-up avenues for their engines through performance equipment suppliers.

Mechanical repair work is much less pressuresome if you can draw on the experience and expertise of a seasoned mechanic when needed. There are several ways to plug into expert help. The easiest, most enjoyable way is to join a local club where you can meet others who have an interest in older vehicles. In this group will be those with strong mechanical skills who will take an interest in your project and be willing to lend advice, if not help. Another avenue is to sign up for an auto mechanics course taught at a local vocational-technical center. You won't become a master mechanic in ten to twelve weeks, but the course will give you a good foundation and you will be able to draw upon the instructor's skills for questions you may have with your restoration project. Another way to get help when your mechanical projects have you in over your head is to cultivate a friendship with a retired mechanic. More than likely, assisting you with your questions will be as important to the mechanic as his answers are to you.

The experience of overhauling your truck's mechanical components can be richly satisfying. Beyond the inclination and access to help when needed, you will need a mechanic's tool set, plus

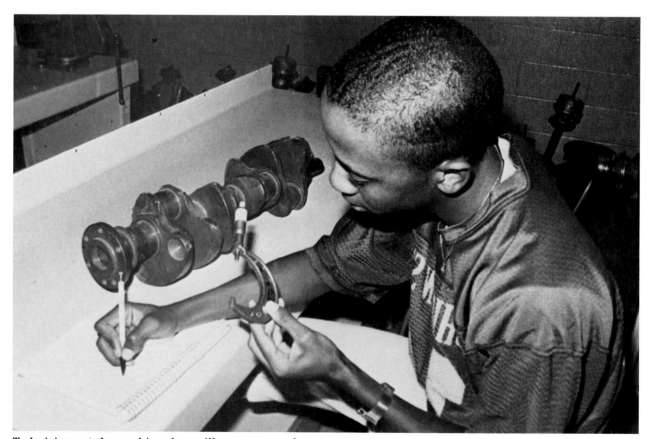

Technicians at the machine shop will measure crank-shaft journals for wear. Ferris State University Public Affairs Office

some specialty items such as pullers that will be listed as called for. The other essential resource for mechanical work is a collection of shop manuals. Besides the service manual for your truck, it also helps to have a *Chilton* or *Motor* manual that covers your year truck. Instructional manuals on engines, drivetrain components and electrical systems are also helpful. You can sometimes find these instruction manuals at used book stores or swap meets. One benefit of the instruction manuals is that they give you the theory behind the component's operation that is missing from a service manual. The reason for gathering several service manuals (a *Motor* manual plus the Chevrolet shop manual, for example) is that you're likely to have more photos of the disassembly, repair and reassembly steps. Also, different manuals are likely to approach the repair sequence somewhat differently, giving you a more thorough understanding of what you are setting out to do.

If you're just starting to develop your mechanical skills, the place to start is with the smaller components presented first in this chapter. An advantage of working with the carburetor, generator and starter is that these assemblies can be dismantled and overhauled inside the house if need be, as cold weather projects. There's also no set time in the restoration sequence that these components need to be overhauled, providing the work is done before final assembly. Unless the truck has exceptionally low mileage or these components have recently been rebuilt, most likely their maintenance or repair is in order. Follow the guidelines presented below and refer to the step-by-step overhaul sequences in your truck's shop manual and you will soon find your mechanical skills and confidence growing to the point where you are likely to be ready for the challenge of bigger mechanical projects—like overhauling the engine.

Engine Rebuild

So the old truck doesn't run like it used to; light blue smoke billows out the tailpipe when you accelerate and the oil level drops a few notches on the dipstick after you've made just a few short trips around town. Maybe it's time to consider having the engine rebuilt. If you're thinking in this direction, a question that may play on your mind is whether you can tackle the engine rebuild. If you think that rebuilding an engine is outside your skills, then you'll need to know what to look for in an engine rebuilder, how to gauge the fairness of the prices you're quoted, and any tips for ensuring a quality job.

You may also be wondering whether the engine needs a complete rebuild or if a partial overhaul will restore the engine's health for several thousand more miles. This question is answered in part by your goal and purpose for the truck. If it is to be a driver, fixed up to be presentable, you may

be satisfied with an engine that runs strong enough to get you to your destination, maybe burns a little oil but not so much as to be a major nuisance and is free from worrysome noises. If your desire is that the repair work you're doing now be permanent—so that you can drive the truck reliably for many years to come—you'll probably not be satisfied with anything less than a completely rebuilt engine.

Engine Inspection

Performing a few simple tests can give you a good indication of the engine's condition. The starting point is to check the compression. From this test you will have a good indication of condition of the valves (whether or not they are seating well or burned) and piston rings (whether or not the cylinders are worn or scored and if the rings are seating snugly against the cylinders). This check is made with a compression tester, available from auto parts stores. The engine section of your shop manual should indicate "in spec" compression readings. Chevrolet 235 ci six-cylinder engines, for example, should show a compression reading of 130 lb. or better and all cylinders should be within 5 to 10 lb. of each other for satisfactory engine performance. If the compression readings are substantially lower, chances are you've already observed the engine to burn oil, idle roughly and perhaps even heard a sucking sound at the tailpipe (an indication of a burned valve). Be sure to write down the compression readings because they will help a rebuilder, or the machinist if you decide to do the rebuilding yourself, to determine the engine's condition.

Other indications that an engine is in poor health are knocks (indicating worn bearings), low

Reassembling the engine is a precision job that requires careful measurement and extreme attention to detail. This photo shows Plastigage being used to check bearing fit.

oil pressure (below 10 psi once the engine has been warmed up) and oil blow-by (seen as a heavy oil film around the crankcase breather cap). Blow-by is a sign of poorly seated rings or tapered cylinders. Chevrolet's long-stroke six-cylinder engines, used until the modern short-stroke six appeared in 1962, have a relatively rapid wear cycle—particularly in pickup trucks where they are coupled with low-geared rear ends. This means that by 80,000 miles, enough cylinder and bearing wear will have occurred so that a major overhaul is in order.

Engine Removal

Although the cylinder head can be removed to overhaul the valves and crankshaft and rod bearing, work can be done with the engine in the truck, in most situations, and certainly for restoration, the engine will be removed. On older vehicles this is a pleasantly straightforward job that begins by removing the hood and radiator. If the truck is coming apart for restoration, it also helps to remove the grille assembly. Next, all wiring leads to the engine's electrical components are disconnected. If new wiring will be installed, it isn't necessary to label the leads, but if the existing harness

will be reconnected you should tag all leads so that you can put them back correctly later. You will also disconnect the fuel line, carburetor linkage and choke cable. The exhaust pipe needs to be disconnected at the manifold (often these bolts are rust-frozen and have to be heated with a torch to prevent breaking).

Now the motor mount bolts can be loosened and the bolts removed that attach the transmission to the engine bellhousing. This done, you are ready to pull the engine. The best way to lift the engine is by a sling that attaches to the head bolts. Rigging a sling from a length of heavy chain is not recommended because it does not ensure stable control of the engine during lifting. Either an overhead chain fall or a cherry-picker engine hoist, available at most rent-all stores, can be used to lift the engine out of the truck.

Engine Cleaning

With the engine removed, the next step is a thorough cleaning. The easiest way to clean off years of accumulated grease and grime is with a steam cleaner—a tool that can be rented from most rent-all stores. The other option is to clean the engine using Gunk (a degreasing cleanser), hot

As part of the engine overhaul process you will want to paint the engine block and all related components and assemblies. Castings that were not painted at the factory can be given the appearance of fresh parts with a coating of Cast Blast. Mike Cavey

water, a putty knife and scrub brush. This approach is time consuming and tedious. Once the engine is cleaned, it is ready to be disassembled. The shop manual for your year truck will outline the sequence to follow in disassembling and rebuilding the engine. It's also helpful to have a *Motor* or *Chilton* manual covering your truck as well. To do an engine overhaul you will need a moderate level of mechanical skills, and if you are tackling an engine rebuild for the first time, you should also have someone with experience who you can call on for help or advice. Although rebuilding an engine sounds like a major mechanical challenge—and it does require great attention to detail—older engines, particularly the venerable Chevrolet 216 and 235 ci, are the essence of mechanical simplicity. One thing is sure, if you rebuild your truck's engine yourself you will receive great satisfaction every time the engine spins to life.

Organizing Parts

In preparation for the engine's disassembly you should gather a dozen or so Manila envelopes, empty coffee cans or plastic milk cartons with the necks cut off, plus several cardboard boxes to hold bolts and the engine's internal parts. The envelopes can be used to separate the bolts for the oil pan, timing cover and other assemblies so that when you are ready to put the engine back together you will be able to quickly find the right bolts for each step. You will want to wash the bolts in solvent and dry them before placing them in the envelopes. Be sure to label each envelope. It is also important to identify the location of many of the engine's internal parts. The pistons and rods, for example, should be clearly marked as to which cylinder they came from. This can be done with a file, punch or marker. Likewise the valves need to be marked for their location. An easier way to do this is to place the valves in a rack consisting of a length of wood with holes drilled large enough for the valve stem to fit through. The Eastwood Company markets an inexpensive parts tray that is ideal for organizing the pistons, rods, cam, lifters and pushrods.

Tools

You'll need a few specialty tools to take the engine apart and a few more to put it back together. Some of these tools can be rented, or possibly borrowed, if you want to hold the line on tool investment. For convenience working with the engine, and so that you won't be wrestling with it on the shop floor where it is likely to pick up dust, you should plan on buying an engine stand. If your welding skills are up to par, you can make a stand for a small investment in steel. Otherwise, sturdy engine stands are available from specialty tool suppliers, auto parts stores and discount marts.

For disassembly, you will need a puller to remove the harmonic balancer and a valve spring compressor to remove (and remount) the valves. For reassembly you will need a ring compressor, a brass drift and a torque wrench. This tool list assumes that you will have a machine shop fit the wrist pins in the pistons and perform other specialized assembly steps of that nature. Prior to starting the engine, you will want to buy or make an oil pump primer. This tool is used to spin the oil pump and fill the empty oil lines and galleys. As an alternative to purchasing this tool, you can make a primer rod by welding an extension onto an extra distributor shaft.

Machine Shop Selection

Regardless of whether or not you decide to rebuild your truck's engine, the machining work should be done at a machine shop. Selecting the shop to do the machining involves more than just opening the phone book to the Yellow Pages. It helps to make inquiries on the shop's reputation for quality, and get recommendations from friends who have had engine machine work done at rebuilding shops in your area. Most machining facilities are small, so satisfied customers are their only means of advertisement.

Your best approach will be to disassemble and clean the parts needing machining before taking them to the machine shop. Once they are delivered, you will get a price estimate on the work and a time frame in which you can expect the work to be done. Sometimes this time frame is met and sometimes it isn't.

To understand why the shop is not always as prompt as you would like, it helps to understand how items progress through the shop. In most machine shops, jobs are done in such a way to provide the machinist with a step-by-step work

If you are doing a frame-up restoration, the engine will go back in the chassis before the sheet metal is replaced.
Mike Cavey

flow. Each operation takes an unspecified amount of time because of individual problems or unique situations that may occur during a particular process. For example, getting a crankshaft ground takes one to three hours depending on the amount of preparatory work that is needed and how many other crankshafts are ahead of yours. Preparatory work may include further cleaning, Magnafluxing (crack detection), checking straightness and measuring of each bearing surface. If the crankshaft needs repairs, the time involved increases, as does the price. When the parts are ready for pickup, be sure to check them against the work order to ensure all parts are there. The work order also gives you a breakdown of each machining process and its individual cost. You should look over each machined part to make sure the things you wanted done have been done. It's important to realize that this visual check does not guarantee your parts were machined correctly, however. As an example, a crankshaft that has been ground with a dull grinding wheel can have a slight curvature at the ends of each journal instead of a straight cut. The curvature can grip the bearings, causing the crank to seize. Unfortunately, an improperly ground crankshaft cannot be touched up. When a flaw like this is discovered, the crank will have to be reground to the next smaller size and new bearings ordered. The final test of the machine work will be when the motor is being assembled, and this should be done carefully. An ample amount of time and money will have been spent by this time and shortcuts can undo work that has been done.

Engine Disassembly

Typically, an engine rebuild begins by boiling out the block. This is done to remove sediment that may be clogging the oil passages and rust scale and other debris from the water passages. In a Babbitt bearing engine like the 216 ci six used until 1953, hot tanking (as the boiling process is called) can soften or destroy the bearings. Usually in a rebuild, the bearings will be repoured (or replaced if insert-style bearings are used) so no real damage is done.

After the block is cleaned inside and out, the cylinders are checked for taper (a larger diameter at the top than the bottom) or elongation (an egg-shape wear pattern). Cylinder taper occurs through as the rings rub up and down the cylinder walls. If you are restoring your truck, taper in excess of 0.005 in. will indicate a need to rebore the cylinders and install oversize pistons. (Honing the cylinders will remove taper to 0.005 in.) Since pistons are sized in increments of 0.015 in. over standard, the cylinders will be enlarged to match the closest piston size.

Cylinder taper often exceeds 0.005 in. If the cylinder taper in your truck's engine is in the 0.010 to 0.012 in. range and your purpose is to overhaul the truck to make it serviceable (with cost being a consideration), you could have the cylinders honed and the pistons knurled. This will avoid the cost of having the block bored and buying new pistons (most likely you will replace the rings). The combination of honing and knurling will eliminate half of the taper and expand the pistons slightly. A good machine shop can advise you on the seriousness of the taper and whether the block needs to be rebored. Problems resulting from cylinder wall taper are premature ring failure and power stroke gases blowing into the crankcase. When cylinder taper allows combustion gases to escape past the rings, a condition called blow-by can be seen. You may have noticed this in seriously worn engines where the crankcase breather cap "exhales" an oily smoke.

The block typically receives one other machining operation called "decking," which consists of grinding the surface at the top of the cylinders that mates with the head so that it is perfectly flat.

Although machining work on the block is now complete, other machining operations remain before the lower end of the engine can be reassembled. These include grinding the crankshaft to make sure that the journals for the rods and main bearings are perfectly round and without any surface irregularities that would cut into the bearings. The camshaft must also be inspected for wear on the lobes (the triangular extensions off the center of the shaft) which can cause the valves to open only partially.

Although not a machining step, if the original connecting rods are to be reused, they should be checked at the machine shop for trueness. A bent rod will bind on the crankshaft journal as it revolves, making the engine difficult to turn over initially and if it is possible to start the engine, that rod's bearing will be short-lived. If the engine is of the older Babbitt bearing type, new bearings will also need to be poured and bored to size before the engine is brought home for assembly.

At this stage you can make a list of the parts that are needed to complete the rebuild and start locating them. You will also need a set of engine overhaul gaskets. The first place to shop for parts is your local auto parts store. Chevrolet is such a popular make and used the same engines for so many years in both cars and light trucks that many mechanical parts are still in production. For those items not available at the auto parts store, you can try the specialty parts suppliers for vintage Chevrolet trucks. Presumably you have already ordered their catalogs. Along with the needed mechanical items (new pistons, rings, bearings and so on) you will also want to order the correct paint for your truck's engine and decals for the valve covers. When Chevrolet painted its engines in the factory, everything (except the carburetor and accessories like the generator and starter which had not been mounted yet) got a coating of paint. This means that the exhaust manifolds were painted, too, but that the paint quickly burned off. However, if you look carefully around the manifold flanges, where the metal does not get as hot, you are likely to see traces of the original paint. If you're a stickler for authenticity, you will apply a touch of paint to the manifolds in these cooler locations.

Engine Block Rebuild

Refitting the internal parts into the block is a precision job that requires extreme attention to detail. The steps for this sequence can be found in a Chevrolet shop manual. A major precaution to observe during reassembly is to oil everything well. This is especially critical of engine bearing surfaces. A low-friction oil like STP will give good protection against metal-to-metal contact for the bearings and other rotating parts until the engine is pre-oiled by spinning the oil pump prior to start-up.

If you attempt to rebuild the engine from an older gasket set (which are sometimes available at swap meets), you may find that the cork gaskets have dried and shrunk. When this is the case, the gaskets should be soaked in water for an hour or so before using to allow them to stretch back to shape. Don't soak paper gaskets, though. Many engine rebuilders advise laying a thin bead of Permatex Blue gasket sealer on all gasket surfaces (both sides of the gaskets) to ensure a leak-free engine.

When you have finished assembling the block, you can install the oil pan and set this unit aside. Be sure to cover the engine block well to prevent dust from settling in the cylinders and other moving parts.

Cylinder Head Rebuild

All Chevrolet engines use the valve-in-head design. This means that the valves and valvetrain are serviced with the cylinder heads. As with the block, the cylinder head will also be taken to a machine shop for several checks. The head (two heads on a V-8) should be cleaned first; otherwise the machine shop will charge you for this preparatory step. You should ask the machine shop to Magnaflux the head for cracks. Cracks that develop across valve seats are sometimes visible, sometimes not. It is important that all cracks be detected and repaired. Otherwise, the engine may leak coolant into the cylinders, quickly resulting in a ruined engine. The head will also be machined to make sure it rests flat against the block. In addition, the machine shop can press out the old valve guides and install new ones, as well as seat the valves.

Besides these standard machining steps, on pre 1969 engines, it is strongly advisable to have the valve seats cut out and hardened seats installed. The tetraethyl lead additive that was used quite liberally in leaded gasoline when these older engines were built provided lubrication that pre-

vented valve-seat wear. The absence of lead in any but the most minute quantities in today's gasoline poses the threat of significant premature valve-seat wear in engines that were designed to operate on leaded gasoline. This can be prevented by having the machine shop fit your engine's head with hardened valve seats and also purchasing hardened valves. The expense of this changeover is well worth the freedom from concern about future valve wear.

After following instructions in the shop manual for installing and adjusting the valves, a fresh head gasket is placed on the block and the head is bolted in place. Be sure to follow the tightening sequence for the head bolts as shown in the shop

For trucks that will enter show competition, detailing the engine becomes a very important step. Note the careful routing of fuel and vacuum lines on this national prize-winning Advance Design. For a prize-winning truck, it's also important that the engine and accessories be painted the correct color scheme. Mike Cavey

Decals are available from vintage Chevrolet parts suppliers to recreate the original lettering on the valve covers.

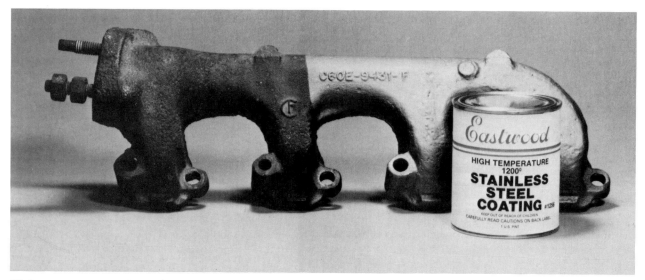

High-temperature paints like this product from The Eastwood Company can be applied to exhaust mani- *folds to give this part a finished look.* The Eastwood Company

manual, and tighten the bolts to the specified torque. Now the manifolds and accessories can be fitted and the engine replaced in the truck. This done, the fuel lines will be reconnected and the wiring harness hooked up to the engine's electrical connections. New spark plugs will be used, along with new spark plug wires run from the distributor cap to the spark plugs. Be sure to follow an electrical diagram for the engine to make sure that the wires to each spark plug are inserted in the correct sockets in the distributor cap.

Carburetor Overhaul

Single-throat carburetors, used on Chevrolet six-cylinder trucks into the 1970s, are the essence of simplicity. But, as is common with low-tech designs, these simple fuel-metering devices can appear to operate just fine while actually disguising problems warranting a rebuild. Usually engine performance deteriorates slowly—the points wear, the ignition timing slips, the carburetor begins to

---

How to Check for Carburetor Air Leaks

To check for air leaks at the flange base gasket, around the throttle shaft or the intake manifold gaskets, with the engine running spray carburetor cleaner around these areas. If the engine speed picks up, an air leak is present. Signs suggesting an air leak are a rough or fast idle. If an air leak exists around the manifold or carburetor base, the gaskets in these areas will probably have to be replaced. On most carburetors that have seen extensive use, an air leak at the throttle shaft can be anticipated.

---

operate a little rich, the engine may begin to start a little hard and fuel economy drops off.

If you are overhauling your truck's engine, or doing a complete restoration, rebuilding the carburetor is part of the process. Although this chapter concentrates on the simple, one-barrel carburetor layout, rebuilding a two- or four-barrel carburetor follows the same principles. In this section you will get an overview of the rebuilding process and an insight into how a carburetor works. Regardless of the carburetor you're rebuilding, you'll want to open the Chevrolet shop manual for your truck and follow the step-by-step instructions.

Carburetor Removal

In order to overhaul the carburetor you've got to remove it from the engine. This is a straightforward process that starts by taking off the air cleaner, disconnecting the gas line, accelerator linkage and choke cable, then unbolting the carburetor from the intake manifold. To remove the gas line, you will need two open-end wrenches; the wrench sizes are usually ½ and ⁹⁄₁₆ in. One wrench will be used to hold the carburetor inlet fitting while you loosen the gas line fitting with the other. Adjustable wrenches should not be used because they can easily slip off the soft brass fittings, rounding the edges. The throttle linkage may be held in place by tiny clips. If so, be careful not to break or lose these fasteners. The choke cable usually pulls free after loosening a clamp and set screw.

When removing the carburetor, be careful not to drop the carburetor nuts or lock washers down the hole in the intake manifold. As soon as the carburetor is off the engine, plug the inlet hole in the manifold with a clean rag to prevent dust or stray parts from entering. If the engine has been operated recently, the float bowl will still contain gas, most of which can be poured into a suitable container by turning the carburetor on its side. Before taking the carburetor apart, you need to locate a new set of gaskets.

Rebuild Kits

Carburetor gaskets are included in what is called a carburetor kit. Actually, there are two types of carburetor kits. One is intended for a complete rebuild and, in addition to gaskets, will contain a new needle and seat, accelerator pump, and numerous small parts such as the check ball, springs, clips and fasteners. The other, called a jiffy kit, will include gaskets plus a few basic tune-up parts. For a carburetor rebuild you should have the complete kit.

In order to cover a broad range of model applications, some rebuild kits include extra gaskets and small parts not needed for your repair job. To make sure you use the right parts, you will sometimes need to compare old parts from the carburetor with new parts from the kit. Often, the rebuild kit will include an instruction sheet for servicing the carburetor. This sheet is useful, but should be considered a supplement to the carburetor overhaul instructions in the service manual.

Just because the carburetor is sitting atop a thirty-year-old engine is no reason to think that the kit will be hard to find. The first place to look is a local auto parts store. I have found NAPA parts stores to be unbeatable in their ability to supply parts I would have considered to be long out of stock. In many cases, your local NAPA auto parts store will have parts for a thirty- or even forty-year-old Chevy truck on the shelf.

When the auto parts store does not have and cannot order a carburetor kit for your truck, the next step is to contact a specialty supplier that specializes in carburetor repair (see appendices for listings). Note that before contacting the supplier, you should find out the carburetor's manufacturer and model number and write down the data so that you have it available when you need it. This information is usually contained on the metal tag attached to the float bowl and may be embossed on the carburetor casting. If the tag is missing (probably discarded in an earlier rebuild) and no information can be read from the casting, the make and model information will be listed in the service manual.

Carburetor Disassembly

Taking apart a single-barrel carburetor is a simple process. Basically, the carburetor casting consists of three parts: the air horn assembly at the top, the body which contains the float bowl, and the flange base which holds the throttle valve and is sometimes cast integral with the body. Screws hold the air horn and the flange base to the body.

The choke linkage, which runs up the side of the carburetor, will have to be disconnected in order to separate the casting elements. Before undoing the linkage, take a close look at how it functions and fits together. If you have a service manual, you may be able to refer to photos showing the linkage when reassembly time comes. Lacking a manual or a clear view of the linkage, it is a good idea to take several photos of the carburetor with linkage intact, or draw a schematic of how the pieces fit together for future reference.

While the carburetor is still in one piece, the choke and throttle shafts should be checked for

A carburetor may be made up of two or three casting elements. The cast iron style carburetors used on Chevrolet trucks into the 1940s had consisted of two castings: the airhorn (top) and the body and flange base (bottom). Later die cast carburetors used a separate (third) casting for the flange base.

wear, felt as slop or play where the shaft passes through the casting. The choke is the large valve at the top of the air horn. The throttle is located in the flange base casting. On some earlier carburetors the choke and throttle shafts are made of brass. More commonly, though, the shafts are made of soft steel. Both the choke and throttle shafts turn in holes drilled through the carburetor casting, another soft metal. In normal operation, wear occurs on both the shaft and casting. The shaft wears undersize where it passes through the carburetor casting, and the holes in the casting wear oval-shaped. Because the throttle is in relatively constant movement while the engine is running, wear is far more likely to be found on the throttle shaft than on the choke shaft which moves mainly when the engine is being started. Signs of a worn throttle shaft are erratic idling and a whistling sound sometimes heard on acceleration. If the throttle shaft has worn to the degree that it slops around in the housing, a less worn carburetor should be used.

If the throttle shaft fit is very loose, and a carburetor body with less wear cannot be located, you'll need to consider resizing the shaft. The simplest approach is to locate a slightly oversize shaft and rebore the holes in the carburetor base to fit. Although this repair is relatively simple, this solution is usually impractical because finding a new shaft for most older carburetors is nearly impossible. As a result, if throttle shaft wear is severe enough to require repair, you'll probably have to send the carburetor away to a repair service.

It's important that the throttle valve (at the base of the carburetor, shown here) and the choke valve (in the carburetor air horn) move freely and close tightly. If the throttle or choke valves bind or do not close tightly against the opening, some troubleshooting and repair is necessary.

To take the carburetor apart, simply remove the screws holding the air horn and flange base to the body. As these components are separated, you'll also have to detach portions of the choke linkage—a process that can be something like working a Chinese puzzle. When the air horn is removed, you will see the float and nearby (in what appears to be a narrow well) another mechanism that looks like a plunger. This is the accelerator pump that provides the engine's fuel needs when you tromp down on the throttle. At the bottom of the float bowl you'll also see what appears to be a copper screw. This is a jet that passes a metered amount of gasoline into the air stream that is drawn down through the carburetor and into the engine.

Carburetor Cleaning

The carburetor should be cleaned of grease and grime that has accumulated from its years of service, but first you should remove the float accelerator pump and other internal parts. The float is removed by slipping out the thin copper pin that acts as a hinge. Always check the float for leaks by shaking it beside your ear. If a slight sloshing noise is heard, the float may have a pinhole in a seam or other spot that is letting gasoline leak into the hollow interior. A leaking float will fail to keep the gasoline level in the float bowl at the proper height, resulting in a richer mixture as well as possible flooding. If the leak is severe and the float becomes filled with gasoline, the carburetor could overflow, sending a stream of gasoline down onto the intake manifold.

The accelerator pump is removed by disengaging the plunger from its linkage. Other parts—the main jet, check ball, fuel-metering rod and idle-adjusting screw (located in the flange base)—should also be removed prior to cleaning. Instruction in the carburetor kit should show these parts; if not, they will be identified in an exploded diagram of the carburetor found in the service manual.

Several methods can be used to clean a dirty carburetor. A good noncaustic cleaner is an industrial-strength detergent such as Trisodium Phosphate (TSP), which can be purchased at most discount marts. The detergent is mixed with hot water, and the carburetor is left to soak in it for several hours. After soaking, the parts are washed with clear water. At this stage any remaining grime can be scoured off with a vegetable scrubber or toothbrush.

Another cleaning method is to soak the castings in mineral spirits to remove grease and grime, then clean the outer and inner surfaces with carburetor cleaner or a strong solvent like lacquer thinner. Both carburetor cleaner and lacquer thinner are highly flammable and should be used with caution and disposed of properly. Carburetor cleaner in a spray can is probably the wisest choice, since the quantity needed to soak the castings in it would be moderately expensive. If the spray-can approach is used, you can give the castings a good soaking with cleaner, allow the solvent to work a few minutes, then scrub any caked-on grime with a parts cleaning brush. Rubber gloves should be worn in this operation since carburetor cleaner is a strong solvent. The housing can be rinsed with clean water after each scrubbing. If any gasket material remains on the mating surfaces, these machined surfaces need to be scraped clean with a single-edged razor blade or Xacto knife.

When the carburetor is thoroughly cleaned outside, blow carburetor cleaner through all holes and openings, then visually inspect these passages to ensure that all are free of buildup and residue. Blow all passages clean with an aerosol air gun of the type used to clean photographic equipment (available in photo supply stores), or a needle-tip blow gun from an air compressor, to make sure that no obstructions or residue remain.

Troubleshooting Throttle and Choke Shaft Problems

Before reassembling the carburetor, check the throttle and choke assemblies for bent shafts. Bent shafts are not all that unusual on a carburetor that has seen much use and some abuse. A bent choke shaft can be caused by a mechanic sticking a screwdriver down the air horn to hold open the choke. A bent throttle shaft is likely to be caused by a severe backfire or someone jamming the gas pedal to the floor, causing the linkage to kink the shaft on the end. Signs of a bent choke or throttle shaft are failure of the butterfly valve to seat properly against the housing, or a visible kink in the portion of the shaft that sticks out of the housing.

Often a bent choke or throttle shaft can be straightened without removing the shaft from the carburetor housing. This operation is somewhat delicate and requires care. If the shaft is bent inside the housing, tap against the bend with a light hammer and brass drift until the butterfly valve seats evenly. If the bend is outside the housing, the shaft may be straightened with pliers. Be sure to wrap a piece of cloth or paper towel around the end of the shaft to prevent the plier teeth from chewing into the shaft.

If the shaft has to be removed to be straightened, the first step is to turn out the screws holding the butterfly valve to the shaft. Sometimes the ends of these screws have been peened over to prevent their loosening. If that is the case, remove the peened area with a small file, then turn out the screws. Before removing the butterfly valve, note that the lip that closes down on the housing is beveled on the bottom side while the lip that closes up on the housing is beveled on the side facing you.

Making a Carburetor Drip Pan

by Dick Matott

After rebuilding two Carter W–1 carburetors for my 1947 Chevrolet half-ton with a 216 ci engine, I have come to the conclusion that it is nearly impossible to stop all gasoline leakage from this model carburetor. Even though the amount of gas leaked is very small, it makes it difficult to keep a good-looking finish on the manifolds.

To solve the problem, I fabricated a simple drip pan out of 26 gauge sheet metal and installed it between the carburetor and insulating block with an extra gasket. I brazed the corners to make a leak-proof assembly, but solder would work as well. The final finish is a coat of flat-black high-temperature paint. An 18 in. length of steel brake tubing brazed to the front corner of the pan directs gasoline to the ground (or a container). I have found that the little bit of gas my truck's carburetor leaks evaporates in the pan and never reaches the drain. With the pan in place, the manifolds stay looking great.

I used a hole saw to make the hole for the carburetor throat opening, but an electrician's knock-out punch would work as well. Use your carburetor gasket as a template for the mounting holes.

It is important to use a new gasket between the carburetor body and air horn to avoid fuel and air leaks.

In order to seat properly, the valve will have to be reinstalled with the bevels in this same orientation. So that you do not mistakenly reverse the orientation of the valve (with the result that both bevels would face the wrong way and the valve would not shut off the airflow), you should mark the top of the valve with a piece of chalk or a marker. Sometimes the valve will slip out of the slot in the shaft by hand. If not, it can be pulled loose with a pliers. Often the butterfly valve will have to be rocked back and forth in the shaft slightly to pull it free. With the valve removed, the shaft will slide out of the housing. Now the bent shaft can be straightened by rolling it on a flat surface and tapping against the bend with a brass drift.

When the shaft is ready to be reinstalled, coat it with light grease (Vaseline works well) so that it will slip easily through the holes in the carburetor. Likewise coat the butterfly valve so that it will slide easily into the slot in the shaft. It may be necessary to shift the valve in the shaft until it seats evenly on the carburetor housing. Remember to reinstall the valve with the beveled edges facing the housing. To check for proper fit, close the valve and hold the carburetor housing to the light. If no light can be seen around the edges of the valve, it is seating correctly. Continue to hold the valve closed and replace the screws that attach the valve to the shaft. Either peen the screw ends or place a drop of Loctite on the threads to prevent the screws from loosening and dropping into the intake manifold. If you decide to peen the threads, be sure to support the shaft while tapping on the screw ends.

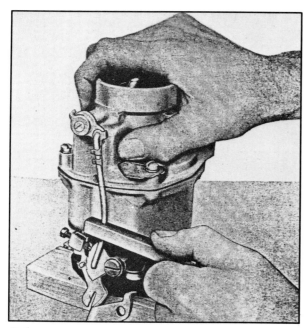

Before installing the reassembled carburetor on the engine, the choke rod is adjusted to ensure that the choke closes properly. Chevrolet Division, General Motors

Carburetor Rebuild

Clean, smooth surfaces on the needle and seat are critical to a carburetor's operation. Because these tight-fitting parts can become worn, the carburetor kit typically contains replacements. The needle and seat control fuel flow and are located behind the float. The seat threads into the outlet hole on the float bowl and becomes the attaching point for the fuel line. Since the needle (the cone-shaped part) is held in place by the float on many carburetors, you won't slip it into the seat until just before replacing the float.

On most carburetors that have been sitting for years on an older vehicle, the accelerator pump will have dried out, causing the engine to sputter and spit when the gas pedal is tromped for fast acceleration. To remedy this problem, the repair kit also includes a new accelerator pump (this is the plunger that fits into the well beside the float bowl), as well as a replacement for the check valve at the bottom of the well. The check valve (which is often nothing more than a tiny steel ball about the size of a BB and a clip) prevents fuel from running back out of the well, causing a hesitation on acceleration and raising the gasoline level in the float bowl. In replacing the accelerator pump, the spring and arm will have to be removed from the old pump and fitted to the new. Then the pump can be slipped back into the well and the arm fed down through the hole that exits through the bottom of the casting. Later, this arm will be connected to the throttle linkage.

A carburetor rebuild kit should show the procedure for replacing the check valve and accelerator pump as well as the main jet, metering rod and other internal parts. If new springs and gaskets are supplied with the kit, substitute these for the originals. Some adjustment may be called for in replacing the metering rod. If so, these instructions should also be contained in the kit's procedure sheet or the service manual.

The last step inside the carburetor is to replace and set the float. This procedure is critical to the carburetor's proper operation and must be done accurately and correctly. Remember that if the needle fits into the seat from the bowl side, it must be inserted before replacing the float. Wipe the needle with a dry, soft paper towel before slipping it into the seat.

It is essential that the float be installed right-side-up. Looking at the float, no side may appear to be the top, but the orientation of the hinge gives the float a top and a bottom. Normally, the loops for the hinge face the bottom of the float bowl. If in doubt, the kit instruction sheet or parts diagram from the service manual should show the proper float orientation. Now the float can be slipped into the float bowl and held in place by inserting the pin through the hinge.

The float must be set to the ride at the correct level. Most carburetor kits will supply a paper gauge to set the float. If a gauge is not included, measurements for the proper float setting can be found in the specification sheet with the kit or the service manual. Typically the gauge with the carburetor kit will look like a short ruler with two tabs protruding on one side. This type of gauge is placed across the top of the float chamber so that the tabs hang down toward the float. In raised position, the float should just touch the tabs.

The float's purpose is to control the fuel level in the float bowl. As the fuel is drawn into the carburetor's air stream the float drops, and when the float drops low enough to release the needle, more gasoline flows into the bowl. This raises the float and cuts off the fuel supply. The float is adjusted to the correct height by bending the arm or tab on the hinge slightly until the top of the float reaches the required level. This is a simple procedure, but one that demands accuracy.

Before reassembling the carburetor, make sure the float drops easily and does not bind on either the hinge or the needle. To check the float action, tip the bowl assembly back and forth in your hand, watching the movement of the float. Old gaskets, found in carburetor kits that have sat on a supplier's shelf for many years, usually have shrunk from their correct size. Assembling the carburetor with these undersized gaskets can also bind the float. To make the bowl gasket pliable so that it can be stretched to its original shape, soak the gasket in water for an hour or so before installing.

In addition to making sure the gasket between the body and air horn fits the outline of the float bowl and does not interfere with the operation of the float, also check the gaskets between the body and flange base to be sure that all holes align properly. At this point, a reminder is in order to never discard any parts until you are finished with the rebuild and are sure the carburetor operates properly. In the event that the flange base gaskets supplied with the kit are for a different application, you can—if necessary—reuse the old gaskets. Now you will insert and tighten the screws holding the air horn and flange base (or base and spacer) to the body. With the carburetor reassembled, you're faced with putting together that Chinese puzzle—the linkage. Chances are you'll need to refer to the photos taken or diagrams made before disassembly, or to an illustration in the service manual as a guide in putting the linkage together.

Carburetor Adjustment

Since the idle screw was removed for cleaning, it will have to be adjusted. Specifications call for rough-adjusting the idle screw between a half and one-and-a-half turns off the seat. If the throttle screw has not been tampered with in the rebuild, it can be left where it is and the engine should run. If the throttle screw has been removed and replaced, turn it in enough to keep the engine running. Final adjustments can be made under the hood. What you're aiming for in fine-tuning the carburetor is the highest vacuum or rpm at idle. To achieve this, you will adjust the throttle and idle settings in tandem, often turning in the throttle screw slightly, backing off the idle and so forth until the optimum setting is reached.

Air Cleaner Servicing

The last step in carburetor overhaul is servicing the air cleaner. Old-style oil-bath air cleaners should be washed out and refilled with clean oil (the owners manual for your truck may call for doing this each time the engine is serviced). Dry, wire-mesh air cleaners should also be washed with solvent and blown dry with an air hose. A light coating of oil sprayed into the mesh increases this type of filter's effectiveness. Modern paper filters are simply replaced.

Carburetor overhaul can make a dramatic difference in an engine's responsiveness, economy and overall performance. The process is simple enough for any old-truck owner to perform successfully, and applies with little increase in complexity to two- and four-barrel carburetors as well.

Generator Rebuild

Although considered part of the electrical system, both the generator and starter attach to the engine and are discussed in this mechanical overhaul section, since rebuilding these two components is more mechanical than electrical in nature.

Restoring Choke and Throttle Cables

by Everett Hanson

Remove the original cable from the vehicle and purchase a new cable to replace the wire and cable housing. Now remove the head with the wire from the old unit and cut off about ½ in. of the head where the wire is attached. Drill a ¹⁄₁₆ in. hole ½ in. deep in the head to accept the new wire, and silver solder in place. Do not use too much heat or the wire may burn off.

Next, put the cable housing head in a vise just so that it does not turn. Use pliers to turn out the old cable housing. Install the new cable housing and tighten with pliers. Measure the length of cable housing needed and grind off excess with a grinder or cutting wheel. Do not try to pinch off the extra cable housing as this will close in the end of the housing so that the wire will not go through. Now insert the head and wire into the cable housing. Trim the wire after it is installed on the carburetor. If the cable housing does not accept the wire, use a ¹⁄₁₆ in. drill to reopen the end of the housing.

A GM generator. This component, which is obsolete as far as modern vehicles are concerned, can be rebuilt quite easily by the handyman hobbyist.

Despite their dissimilar functions, a generator and starter are mechanically similar devices having much the same parts: a heavy steel housing (called a frame) and end caps, a set of electrical coils that attach to the inside of the frame, an armature that turns inside the coils, and brushes that attach to one of the end frames and rub against the armature. The basic difference between the two components is that the generator is an energy converter which changes mechanical energy (supplied by the engine) into electrical energy to recharge the storage battery and to power the truck's electrical system, whereas the starter operates as an electrical motor to turn the engine for starting.

Although generators and starters were built to last the life of the truck, both required periodic service which often got overlooked. So, because previous owners probably overlooked applying a few drops of oil to the armature bushings every six months or so (as called for in the owners manual), and neglected to replace the brushes at 50,000 mile intervals, or thereabouts, it's likely that the generator and starter on your truck are candidates for cleaning, inspection and overhaul. If your truck is undergoing restoration, these components, like everything else on the truck, will be completely disassembled and rebuilt.

Generator Troubleshooting

Even though generators and starters are mechanically similar, their functional differences require that they be diagnosed and overhauled separately.

Generator problems are noticed in three ways: either there is no charge, too much charge or not enough charge. Usually, when the generator is not putting out any current, the generator itself is the problem. If the charging rate is excessive or inadequate, the trouble may lie with the voltage regulator or the wiring.

Assuming the truck runs and the wiring is intact to the ammeter, a nonfunctioning generator will be readily apparent by the ammeter's needle never moving into the positive (or charging) zone. When this occurs, first check that the generator belt is tight and actually turning the generator pulley. If this is the case, and the ammeter circuit is functioning, as shown by the needle moving into the negative (or discharging) direction when the lights are turned on, here are a few simple tests you can perform to see if the problem lies with the generator.

First, make sure that all electrical connections are in good condition (that the connections are clean and tight) and that you have a good battery in the system. On early trucks using only a cutout relay, problems can occur in either the generator or the cutout. To isolate the cutout, put a jumper wire between the output lead of the generator and battery terminal on the cutout. With the engine at fast idle, the charge rate should be indicated on the ammeter if the generator is functioning normally. A word of caution: The jumper wire must be disconnected when the engine is not running to prevent battery discharge through the generator!

On the later systems using a conventional voltage regulator, problems can again occur in either the generator or control unit. To isolate the control unit, you must first determine if you are dealing with a Type A or Type B circuit. If one terminal from the field coils is connected to the insulated generator brush, the generator is the A circuit type. If one terminal from the field coils is grounded inside the generator it is a B circuit. Note: Ford circuits are all B type while the others were almost always A type, unless classified as heavy duty. The charging circuit on your truck should be a Type A, but if you are uncertain, check the field connections or the service manual.

On the Type A circuit, disconnect the field wire at the F terminal of the regulator and ground it to the regulator base. Now run the engine at fast idle, and a good generator will produce current flow that should be indicated by the ammeter.

On the Type B circuit, the same procedure is followed except that the field wire is disconnected from the F terminal on the regulator and is reconnected to the A or armature terminal on the regulator. With this test, if the generator produces, the regulator is usually at fault. If the generator does not produce with this test, the fault is most likely in the generator, but the regulator could also have a problem.

Another word of caution: The engine should be operated only for a short period in the test mode, as the generator armature will quickly overheat when forced to produce full electrical output—which is the case when the regulator is removed from the system.

Generator problems are usually traceable to worn or sticking brushes, a dirty or worn commutator, worn bearings or an internal short. A generator overhaul addresses all these problems collectively.

Generator Removal

In order to overhaul the generator, you need to remove this component from the engine. Thankfully, we're looking at vehicles with abundantly-sized engine compartments that aren't covered with a tangle of hoses. The generator is held in place by mounting brackets. Before removing the generator, be sure to disconnect the ground cable to the battery. Now remove the wires that attach to the armature, field coil and ground lugs. Unless the wiring will be replaced, mark each wire as it is removed with its attaching point on the generator. With a new, correctly color-coded wiring harness, the generator wires can be attached correctly by referring to a wiring diagram.

Now loosen the bracket bolt that holds the generator pulley tight against the fan belt. Loosening this bolt allows the generator to be pushed against the engine and the belt to be slipped loose of the generator pulley. The generator is now held in place by a mounting bracket bolted to the engine block, and holds the generator from the underside. To gain access to this bracket it is best to swing the generator as far away from the engine as it will go. This should give easy access to the bolt that holds the generator to its mounting bracket. With this bolt removed, the generator can be lifted out of the engine compartment.

Generator Disassembly

To open up the generator, simply remove the cover band, if present, and the bolts holding on the end frames. The armature (with the end frame and pulley attached) will then pull out of the frame. Now the brushes can be pulled out of their holders and their wire leads disconnected from the frame.

This is normally the extent to which the generator will be disassembled. Removing the field coils and pole shoes (the large internal parts that line the inside of the casing) is difficult because the screws that hold these parts in place are often hard to loosen and usually require a special tool. There is also a chance of damaging the parts in their removal and replacement. Unless they are defective, the field coils and pole shoes are better left in place. This is also true for the generator pulley. Unless the front bearing is defective, there is no need to remove the pulley and end frame. A worn bearing should have made itself known by a squealing or chattering sound when you ran the earlier generator tests.

Loosening the through bolts is all that's necessary to take the generator apart. The starter is disassembled the same way. In most cases, disassembly need not proceed beyond this point. The generator can now be cleaned and checked for internal shorts.

If the earlier tests showed the generator to be defective, you will want to test the field coils for a possible short. First, though, you will want to clean the generator and its parts.

Generator Cleaning

Most likely the generator frame is covered with caked-on dirt and grease. This buildup should be scraped off external surfaces with a putty knife before washing with parts cleaner. The frame, end frames, armature, cover band and pulley can now be washed in cleaner solvent. Since these instructions have not advised completely disassembling the generator, you should not immerse the generator frame in the cleaner. Instead, use a parts cleaner brush to scour away grease that may have collected inside the frame. Likewise, you will use the parts cleaner brush to get at grease on the backside of the pulley and front end frame. Gunk degreaser is also an effective cleaning agent. This product, which is available at discount marts as well as auto parts stores, comes in aerosol cans and is sprayed onto the grease-coated surface, allowed to work for a few minutes, then simply washed off with a garden hose. Stubborn grease coatings may require a couple of applications.

If the exterior surface of the frame is rusted, it can be sanded or cleaned using an acid gel like Naval Jelly or Jenolite.

Generator Testing

If the generator did not put out current during the earlier test, you will need to run another set of tests now that the unit is disassembled to pinpoint the problem. With these tests, you will be checking for open or grounded circuits in the field coils, armature and brushes. These tests require that you have a VOM (Volt-Ohm) meter. This electrical test device can be purchased at electronics stores like Radio Shack for under $25. If you have not used this test device before, be sure to read the instructions to become familiar with the instrument.

Field Coil Testing

Two tests are involved in testing the field coils. The first test checks for an open circuit. On the ohmmeter position, place one lead from the VOM meter on the field coil terminal (the insulated bolt that sticks out of the generator frame) and the other lead from the field coil that attaches to the brushes. If the needle on the meter does not move, the field coils have an open circuit (electricity is not passing through). An open circuit requires that one or both of the field coils be replaced. Separating the field coils electrically and checking each should indicate the problem.

This view shows the generator end frame with the brush holder. The bushing in this end frame is usually replaced, as are the brushes.

Several tests are performed on the disassembled generator to make sure there are no internal shorts. The test shown here checks to make sure that the field coils are not grounding to the generator frame. For this test, one lead of a VOM meter is placed on the field coil terminal and the other on the frame. The meter should not register current flow.

The second test checks for a ground between the field coils and the frame. For this test, place one lead from the VOM meter on the field coil terminal and the other on the generator frame. Make sure the field coil terminal which connects to the insulated brush holder is disconnected and does not touch the frame. If the needle moves, the field coils are shorted to the frame. To make sure the problem is not at the field terminal, disconnect the field terminal from the frame and try the test again. If the needle does not move this time, replace the insulating washers on the field terminal. This should correct the problem.

Armature Testing

Again, two tests are involved in testing the armature. The first checks for a short in the armature terminal. This is done by placing one lead from the VOM meter on the armature terminal and the other on the generator frame. If the needle moves, a short exists and the insulating washers on the terminal shoud be replaced.

The second test checks for a ground inside the armature. This is done by placing one test lead on the armature core or shaft and the other on the commutator (the smaller diameter copper section against which the brushes ride). If the needle moves, a short exists in the armature and this component will have to be replaced. Further testing of the armature would have to be done at a repair shop using an armature growler.

If the commutator is dirty (lacks a bright copper finish), it can be brought back to a shiny copper surface by spraying with carburetor cleaner and wiping with a paper towel. Several applications of cleaner may be necessary to restore the copper sheen. If the commutator has a worn or rough feel, or if one or more segments appear to be burned, it will need to be turned and the mica (the separators between the copper segments) undercut. This can be done at a generator or starter repair shop. A more serious problem is solder melted out of the winding to commutator connections due to past overheating in the generator or starter. (Solder will be found on the inside of the frame near the brush holders.) If the overheating caused some of the armature windings to separate from the commutator, the armature should be replaced.

Brush Testing

As you look at the end of the generator that has brush holder brackets, you will notice that one set of brackets is insulated from the plate. To check for a short in this insulation, place one lead from the VOM meter on the brush holder and the other on the end frame. If the needle moves, a short exists in the insulation. If the generator passes all these tests, new brushes and a cleaned commutator should restore it to working order.

Generator Painting and Assembly

Painting is best done while the generator is still apart. Be sure to mask the Delco Remy plate and terminals. For a quality finish, prime and paint using a professional-style spray gun.

As you reassemble the generator, you will also want to inspect and replace the bearing and bushing, if needed. If the bearing on the end frame with the generator pulley is worn, you should have heard a howl, whine or chatter in the earlier diagnosis when you were running the engine. Discoloration due to heat or a rough feel when the bearing is turned are other signs that this bearing should be replaced. Doing so will necessitate removing the drive pulley, and this will require a puller.

The bushing in the end frame that has the brush holder is likely to be worn, particularly if previous owners failed to squirt a few drops of oil onto this bushing from time to time. You can check for wear by inserting the armature shaft into the bushing and measuring the clearance. If a gap of more than 0.004 in. exists, the bushing should be replaced.

Bushings and bearings are available from vintage Chevrolet parts suppliers like Jim Carter's Vintage Chevrolet Parts (see appendices for address) and can often be purchased at the local NAPA parts store. When attempting to find these items at the parts store, it's best to measure the width of the old bushing or bearing as well as the inside and outside diameters. These measurements can be taken with a micrometer from the depth of the bushing inset in the end cap, the diameter of the inset and the diameter of the armature shaft. If you lack a micrometer with which to make precision measurements, just take the unit to the parts store and the counter clerk should be able to do the measuring. When these trucks were in regular service, rather than replace the bushing, repair shops just installed a new end frame. You might ask the parts store if they have an end frame with bushing in stock. If they do, you will be saved the job of replacing the bushing. Plan to buy new brushes when picking up the bushing, bearing or end frame.

The old bushing can be removed from the end frame by turning the bushing out with a tap. First you will need to select a washer that will fit inside the bushing. The washer's purpose is to support the tap. Drop the washer into the bushing hole, then select a tap large enough to thread into the bushing. Insert this tap into the bushing and turn it until the tap seats against the washer at the bottom of the bushing hole. Continue to turn the tap and the bushing will climb up out of the hole. The new bushings should be installed with a driver. Lacking this, you can use a socket.

The next step is to connect the leads from the field coils to their attaching points and insert the brushes into their holders on the end cap. The clips that hold the brushes against the armature when the generator or starter is operating will have to be pulled back in order to insert the brushes into the holders. You can pull back the clips with needle-nose pliers, but a better tool can be made by cutting about a 4 in. piece of coat hanger wire and bending one end into a hook. Make a 90 degree bend about 1 in. from the other end to form a handle to use in pulling against the spring's tension.

Instead of letting the clips snap back against the brushes, try to rest each clip against the side of the brush which is just started into the holder. If you are able to do this, you can slip the armature through the frame and into the end containing the brushes. When the armature is in place, push the brushes down against the commutator and position the clips on the brushes.

Before attempting to insert the armature into the frame and end cap, place a dab of high-temperature grease into the end-cap bushing. This will ensure that the armature is well lubricated for many, many miles. Now the generator is reassembled and you can replace the through-bolts to hold the parts together.

Generator Polarizing

When a generator has been off the vehicle for testing or repair, it may lose its residual magnetism. This magnetism will need to be restored to the correct polarity before the generator will charge. This must be done before the engine is operated. The process of repolarizing the generator differs, depending on whether the generator is of the A (externally grounded) or B (internally grounded) type. Most GM generators are Type A. Check the service manual for your truck if you are not sure whether the generator is internally or externally grounded.

To polarize a Type A (externally grounded) generator, disconnect the field terminal at the regulator and ground it, then momentarily connect a jumper wire between the battery and generator armature terminal. This brief surge of current will polarize the generator.

To polarize a Type B (internally grounded) generator, disconnect the wire to the field wire at the regulator terminal and momentarily connect it to the battery terminal.

Generator Bench Testing

Before reinstalling the generator on the truck, it's a good idea to test it for current draw. In this test you will be operating the generator as a motor. It will be drawing, not producing, current. To motorize the generator, connect the battery and an ammeter in series between the generator armature terminal and proper battery post (positive post on negative ground systems, negative post on positive ground systems). Ground the field terminal to the generator frame with a jumper wire.

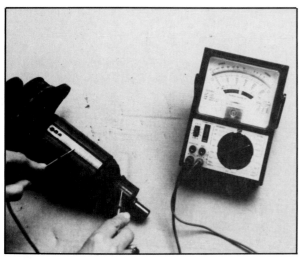

Another test checks for an internal short in the armature. As shown here, one lead from the VOM meter is placed on the armature core and the other on the commutator.

A GM starter. The design and construction of this component closely resemble the generator.

Next attach a ground cable to the generator frame and other battery post. The generator should now operate as a motor (it should spin) and on most generators the ammeter should register between 4 and 6 amperes. If the current draw is not within this margin, check for poor connections. If the connections are good, the problem could be a faulty armature or field coils, or possibly poor brush fit on the armature. If you suspect that the brushes have not conformed to the surface of the armature, you may want to run the generator as a motor for a short period to let the brushes wear in. Then give the generator time to cool to room temperature and repeat the test again, checking current draw. If it is within the acceptable range, the generator is ready to be installed on the truck.

This motorizing test also polarizes the generator.

Reinstalling the Generator

After replacing the mounting bolts at the bottom of the generator, slip the belt over the generator pulley and pull the generator tight on the belt. Now screw in the clamp bolt on the generator bracket and check the belt for correct tightness (usually 7/16 to 1/2 in. deflection of the belt at a point midway between the fan and generator pulleys). Retighten or loosen the generator as needed. Now reconnect the wiring leads to the generator. It should be in sound operating condition.

Starter Rebuild

Starter problems are noticed when the starter turns sluggishly, if at all, on a well-charged battery. When poor starter response occurs, you will want to determine whether the source of the problem lies in the wiring or the starter. A simple way to do this is to turn on the headlights and crank the starter.

If the lights go out, there is insufficient voltage to operate the lights and starter motor. This can be caused by a battery in poor condition or bad electrical connections or cables. A poor connection almost always can be traced to corrosion on the battery terminals or a loose cable clamp. This is corrected by removing the battery cables, cleaning the posts and cable clamps with a solution of baking soda and water (be careful that none of this solution runs into the battery cells), then scouring posts and cable clamp holes with a battery post brush. To prevent the terminals from re-corroding, replace and tighten the cable clamps, then spray the clamps and terminals with Plasti-Dip, a spray plastic coating available in auto supply stores and discount marts. Now make sure the battery has a good charge and try this test again. In most cases the starter will now spin normally.

If the lights dim substantially and the starter turns very slowly or not at all, either the battery is in a run-down condition, or the engine or starter has some mechanical problem that is throwing a heavy load on the starter. The battery's condition can be checked with a hydrometer. Lacking this inexpensive testing device, you can put a charger on the battery and give it a charge. If it takes the charge, bring the battery to a fully charged state and try this test again. If the problem was a discharged battery, the starter should spin normally.

Mechanical problems with the engine that could cause the starter to turn sluggishly or not at all are water in the cylinders, a bent rod, seized piston rings, seized bearings—to name the most common. If the starter itself is failing to operate normally, possible problems include a bent armature, loose starter screws or worn bearings. Of these, on an older truck worn bearings are the most common.

If the lights stay bright and the starter fails to crank, there is an open circuit in the starter, the starter switch or the control circuit. If the starter is equipped with a solenoid, this control device can be bypassed with a heavy jumper to remove this possible problem component from the circuit. The entire starter control circuit can be bypassed by connecting a heavy jumper (a battery jumper cable works well) directly from the hot battery post to the starter terminal. If the starter turns over, the problem is in the control circuit which will have to be checked out component by component. If the starter does not operate by the jumper, it either is not receiving a good ground or has an internal mechanical problem. To check for a good ground, first make sure the starter is bolted tightly against the bellhousing. If this is the case, you can clamp one end of the jumper cable to the starter case and the other end to the ground terminal on the battery. If the starter still fails to respond, it definitely has a mechanical problem and will need to be removed from the truck for repair.

Starter Removal

To remove the starter, first disconnect the ground cable from the battery, then loosen and remove the large brass nut that attaches the heavy cable to the starter. If the solenoid mounts to the starter housing, you will also need to remove and label the small wires that enable the ignition key to activate the starter. Now you can loosen the bolts that hold the starter to the bellhousing and remove the unit. Some starter bolts are accessed best from underneath and the starter can generally be removed easiest from this direction. Note the position and save any shims found between the starter and bellhousing. They will be needed for reinstallation.

Starter Disassembly

A starter comes apart in much the same way as a generator. As with the generator, it is inadvisable to disassemble the starter more than necessary. This means that unless the starter needs to be totally disassembled, it is advisable to leave the field coils in place.

Cleaning and painting the starter is the same as for a generator.

Starter Testing

Inspect and test the armature, following the steps described for testing the generator. If the armature is bent or shorted, it should be replaced. If the armature is OK, clean the commutator. And if the copper surface is rough or out of round, have it cut smooth at a machine shop.

The starter terminal (this is the copper bolt to which the starter cable attaches) should also be

As you look at the starter or generator end plate that has the brush holder brackets, you will notice that one set of brackets is insulated from the end plate. To check for a short in this insulation, place one lead from the VOM on the brush holder, and the other on the end plate. If the needle moves, the insulation is allowing current to pass and the end plate will need to be replaced.

inspected for stripped threads. If the threads are damaged, the bolt should be replaced at this time. If the bolt is replaced, it will be necessary to resolder the connections to the field coils. Next the field coils are tested, following a procedure similar to that used to test the generator field coils.

To test for an open circuit, place one lead from the VOM meter or test light on each field coil lead (these wires attach to the brush holder when the starter is assembled). If the meter does not show current flow (or the test lamp does not light), the field coils do not make a complete circuit and should be replaced.

To test the field coils for a ground, first make sure the field coil terminals inside the housing are disconnected. Then place one lead from the VOM meter or test light on the starter terminal and the other on a clean, unpainted surface of the starter frame. If the meter shows current flow or if the test lamp lights, a ground exists in the field coil circuit and must be isolated to determine what repairs are needed. Note that false ground readings may be obtained if the brushes are not all the way out of the brush holder or if the field coils or terminals are touching the housing.

The starter brush holder is tested for grounds following the same method outlined for the generator.

Starter Assembly

Before reassembling the starter, check and if needed replace the bushing and bearing as described in the generator reassembly section. Also install new brushes in the brush holder.

If a solenoid mounts to the starter, also bolt this component in place and connect the solenoid cable to the lug on the starter frame. The amount of clearance between the starter gear (pinion) and its retainer now has to be checked and the location of the solenoid adjusted, if needed, to ensure the correct amount of clearance. Instructions for making this clearance adjustment are found in the Chevrolet truck shop manual.

Reinstalling the Starter

The starter can now be replaced on the truck in the reverse order that it was taken off. Be sure to match the wires to the correct terminals on the solenoid and tighten the nut holding the starter cable to the terminal post. Assuming all wiring connections have been made correctly, that all wiring is sound and the battery is charged, the starter should spin the engine briskly.

If the generator and starter have been restored for later use, they should be wrapped (a plastic or paper grocery bag works well), labeled and put aside for later installation.

Running the Engine

Before starting the engine, it's essential to prime the oil pump to prelubricate the engine. This is done either by purchasing an oil system primer that is inserted through the distributor hole and spun by a ½ in. electric drill, or by making a primer by removing the cap and rotor and any other internals from a scrap distributor. Next, braze a bolt to the top of the distributor mainshaft (with the threads sticking up). If the distributor shaft meshes with the camshaft, grind off the teeth on the distributor shaft using a bench grinder. Insert the distributor shaft into its hole and spin the bolt by hand to check for any binding that would not

To test for an open circuit inside the starter, place one lead from the VOM meter on each field coil. The meter should show current flow.

allow the mainshaft to turn freely. Now use a ½ in. electric drill to spin the shaft and prime the pump. This will take a few minutes. Air must be expelled from the pump for the lubrication system to become functional. You will feel when the system becomes active by a slight shift of the drill in your hand.

The carburetor should be primed with gasoline to avoid the cranking time that will be needed to fill the fuel line, but other than this, if the engine has been put together carefully it should start right up. If the engine refuses to start, check the ignition timing and other tune-up steps to make sure the engine is delivering a hot spark.

For more modern trucks, specifically those built since the late 1960s, rebuilt engines are available either in short-block (this is the block assembly and internals only, without the oil pan or heads) or long-block (complete engine). Buying a short-block is typically less expensive than the cost of machining work and purchasing new internal parts separately. The advantage of a long-block unit is cost savings over hiring someone else to assemble the engine. The disadvantage of this approach is that the truck now has a nonoriginal engine. Also, depending on the camshaft and compression ratio, the rebuilt may either be a stronger or less powerful engine than the original.

Engine Detailing

Besides painting the engine and accessories in keeping with the original color scheme, engine detailing consists of running the spark plug wires through the proper guides or tying the wires together with retainers, replacing the decals on the valve covers, and placing the fuel and vacuum lines in their proper path and securing these lines with the correct clips installed at the original positions on the engine. For the perfectionist who is preparing a truck for show competition, illustrations in the factory assembly manuals show the factory routing of the spark plug wires, the orientation of the bolts holding the generator to its mounting bracket, and other details of this sort.

It's also possible that you may want to dress up the engine with accessories that were available during the period. These options make your truck a livelier performer and give the engine a performance look as well.

Stovebolt Performance

If you're looking for more power and performance from that Advanced Design or earlier Chevrolet truck, but don't want to shoehorn in a V-8 (with all the modifications that implant would require), there's plenty you can do to build excitement into a Chevrolet or GMC Stovebolt six. The only hitch here is that the original 216 ci engine with its Babbitt bearings and low-pressure oiling, which Chevrolet installed in its light trucks up to 1954, is not a good place to start. Six-cylinder engines suited to performance treatment are the pressure-oiling 235s (used in cars and trucks from 1954 to 1963) and the 261 ci six, also introduced in 1954 for heavy-duty trucks, and used in Canadian Pontiac cars from 1955 to 1963.

If you can find a 235 ci that was originally coupled to a Powerglide, you're already a step ahead as it has a small horsepower edge to make up for the slippage of the automatic transmission. The Canadian Pontiac 261 has the advantage of using the same head as the 1953–1955 six-cylinder Corvette. Besides the Chevrolet 235 and 261, the 248 and 269 ci GMC engines have strong hop-up potential. You will find that these 1954 and newer sixes are a bolt-in for the original 216, except that the water pump is longer and needs to be replaced by a special pump sold by Patrick's, of Casa Grande, Arizona, or the Stovebolt Engine Company, located in Corbett, Oregon. All the rest of the accessories from your truck can be used, which means that you can keep the engine looking original. (See appendices for suppliers' addresses.)

The larger Chevrolet and GMC sixes will respond to all the traditional hot-rod tricks. In fact, in the 1950s, before the Chevy 265 and 283 ci V-8s became plentiful, dragsters and stock cars with hot-rodded Stovebolt sixes were formidable competition. You can make that Stovebolt live by doing any or all of the following.

Compression

The compression ratio of a Chevrolet or GMC six can be raised as high as 10.5:1, although at that level you'll be looking for octane boosters to avoid spark knock in today's gasoline. You will probably want to be conservative—say 8:1, which is stock for a 1956-57 235 ci (though this may not be the actual compression ratio of all production engines).

There are two different ways to raise compression on your six. First, you can mill the stock head. Milling 0.030 in. from a stock 235 ci. head from a 1954 or later engine results in a compression ratio of 7.85:1 when the 235 head is installed on a 261 ci engine. To achieve this same compression, the 261 head would have to be milled 0.125 in. It's important to note that when a Chevrolet six head is milled, it is necessary to recess the intake valve into the head by an equal amount so that interference does not occur between the valve and piston.

The second option is to install an aftermarket higher-compression head such as Wayne, Edmunds or Fenton. These are being remanufactured by Charlie Baker Vintage Development and Design out of Nevada, Iowa (see appendices for address). Originals are rare, but not impossible to find.

You'll probably want to polish the combustion chamber in the head. This takes the rough edges off the combustion chamber and valve passages. Pol-ishing is done using a cylinder head porting kit available from The Eastwood Company.

Remember that good gasket surfaces are an absolute must! Check the mating surfaces of the head and block for trueness using a straightedge before assembling. Also, look up the head-bolt tightening sequence in a service manual and re-tighten the head as soon as the engine warms up and again after 500 miles.

Induction

Better breathing really wakes up these engines. Edmunds and Fenton both made dual- and triple-carburetor manifolds for both 235 and 261 ci

Multiple carburetors really make inline Chevrolet and GMC engines come alive.

A four barrel carburetor also boosts engine performance. Larry Hurst

Chevrolet blocks and reproduction copies of these manifolds are now available. Performance intake manifolds set up to take a four-barrel carburetor are available for the 248 and 269 ci GMC engines. You can also make a multiple carburetor manifold using your stock cast-iron one as a base. Sometimes it is possible to locate a triple-carburetor 1953-55 Corvette manifold.

Multiple carburetors can be a real headache to synchronize, so the three-carburetor setup is not necessarily an improvement over the dual carburetors. Two one-barrel carburetors, or a four-barrel, make a simpler setup.

Valves from a 1987 Chevrolet six are an exact fit for the Chevy 235 and 261 ci engines, and are designed to operate on unleaded gas.

Exhaust

Any improvement in a six's exhaust system will help. A simple split manifold is a must. Fenton headers are nice to look at, work well and are readily available in reproduction form. Put on non-restrictive mufflers and a good, clean exhaust system and this part of the job is done. Nothing sounds as sweet as a Stovebolt six with dual pipes—not even a flathead Ford V-8.

Porting

The most significant improvement to be made is the matching of the ports in the head with the manifold passages. Make templates of the manifold and open the ports to match with a rotary file. This is a simple, but exacting, operation. Carelessness can ruin your head. Even a stock rebuild will benefit from porting.

Some performance advantage can be gained by smoothing intake and exhaust passages in the head. Again, this is a simple process, but one that must be done with care.

Slightly greater clearances are desirable in a performance engine to ensure good lubrication and allow for expansion due to greater heat. Allow 0.004 in. for piston skirt clearance and between 0.0015 and 0.002 in. for bearings. Set valve tappets at 0.002 in. over factory specs.

Camshafts

Hotter cams are available and will complement the other modifications on a Stovebolt six. It is advisable to replace hydraulic lifters with solid (mechanical) types in combination with a hotter cam. Mechanical lifters were used in non-Power-

In most situations, certainly for restoration, the engine will be removed from the truck for rebuilding. First the engine will be thoroughly cleaned, then it should be mounted on an engine stand for disassembly. Mike Cavey

glide Chevrolet passenger-car sixes for 1954 and 1955.

Spark

A Mallory dual-point distributor will really put these engines through their paces. At one time, Mallory distributors were quite popular aftermarket items. With luck, you may find one at a swap meet. Patrick's has persuaded Mallory to begin rebuilding the dual-point distributors and is the sales outlet for these new manufactured items.

Dress-up

Wayne finned and polished aluminum valve and pushrod covers look sharp on a performance Stovebolt. They not only look great, but bring back all the nostalgia of the days when a hopped-up Chevrolet or GMC six could blow the doors off a well-tuned Ford. These items are readily available in absolutely authentic, reproduction form.

Interchange Tips

For 1937 and later Chevrolet trucks, the standard 261 ci flywheel, pressure plate and clutch plate may be used. A 1941 or later water pump, 1940 or later crankshaft pulley and 1937 or later generator, voltage regulator, starter and fuel pump can also be used on a 261 ci conversion or a 1955 First Series and earlier 6 volt truck. A 1953 Powerglide or any 1954 or later 235 ci oil pan will fit the 261 and give needed clearance for any 1937 and later front-end components. As mentioned earlier, cylinder heads from a 1953 Powerglide or 1954 and later 235 ci will interchange with the 261.

With performance upgrading, you will find the 235 or 261 ci Chevrolet, or the 248 or 269 ci GMC sixes have plenty of power for hills and to keep up with today's traffic. You'll welcome the extra responsiveness and probably find yourself putting more miles on your older truck, and enjoying it far more than frumping from place to place with the original engine.

I've ridden in a one-ton GMC panel truck, owned by *Trucks* magazine publisher Chris Krieg, which has been upgraded with a performance 248 ci Jimmy six. Krieg drives his GMC daily, for both work and enjoyment. The engine, which has been modified with a four-barrel carburetor and split-exhaust manifold, moves the truck through a set of higher speed rear-end gears from a later-model Chevrolet one-ton pickup. Although the drivetrain is nearly stock appearing, the truck shows plenty of scat and cruises easily at 55 mph. If you are among the old-truck lovers who picked your Chevrolet or GMC for driving, you'll find a Stovebolt upgrade has plenty to offer—and most performance parts are readily available.

9

Transmission and Drivetrain Rebuild

Few hobbyist mechanics possess the skills and specialized tools needed to rebuild an automatic or manual transmission or a light-duty truck rear end. However, these units need to be inspected for wear and problems like worn bearings and leaking gaskets that could cause a breakdown on the road. In the first part of this chapter you'll learn about noises and other indications of transmission and rear drive problems, as well as guidelines that may save you money and prevent the headaches that can occur when you're trying to find a reliable shop to rebuild major mechanical assemblies from an older truck. There'll also be tips for removing the transmission and driveline from the truck. For step-by-step instructions on these removal procedures you'll want to refer to the Chevrolet shop manual for your year and series of truck.

Later in this chapter you will find instructions on how to install an overdrive transmission in a

Pictured is the cluster gear set which spins around a sun gear driven from the output shaft of the three-speed transmission. This cluster gear set fits into a ring gear which rotates at a speed one-third greater than the transmission mainshaft. The result is higher comfortable cruising speed, decreased engine wear and greater fuel economy.

vintage Chevrolet or GMC truck. Overdrive, which was a factory accessory most years between 1955 Second Series and the mid 1960s, has advantages in fuel economy, reduced engine wear and higher highway cruising speeds.

Toward the end of the chapter there is information on the extremely rugged four-wheel-drive conversions for 1950s and early 1960s Chevrolet trucks supplied by NAPCO. Until 1958, the NAPCO 4x4 driveline assemblies were retrofitted to two-wheel-drive trucks, which means that if you own an early to mid 1950s Chevrolet truck and come across a NAPCO setup, you could swap the parts to your truck. That's what Chevrolet dealers did for customers who ordered four-wheel-drive when the trucks were new.

Automatic Transmission Problems

By the nature of their design, automatic transmissions—available on Chevrolet and GMC trucks beginning in 1954—are subject to different kinds of wear and failure than manual transmissions. If your truck is equipped with an automatic, three quick checks (checks you're advised to do when purchasing an automatic transmission truck) are to look underneath for signs that the transmission is leaking fluid, notice whether the truck slips in gear or slams into gear, and inspect the color of the transmission fluid.

Leaking fluid can usually be seen in puddles on the ground or garage floor, or in traces of dripping fluid at the end of the transmission case or front of the driveshaft; leakage from the rear of the transmission is more likely to occur when the truck is parked on an incline. Leakage around the pan at the bottom of the transmission or the rear seal is relatively easy to fix with the transmission in the truck. Slippage and hard shifting can be signs that the transmission needs to be rebuilt.

Fluid is checked in an automatic transmission with the truck running and the engine warmed up. In this setting the fluid should reach the full mark on the dipstick. The transmission fluid should be dark red. A brownish color, typically coupled with a burnt smell, means that the transmission is slipping and is a sign that the automatic transmission is in need of a rebuild.

Manual Transmission Problems

Manual transmission problems are identified by noises. A rumbling noise coming from the transmission location under your feet with the engine idling and the clutch out probably is coming from a worn front transmission bearing. A similar noise from the same location when the truck is being driven in third gear and that isn't heard with the transmission in neutral probably indicates a worn rear transmission bearing. A chipped or missing tooth on first or second gear can often be heard as gear noise when the truck is operated in either of these gears, although you can expect to hear gear noise from any high-mileage transmission.

Besides worn bearings and worn or chipped gears, manual transmissions can also develop excessive end play (movement of the gears and shafts inside the case) due to normal wear of the thrust washers and synchronizer clutches, and possibly broken snap rings that are used to hold the bearings in place. End play becomes most noticeable when the transmission jumps out of gear. What happens here is that you are driving along and let up on the gas momentarily and the transmission shifts itself into neutral.

Although abusive driving and running the transmission low on gear oil can cause the problems described above, these are also natural signs of wear that result from high mileage. If the truck you are restoring or overhauling has worked a long, hard life, you should plan on a transmission rebuild or look for a low mileage replacement unit.

If the truck is being disassembled for restoration, the transmission will be removed after the engine. If you are taking the overhaul approach—and the transmission shows signs of needing to be rebuilt—it can be removed without disturbing the engine by uncoupling the driveshaft on mid 1955 and later Chevrolet trucks or by loosening the rear spring bolts and sliding back the rear end and driveshaft on light-duty Chevrolet trucks built through early 1955.

When selecting a transmission rebuilder, look for a shop or repairman with experience on transmissions of your truck's vintage. Gasket sets and bearings for Chevrolet manual transmissions are readily available from specialty suppliers such as Jim Carter. Replacement gear sets may be expensive and difficult to find. For this reason, it's probably wiser to replace a worn, high-mileage manual transmission with a better condition unit. In later-model trucks with PowerGlide and Turbo Hydramatic transmissions, truck and car units interchange, making parts and service quite plentiful.

Clutch and Pressure Plate Problems

The clutch provides a coupling that is used to disrupt the power flow from the engine through the transmission to the rear end. When the clutch is engaged and the pedal is released, power from the engine flows through the driveline. When the clutch is disengaged and the pedal is depressed, the engine is disconnected from the driveline. The clutch itself consists of a disc-shaped plate containing friction material. When engaged, the clutch's friction surfaces are pressed tightly against the flywheel by the pressure plate. This allows the input shaft of the transmission to turn at the same speed as the engine.

Basically three types of problems can occur at the clutch coupling. The first is clutch wear, which leads to slippage. The second is clutch chatter, an annoying jumping motion as the clutch is engaged. The third is wearing of the clutch mechanism rather than the clutch itself.

Clutch wear and slippage are easy to recognize. When slippage occurs, the engine's power isn't being transmitted to the rear wheels. If the truck is operated in this condition you may notice a burning smell. Slippage is a sure sign that the clutch needs to be replaced.

Chatter can be caused by several factors. If the engine has an oil leak through the rear main bear-

---

Coupling an Automatic to a Stovebolt Six

The aluminum-case Powerglide, Turbo Hydra-matic 350 and Turbo Hydra-matic 400 and 700 Chevrolet transmission can be bolted to Chevrolet's 216 ci engine for 1937–1953; the 235 ci from 1941–1963; the 261 ci from 1954–1963; and the GMC 228, 248, 270 or 302 ci from 1939–1962.

You'll need to use a ⅝ in. steel plate adapter from the Stovebolt Engine Co. The adapter is precision-cut with all holes drilled and topped for easy installation. The automatic transmission conversion requires a 12 volt starter from a more recent Chevrolet 250 ci six-cylinder engine, which installs by bolts installed with the adapter kit.

The adapter is designed for use with stock Chevrolet anti-rocking mounts which are usually on the front of stock bellhousings. The mount hole on the passenger side is moved over slightly to make room for the starter, requiring a new hole be drilled in the frame.

The kit comes with a Chevrolet 350 ci V-8 flywheel which has been modified to fit either the earlier Chevrolet or the GMC flywheel flange bolt pattern. The flywheel is also drilled for a timing mark which is in the same location as the ball bearing on the stock iron flywheel.

ing seal, the clutch facing could be picking up oil, which can cause the friction material to slip then grab several times before seating tightly against the flywheel. If the clutch has worn so that its friction disk has developed hard spots, this can also cause chatter. In addition, chatter can be caused by a flywheel that has high spots on its face or is not seated squarely on the end of the crankshaft.

Wear in the clutch mechanism is most readily noticed as a high pitch vibration or chatter heard with the clutch disengaged that indicates a dry or worn pilot bushing or throw out bearing. Any of these conditions will require removing the engine or transmission to access the clutch mechanism. On a Second Series 1955 to present day Chevrolet truck with Hotchkiss drive it's easiest to reach the

Borg-Warner overdrives, which Chevrolet installed in its cars and light trucks, were activated by an electric solenoid. When supplied with current, the solenoid extended a lever (as shown) to shove a pawl into the sun-gear control plate and lock the overdrive into action. This solenoid is the Achilles heel of these overdrive units. Replacements are not being made, and workable original solenoids are in short supply. If you are considering retrofitting overdrive into your truck, the decision as to whether or not to use the original electrical control will depend on locating a workable solenoid.

clutch by disconnecting the universal joints and removing the driveshaft and transmission.

While servicing a worn clutch, it's advisable to remove the flywheel and have the face checked for trueness and surface condition at a machine shop. If problems are noted, the flywheel should be machined to a true, smooth surface. The pressure plate should also be inspected for worn fingers (the prongs that contact the throw out bearing when the clutch is disengaged), grooves and other signs of wear on the contact surface, or warped or broken springs (a sign of severe abuse). The pilot bushing should also be checked for wear and replaced if necessary. It is important to remember to lubricate the pilot bushing before installing a new clutch.

Replacing a clutch is within the skills of most hobbyist mechanics. The only specialized tools required are a torque wrench and an alignment shaft to center the clutch disc on the pressure plate. The service manual for your year of Chevrolet truck gives a good step-by-step guide to follow if you're replacing a clutch for the first time.

Universal Joint and Driveshaft Problems

Universal joints are inserted into the driveline to change the angle of the powerflow from the transmission to the differential rear end. When kept properly lubricated, universal joints will last indefinitely. When lubrication is overlooked these constantly moving parts can wear rapidly. The first sign of universal joint wear is usually driveline vibration. This occurs because the needle bearings in the universal joints have worn sufficiently to throw the driveshaft slightly off center. When the universal joints wear to the point where they are making noise, the bearings are gone and you're not going to be driving your truck many miles before the universal joints fail and the driveshaft drops onto the road.

It's possible to replace the universal joints and still experience driveline vibration. The cause in this case would be an out of balance, bent or improperly installed driveshaft. You can have the driveshaft balanced at a machine shop. When installing the driveshaft in the truck, the sliding yoke goes at the upper end, behind the transmission.

Differential Problems

Like other parts of the drivetrain, wear in the differential rear end is also signaled by noises. Basically there are three kinds of noises that indicate rear-end problems. A howling sound (not a scream, but a noise that sounds like poorly meshing gears) indicates gear wear in the differential. This noise will normally change as you accelerate and decelerate, thereby altering the load on the ring gear and drive pinion. A rumble or rougher sound points to worn bearings. A clunk, heard when starting to back the truck up, is a sign of backlash or wear which may be occurring anywhere in the drivetrain but is often located in the rear end.

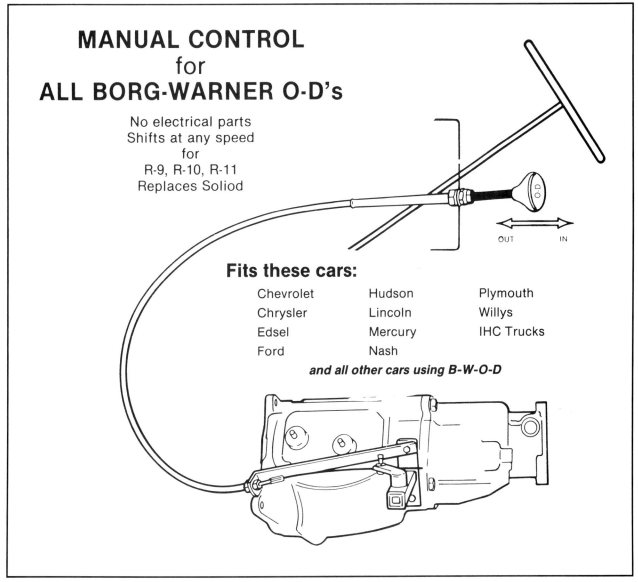

MANUAL CONTROL
for
ALL BORG-WARNER O-D's

No electrical parts
Shifts at any speed
for
R-9, R-10, R-11
Replaces Soliod

OUT   IN

Fits these cars:

Chevrolet	Hudson	Plymouth
Chrysler	Lincoln	Willys
Edsel	Mercury	IHC Trucks
Ford	Nash	

and all other cars using B-W-O-D

As an alternative to the electric solenoid you can operate the overdrive with a manual control engineered by OverDrive Inc. The manual control gives the extra advantage of enabling you to use the overdrive as a gear-splitter transmission so that instead of the standard three-speed plus overdrive, you now have six forward gears.

The other problem to look for is oil leakage. This may be seen around the differential gear housing in the center of the rear axle where the cause is either loose bolts around the differential cover or a bad gasket. Drive pinion seal leakage will sometimes cause oil to be thrown from the rear universal joint yoke when the truck is running. This can cause the oil level to drop below the drive pinion in the differential. Along with looking for signs of oil leakage, always check the oil level in the differential. Oil can also leak past the seals at the ends of the axles. When this happens the leakage is sometimes seen on the rear wheel backing plates or can be seen when the rear brake drums are pulled.

Gear noise can often be reduced or eliminated by adjusting the mesh between the ring and drive pinion gears. The rough use that pickups sometimes receive can cause differential wear that is not normally found in cars. For example, if the truck has been driven extensively with different size rear tires the differential pinion and side gears are likely to show more wear than would be expected for the truck's mileage. This is a common cause of backlash.

When listening for bearing noise, don't get confused with normal tire noise. If your truck is fitted with mud and snow tires or if you are driving on rough pavement, the whine you hear is probably tire noise. To distinguish bearing noise occurring inside the differential from noise being generated by the rear wheel bearings, turn the truck sharply left then right on smooth pavement. Wheel bearing noise gets louder as the truck is turning. Any internal bearing or gear noise means that the differential needs to be disassembled for inspection and repair.

One easy way to tell if looseness or backlash is occurring in the differential is to jack up the rear end and have a friend put the truck in gear and slowly engage the clutch while you watch how far the driveshaft turns before the wheels begin to rotate. Unless you want your truck to be in factory-new condition, some backlash is tolerable as long as the rear end doesn't howl.

Transmission and Rear-End Rebuild

It's possible to overhaul the rear end in the truck, although if you are doing a frame-up restoration you may remove the rear end in preparation for cleaning the frame. Rear-end repair, like transmission overhaul, is work best left to professionals. Since the basic design of light-duty truck rear ends has changed little over the years, any repair shop with experience on Chevrolet trucks should be able to perform this work satisfactorily.

Although gaskets and bearings are readily available—back to the 1940s at least—you may have more difficulty locating replacement gears. In this case, the better move may be to substitute a rear end from a lower-mileage truck.

Overdrives

Back in the days when the light trucks we now enjoy as hobby vehicles were working on farms, lumber yards, construction sites and anywhere else a truck fits in, being able to cruise down an interstate at 65 mph wasn't one of the buyer's prime considerations. The question was, will it haul so many apples out of the orchard without spinning a wheel and bogging down? Low rear-end gearing, combined with stump-pulling first-gear ratios, made a Chevrolet light truck a capable worker, but you wouldn't take the truck on the family vacation unless it was the only vehicle you owned—and you wanted to smell the flowers along the way.

Today, few of us use our trucks for heavy hauling, so now, all that once-helpful low gearing does for us is let the engine roar like a freight train as we're putting down the highway at 45 mph. The freight train comparison fits more than just the engine sound. Traveling 45 mph on a busy road, we'll soon back up enough traffic to look like an iron horse and its string of freight.

Besides increasing the rotation speed of the output shaft of the standard three-speed transmission by thirty percent, the typical Borg-Warner overdrive allows for freewheeling when the throttle is released.

Propeller Shaft Seal

by Dick Matott

In the process of restoring my 1947 Second Series half-ton pickup, I ordered a propeller shaft seal from a supplier who listed this part for 1947–1954 Chevrolets. When I received the seal, it was obvious that it would not fit. I called the supplier and explained what my 1947 seal looked like and found that no seal was available in those dimensions. I tried two large commercial bearing suppliers in my area and determined that no seal of these dimensions was listed by any manufacturer. I was now curious as to what the later shafts looked like, so I tore down the rear end and driveshaft from the 1951 Chevrolet truck I am using for parts. The seal originally shipped fit the 1951 shaft perfectly. The difference is that the propeller shaft from the 1951 is about 1¾ in. shorter than the 1947. The reason for this difference is that my 1951 truck had a four-speed transmission which is longer than the three-speed in the 1947. To make the seal fit, I brought the 1947 shaft and the new rear bushing to a local machine shop and had the propeller shaft machined to match the 1951. Now the unit is assembled and everything seems fine.

An overdrive transmission operates like this: When driving down the road with the overdrive unit disengaged, the transmission mainshaft passes directly through the center of the sun gear so that the overdrive output shaft rotates at the same speed as the mainshaft. When overdrive is engaged, the sun gear slides forward to engage a pinion gear set which rotates an outer ring gear at a speed thirty percent faster than the transmission mainshaft. This step-up rotation passes through the output shaft to the rear end.

On deceleration a freewheeling clutch disengages the driveline. Freewheeling is operative whenever overdrive is engaged and will cause the truck to coast without benefit of engine braking when going down hills. The advantages of freewheeling are greater fuel economy and the possiblity of clutchless shifting from second to third gear. The disadvantages are faster brake wear and the possibility of a run-away if overdrive is left disengaged in mountainous travel.

The freewheeling clutch is located at the rear of the overdrive gear set and consists of a set of twelve clutch rollers which press against an outer ring gear while the mainshaft is receiving torque from the engine. When the engine torque cuts back (by letting up on the accelerator) the clutch rollers disengage, thereby disconnecting the power link between the mainshaft and output shaft. This allows the output shaft to turn with the differential without being restrained by engine braking.

Overdrive Troubleshooting and Repair
by Laurence "Lars" Larson

If you have a 1955 Second Series or later truck with overdrive, it's possible that the step-up transmission may not be functioning. The steps that follow will help you troubleshoot the problem and make the repair.

In retrofitting overdrive to a pre 1955 Chevrolet light-duty truck with torque-tube drive, OverDrive Inc. uses a double chain to couple the overdrive transmission to the propeller shaft inside the torque tube.

Troubleshooting steps

Determine that the overdrive solenoid is OK by applying current to the #4 terminal while grounding the case of the solenoid. This can be done under the truck or you can remove the solenoid and make the check at the battery. The #6 terminal is a grounding circuit to cut out the overdrive so there is no need to check it—except for a possible open or short. If the solenoid operates it obviously is OK. If it doesn't, you need a new one. Replacements are no longer being made and are difficult to find. I tried to get mine rewound but was given figures like $100 plus for rewinding. OverDrive Inc. builds a manual substitute for the solenoid. This device consists of a special lever that replaces solenoid and an appropriate cable to operate same.

Check the fuse on the overdrive relay located on the firewall. Be sure it is good. I found an old fuse that looked good but had a loose end and was not allowing juice to pass through, so looks don't always tell.

A special mounting block allows the overdrive to be bolted to the torque tube, and a sprocket is welded to the input shaft of the overdrive transmission for the chain link.

Higher Gearing for Pickups

by Karl Townsend

I have seen various approaches to increase the road speed on 1947–1954 GMC pickups. Here's what I did with my 1950 Chevrolet 3100 series pickup. The engine and drivetrain consist of a 1962 Chevrolet 235 ci engine, a 1975 GMC transmission and a 1974 Jeep Wagoneer rear end. The clutch housing had to be lathed out to fit the front bearing cap of the GMC transmission. I also used a different flywheel that would fit an 11 in. clutch. The flywheel had a larger crankshaft hole, but it bolted up and the timing marks were in the same place.

The 11 in. clutch is a tight fit, but works well. The cross-member is in the original location with very slight modifications to bolt the transmission mount to it. I shortened a 1965 Dodge panel truck driveshaft and used a new slip yoke and joint to match the 1975 transmission. In the rear, I welded new pads onto the axle tubes with the spring center bolts offset 1 13/16 in. to the rear to center the tires in the wheel openings. Since the Wagoneer rear end is approximately 1½ in. narrower than the original, I reversed the 15x4.5 in. wheels so that there was 2 in. of wheel mounting flange to the edge of the wheel. The tires rub slightly when cornering, but this will be corrected when new spring bushings are installed. The rubbing is also caused by the oversize 7.50x16 in. tires that I run in the rear.

The easiest way to trace overdrive electrical problems is to ground out each unit, starting from the last component, the governor; this is the same principle that you use to test your ignition for weak spark. It is best to use a long wire. Ground at the battery or frame, and use the other end to clip onto the component terminal you are testing. Proceed on, grounding each terminal, working from the rear. For example, if you ground the bottom terminal of the firewall relay and the solenoid clicks, then the wire from the relay to the kickdown switch is open. You may have to isolate the bad component by disconnecting its leads from the circuit to check it out.

Rather than an open, you may have a continuous short, either in frayed wiring or internally in a component. This will show up by the solenoid engaging (clicking—if it is not burned out) each time you turn on the ignition. If this is the case, start from rear again, removing each element in turn from the system. In other words, if you remove the wire from the governor to the rail switch at the rail switch and the solenoid drops out of the circuit (clicks), that wire is grounded and must be replaced. Why not the governor? Because if you are following these instructions you started from the last component and already know the governor is OK.

Note also there are two circuits—the holding circuit and the kickdown (grounding) circuit. These are identified on the diagrams. Each has to be checked out, but the principles are the same.

A useful tool is a 12 volt test lamp with 4 ft. leads and alligator clip on each end. This will allow you to check continuity of individual wires. A cheap 12 volt buzzer will also do and you won't have to watch the bulb—just listen.

After replacing the burned-out solenoid, I also replaced the control wiring with a loom from Rhode Island Wiring Service, in Peace Dale, Rhode Island (see appendices for address). I also replaced the rusty, corroded kickdown switch.

Assuming you have checked everything and the electricals are OK, but there is still no overdrive, the problem has to be in the mechanical end. This is what happened to me, so now on to some greasy work.

Since the overdrive worked earlier, and since all electricals tested out, I decided to remove only the overdrive—if that was possible.

Drain the transmission and overdrive. You should get about 3¼ lb. of transmission lube. Cut off the top of a plastic milk jug and drain the overdrive fluid into it. Use a ⅛ in. drift pin driver to remove the tapered pin holding the overdrive control lever to the overdrive housing. The pin drives up only. Roll or slide to rear of truck and remove the four bolts that hold rear U-joint to the differential flange, then pull the driveshaft. Be sure to protect the driveshaft's machined ends from damage. Tape or use a heavy rubber band to hold the U-joint caps on the differential end so that you don't lose parts.

Remove the speedometer cable and gear. Remove the overdrive cable lever from the shaft, intact, with the wire still attached. Remove the lower and upper solenoid bolts and hang the solenoid with wire or string.

Place the floor jack just under the back of the transmission, drain and raise the transmission about 1½ in. Provide a temporary safety block in case the jack loses pressure or whatever. Pull the stub of the overdrive control lever out as far as it can go, perhaps ½ or ¾ in. Remove the seven cap screws that hold the overdrive to the transmission case and adapter (about 1 in. thick). Slide the overdrive rearward and remove from truck. Remove the overdrive freewheel rollers from their cage. Be sure to catch all the rollers! Using snapring pliers, pull the heavy U-clip from the rear end of the freewheel cage. Pull the cage rearward and remove. Remove the sun gear and fork assembly. Now remove the large (2¾ in. plus or minus) snap ring from the back of the overdrive housing. Remove the control plate and trough. Then remove the balk ring and gear plate with a large screwdriver. Remove the overdrive pawl and plunger and cover the end of the transmission with a plastic bread bag to protect it from dirt. This is it for the overdrive. Any other disassembly relates to the transmission.

Balk Ring Check

The balk ring assembly provides the mechanical lockup to give overdrive action. It has resistance in one direction and little resistance in the other. If you have a fishing scale, accepted pull in one direction is from 3.2 to 5.2 lb. The manual says nothing about the difference in pull in the opposite direction. One of the symptoms my overdrive had earlier was occasional non-kick-in of overdrive. I believe that was because the balk ring was worn and did not have the free movement in one direction.

Overdrive Assembly

After thoroughly cleaning and checking all parts for wear, burning and so on, reassemble in reverse order. When you reinstall the balk ring pawl be sure that you put it in place correctly; that is, with the V or notch facing up. The pawl will not engage fully if it is turned around.

When reinstalling the overdrive you must push the overdrive control lever in so you can get the drift pin back in place. Put the rear lever (first/reverse) of the transmission in the up position; otherwise you probably won't be able to push the overdrive lever in. The other transmission lever should be in the middle (neutral) detent. As the service manual advised, I used a rubber band to hold the overdrive rollers in place on the freewheeling clutch; it works great! The rubber band will dissolve in the transmission lube.

I used Permatex Blue for resealing everything—just don't use too much, only a film. Also, add the transmission lube from overhead so you won't need a suction-type pump to squirt it into the transmission. As the transmission fills, slow down the flow as the lube will run out when full. I found 80/90 wt. multipurpose gear lube, available at a farm-supply store in convenient 2 lb. containers.

While the driveshaft was out, I rebuilt the U-joints and found one completely dry, on its way to failure. When you do this, be sure you put the grease fitting on the forward side of the rear U-joint

Here's what a retrofit Borg-Warner overdrive looks like. Note that the torque tube attaches ahead of the overdrive transmission, allowing the overdrive unit to bolt directly to the differential. In order to make this setup for your truck, you will have to send OverDrive Inc. your truck's torque tube. It is not necessary to supply the overdrive.

A mounting flange is also welded to the rear of the overdrive unit. This flange will bolt to the differential. Note the torque braces welded to the mounting flange and transmission housing.

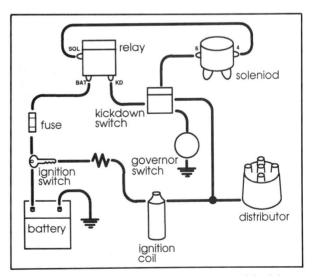

This writing schematic shows the control and kickdown circuits for a Borg-Warner overdrive installed in 1955 Second Series and late Chevrolet light trucks. Mark Tomandl

or else you can't lube it on the truck. When installing the driveshaft, make sure the slip-joint is at the transmission end. This keeps dirt out of the joint.

Adding Overdrive

Going to a modern drivetrain or looking for higher-geared rear end are the solutions usually thought of for the low rear-end gearing problem.

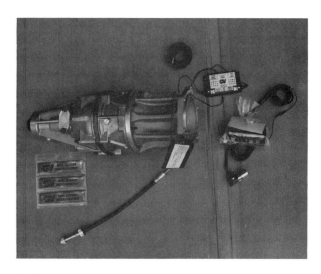

But there's another, often more suitable alternative that can be applied to any year Chevrolet light truck. The low-gearing solution I'm talking about is an overdrive transmission.

Overdrives use a sun and cluster and sun gear arrangement to increase the engine output speed by one third. At the rear wheels, this translates into a one-third reduction in the rear-axle ratio. Let's

---

Retrofitting With a Modern Overdrive

Chevrolet trucks of sixties vintage are becoming enormously popular with collectors and even though these more modern trucks can benefit from the advantages of an overdrive transmission—especially in fuel economy. For these newer trucks, rather than retrofit an old Borg-Warner unit, you have the option of installing a newly manufactured overdrive.

Of the several aftermarket overdrives on the market, the one having the broadest applications for older vehicles, and the best reputation for quality design and workmanship—as well as reliability—is an under/overdrive transmission from Gear Vendors Inc., 1035 Pioneer Way, El Cajon, CA 92020. This auxiliary step-up transmission can be coupled to GM's TurboHydramatic 400 and various manual transmissions installed in Chevrolet trucks over the past thirty years.

Like original equipment overdrives, the Gear Vendors under/overdrive attaches to the back of the transmission, but unlike the factory auxiliary gearboxes, the Gear Vendors product simply bolts to the primary transmission's output shaft through a special adapter that replaces the manual three-speed, manual four-speed, or automatic transmission's tail shaft housing.. (Yes, a Gear Vendors under/overdrive can be used in combination with an automatic—and can even be adapted to four-wheel-drive.)

Gear Vendors under/overdrive transmissions are available directly from the manufacturer or can be purchased from dealers located around the United States. The installation is mechanically straightforward, but does not require that the driveshaft be shortened and balanced by a shop capable of doing this work. The electronic controls are all state-of-the-art and all electrical connections a breeze, thanks to phonejack style plug-in connectors. In operation, a Gear Vendors auxiliary transmissions operates like an 4th or 5th gear, engaging automatically when the vehicle reaches 42 mph and disengaging when the truck comes to a stop. But even more important than effortless operation, a Gear Vendors under/overdrive will extend engine life by cutting rpms and raise fuel mileage by as much as 20-40 percent.

say that the rear-end ratio on your pickup is 3.90:1, the standard ratio of an Advance Design half-ton pickup. With overdrive, the final ratio becomes 2.61 and highway cruising speed increases from 50 to 65 mph.

Although overdrive became popular in the 1930s, Chevrolet didn't offer the step-up transmission in its cars and light trucks until 1955 and the switch to Hotchkiss (open) drive. At this point overdrive served primarily as a fuel economy option. (Decreasing the engine rpms at a given highway speed also increases fuel economy.)

When installed, the overdrive transmission sits behind the standard three-speed and is activated by a combination electrical and mechanical control system. Like other domestic manufacturers, Chevrolet purchased its overdrive units from Borg-Warner. Because car and light truck engine and transmission combinations are so similar, overdrive can be retrofitted to a 1955 and later pickup (Chevrolet made the option available through the mid-sixties) without a great deal of difficulty. If a truck overdrive isn't available, the same unit from a car will work. Even though overdrive was not an option prior to 1955, overdrive transmissions can also be retrofitted to Advance Design and earlier Chevrolet trucks (and cars), though this installation has certain complexities which will be described later.

Even for the years when Chevrolet made overdrive an option, you can't just find an overdrive gearbox and bolt it to the back of your truck's three-speed. The two transmissions were designed as a pair with the overdrive's companion three-speed gearbox having a longer output shaft that turns the overdrive gear cluster. If you're thinking of retrofitting overdrive to a late 1950s, early 1960s

Chevrolet truck, the place to start is to locate a three-speed and overdrive transmission. Scrap yards are a good source, as are swap meets and ads in old car and truck hobby magazines.

If locating an overdrive transmission isn't a problem, what keeps every light truck owner from installing this cure for low rear-end gearing and opportunity for better fuel economy in his or her truck? Lots of things. These overdrives were electrically controlled and the prospect of finding a working thirty- or forty-year-old electrics—solenoid, relay, wiring harness and kickdown switch—discourages most from taking an overdrive swap seriously. The mechanical controls, kickdown switch and so on, are even harder to locate than the electrical parts since the mechanical controls must come from a truck, whereas car electricals will work in a truck as well. Far fewer Chevrolet trucks were fitted with overdrive than cars. However, there is a way to install overdrive without using the electrical controls and kickdown linkage.

Retrofitting overdrive to trucks where this transmission option was available originally (1955 Second Series through the mid 1960s) is relatively simple, providing you are converting a standard three-speed to three-speed and overdrive. The standard three-speed will come out by removing the driveshaft at the universal joints, disconnecting the speedometer cable and shift linkage, and unbolting the transmission at the bellhousing. Installing the overdrive unit should be a simple

In 1957, Chevrolet made four-wheel-drive a factory-installed rather than a dealer-installed option. The transfer case and front-drive mechanism were still built by NAPCO. Carryalls could also be ordered with four-wheel-drive. Trucks with this option are rare and desirable.

A late Advance Design series pickup with NAPCO Mountain Goat four-wheel-drive. This add-on four-wheel-drive setup was so durable that NAPCO advertisements suggested removing the parts at truck trade-in time and installing them on the new truck. Greg Carson

matter of reversing these steps. Unless you also locate a driveshaft from an overdrive-equipped truck of the same model, you'll have to shorten the driveshaft. You'll also have to run a cable from the dash to the overdrive lever to engage and disengage the secondary transmission. It shouldn't be too difficult to find an overdrive lever (stamped OD) and cable in a scrap yard, or you can buy a suitable cable control at an auto parts store. Wiring diagrams for connecting the wiring harness and instructions for hooking up the overdrive are given in service manuals like *Motor* or the Chevrolet service manual for trucks with the overdrive option.

Let's imagine that you've made the overdrive swap. If you're striving for originality, you'll have to scout out the electronics: a functioning solenoid, relay, overdrive wiring harness and kickdown switch. As mentioned previously, some of these items, namely the solenoid and kickdown switch, can be very difficult to find. Depending on the year of your truck, an overdrive wiring harness will be available from one of the wiring harness makers such as Y n Z's Yesterday Parts. The relay is readily available from a number of Chevrolet parts suppliers.

For ease in making the overdrive installation, I recommend replacing the electronics with a manual solenoid available from OverDrive Inc., based in Portage, Ohio (see appendices for address). This unit eliminates the need for the overdrive wiring harness, electronic solenoid, relay and kickdown

switch. The manual solenoid mounts on the overdrive transmission in the same location as the electronic unit and is engaged by a cable control which is supplied as part of the kit. Once the manual solenoid is activated, the overdrive kicks in as though triggered electronically.

Besides lowering the final gear ratio and thereby reducing engine rpm, increasing fuel economy and raising comfortable road speed, a manually operated overdrive also brings the advantage of allowing you to split each forward gear (instead of three forward speeds, your truck can now be driven as though it had a six-speed transmission). You won't shift through all six potential gears each time you pull away from a light (driving in overdrive will be explained in more detail later), but you do have the option of twice as many gear ratios for special purposes. For example, first overdrive is an excellent parade gear.

Retrofitting Overdrive

Through the mid 1950s, Chevrolet used a torque-tube driveline that, because it is incompatible with a normal overdrive setup, makes installation of the extra transmission more difficult. That's the reason Chevrolet was so late in listing overdrive as an option on its light trucks. Torque-tube drive means that the driveshaft is enclosed in a tubular housing which forms a rigid support member for the rear axle. By acting as a brace between the transmission and differential, the torque tube keeps the rear axle from "winding up" on the driveline under acceleration. The disadvantage of the torque-tube arrangment is the difficulty of installing a secondary overdrive transmission. However, just because Chevrolet didn't make overdrive available in its torque-tube-drive trucks from the factory, doesn't mean that overdrive can't be installed in a pre 1955 Chevrolet truck today.

How to Drive in Overdrive

I find that operating an overdrive transmission adds substantially to the pleasure of driving my truck. Not only are cruising speeds in the range of today's traffic, but the overdrive provides just the right gear for any driving condition. In addition, operating the three-speed manual transmission plus overdrive gives me a feeling of activity and control over my truck.

I leave the freewheeling engaged (the freewheeling cable is pushed in). This means that my truck's overdrive transmission is always ready to be engaged. I also find freewheeling comfortable for around-town driving. It allows me to shift from first to second and second to high without using the clutch (if I get the engine revs about right and keep a load off the gearbox) and I can coast up to traffic lights. Freewheeling's disadvantage is that engine compression doesn't assist the truck in decelerating (but the brakes work well, so this is

These parts comprise the complete NAPCO conversion except for the front differential. The rear spring hangers on a four-wheel-drive truck are cast about 5 in longer and have provision for the emergency brake cables. The spring hangers have a 4 in. lift block under them. The transfer case cross-member bolts into four holes in the frame where the center running board bracket is (was) riveted. Greg Carson

not a problem in town where I do most of my driving), and I have to remember to apply the emergency brake when parking (again, no engine compression to hold the truck in gear).

To engage the overdrive, I just accelerate, pull out the manual solenoid control cable and let off the gas. When I resume acceleration, the engine revs have dropped as though I had shifted the transmission into another gear. (I have replaced the electronic solenoid and related wiring, relay and so on with a manual solenoid from OverDrive Inc. One of the benefits of the manual solenoid is that overdrive can be engaged in any forward gear. This is not the case with an electrical solenoid which shifts into overdrive only at speeds above 28 mph.)

Often, for in-town driving, I shift to second, then engage overdrive. It's fun to use the overdrive as a gear splitter for the three-speed transmission (as an over-the-road trucker would use a two-speed rear axle on his ten-speed gearbox). Sometimes, after engaging second-over, I will shift to third and disengage the overdrive (push in the control). Then as the truck reaches the open road, I can pull out the manual overdrive knob and shift into third-over, the cruising gear. The manual control works great, but requires that the driver remember two cautions.

First, overdrive was not designed to start a static load so I must remember to shift out of overdrive (push the cable handle in) when I stop. Second, overdrive must never be engaged when shifting into reverse. This is crucial. If the overdrive is left engaged, it can bind up or destroy the overdrive mechanism. This means that when I come to a stop, I must disengage the overdrive and leave the cable pushed in until I am moving ahead again. There's no problem with leaving freewheeling engaged, either in starting out or backing up. If I were operating the overdrive from its original electronic mechanism, I could disengage overdrive by pushing the gas pedal to the floor (for faster acceleration), or by slowing below 28 mph and easing off the throttle. In this setting, I could not use the overdrive as a gear splitter for the three-speed transmission. A benefit of the electronic control, however, is that I would not have to fear engaging overdrive in reverse as the control would disengage overdrive when the vehicle came to a stop.

For my truck, overdrive easily adds 15 mph to the engine's comfortable cruising speed. Geared as it is, my pickup would be impossible to drive over the highway with any degree of comfort without overdrive, as 45 mph feels to be the engine's top of cruising speed in third gear, direct drive.

Best of all, I like the feel of overdrive. I haven't tired of finding the right gear for the driving condition (first overdrive is ideal for parades) and when I'm using the transmission's flexibility, going, say, from second-under, to second-over, third-under.

NAPCO Four-Wheel-Drive

Many Chevrolet light truck owners are not aware that between 1951 and 1957, GM made four-wheel drive available as an aftermarket add-on. This means that if you own a three-quarter- or one-ton Chevrolet or GMC Advance Design or early Task Force truck (pickup, Panel or Suburban) and would like the versatility and novelty of four-wheel drive (and can find a chassis or parts truck that

---

OverDrive Inc.—The Gearmasters

In a garage-sized shop hidden in the cornfields a dozen or so miles west of Bowling Green, Ohio, maverick engineer Bob Green and his business associate Willis Beckstein, plus a pair of helpers, are fitting Borg-Warner overdrives to practically any vehicle with four wheels.

The overdrive installations performed in this shop differ in two important ways from the factory approach. First, Green and his crew install the overdrive in front of the differential, rather than behind the transmission. For most installations, the reason for this location is space, although on a pickup truck there is usually ample room behind the transmission for the overdrive housing. However, this isn't the case on most cars. Second, Green's installation replaces the electrical solenoid with a manual unit. The reason here is the lack of a supply of dependable solenoids (no one is rebuilding them and the electrical control is missing from about ninety percent of available overdrive transmissions.)

To have Green install an overdrive unit in your Chevrolet pickup's torque-tube driveline, you will need to send the torque tube, plus driveshaft and rear-end carrier to OverDrive Inc. If you also provide the overdrive, you will receive a rebate for that unit. When your parts and order are received, the torque tube will be cleaned, sandblasted and painted. The overdrive to be mated with the torque tube will likewise be cleaned, disassembled and rebuilt. This done, a flange matching the diameter and hole pattern of the differential will be welded to the rear of the overdrive housing. Then the torque tube is shortened the distance of the overdrive unit. The driveshaft is also cut this same amount and a sprocket is welded to the end that will turn the overdrive. A matching sprocket is welded to the overdrive input shaft. A double chain connects the two sprockets and allows for a small amount of play to compensate for any misalignment in the driveline.

Finally, everything is assembled and the flange at the end of the overdrive housing is machined as needed to make sure the overall length is the same as the original torque tube. At this point you can come to the Portage, Ohio, shop to pick up your overdrive unit, or have the assembly shipped to you.

has the 4x4 setup), you can make the conversion to your truck relatively easily.

For its four-wheel-drive conversions, Chevrolet and GMC used a front-drive axle and two-speed transfer case made by NAPCO, a Minneapolis-based company. These NAPCO 4x4 units are reported to be among the most rugged ever built—which means if you find a NAPCO assembly, your chances of its still being usable are good. When this conversion was offered by Chevrolet, a new-truck buyer would select the NAPCO setup when ordering the truck and the 4x4 parts would either be installed at a NAPCO shop or more likely at the dealership. NAPCO sales brochures even suggested that the buyer save the beam front axle and reinstall it on the truck at trade-in time; the 4x4 set up would be removed for installation on the next new truck. That advice speaks highly for the unit's durability. Installation of the four-wheel-drive components is straightforward and really quite simple, and requires no welding or major modification.

Features of the NAPCO 4x4 setup consisted of Rzeppa constant-velocity joints in the front driving axles, Hotchkiss drive axles, a four-speed synchromesh transmission, four-position transfer case and power takeoff.

Converting to NAPCO Four-Wheel Drive

If you desire to convert your truck to four-wheel drive, you will need to start with a three-quarter- or one-ton chassis. NAPCO units were not designed for use on a ½ ton truck. Next, you will need to find a NAPCO setup matching your truck's years and series. Conversion units for Task Force trucks are different from those installed in the Advance Design series. The two different-style front axles are referred to as six bolt and eight bolt. On the six-bolt style axle, so called for the number of lug bolts on the brake drums, the differential is located on the right side of the truck. This axle was used on Advance Design series trucks through 1955. The eight-bolt axle has the differential on the left side of the truck. This axle was used in 1955 and later Task Force trucks. Part numbers are stamped on the right side of the differential.

The third requirement is that the gear ratio must be the same for both the front and rear axles. This means you will need to check the ratio on the NAPCO front differential and make sure the rear-axle ratio matches. The standard NAPCO three-quarter-ton front axle in the Advance Design series had a 4.57:1 ratio, with a 5.14:1 optional. On a 1 ton, the 5.14 was standard. You should be able to find

This restored three-quarter-ton Chevrolet pickup chassis with NAPCO four-wheel-drive will go under a 1955 First Series (Advance Design style) pickup. The four-wheel- *drive setup raises the truck several inches to increase ground clearance. Greg Carson*

NAPCO Parts Interchange with Dodge Power-Wagon

by David Butler

Recently, one of my Dodge customers drove a truck up from Louisiana to visit my shop in Iowa and talk Dodge. He didn't show up in a Dodge, but instead arrived in a very strange looking vehicle. He was driving a 1956 Olden Milk Truck that he had converted to four-wheel drive using a NAPCO drivetrain. I was interested to see how he had installed the front axle, so I crawled under the truck to take a look. He had done a clean conversion, but what really caught my eye was not his conversion but the familiar looking steering knuckle on the front axle of his beast. I looked again, and sure enough it was true. Those steering knuckles were dead ringers to the steering knuckles used on 1941–1942 WC half-ton Dodge military trucks. Close inspection showed that the axle housing, however, was completely different.

In narrowing down the interchangeable pieces, I believe that not only the knuckle, but the knuckle felt retainers, felt, spindle and wheel bearing nuts are identical. All these parts, including new upper bronze cones for the steering knuckle, are currently in stock for Dodge trucks and, as noted, could also be used in a Chevrolet NAPCO installation. (See appendices for supplier details.)

the ratio tag on the axles; if not, turn the driveshaft and count the turns at the wheel hub. When the 4x4 setup is installed, you also need to use the same tire size front and rear. On GMC trucks, some modification to the oil pan may be required to clear the front drive axle.

The NAPCO four-wheel-drive assembly installs as follows: First, elevate the truck and support the frame on jack stands. Then remove the I-beam front axle. Now install the NAPCO front axle. A different pitman arm is also used and needs to be installed in place of the standard Chevrolet arm. The shocks can now be connected to the special mounting plates on the NAPCO front axle and brake hoses attached to the wheel cylinders.

To mount the transfer case, you will need to install a new cross-member (this piece should be on the 4x4 parts truck). First, you need to drop the driveshaft, remove the muffler and tailpipe and disconnect the parking brake rod. The two upper rivets on the running board bracket need to be sheared off and the holes enlarged to $^{15}/_{32}$ in. diameter. The cross-member bolts through those holes. With the cross-member bolted in place through the running board bracket holes, you will see where the remaining holes need to be drilled. As you will see on the parts truck, rubber cushions are used where the cross-member attaches to the frame mounts. In most cases these cushions will be hardened and you will have to locate replacements (body cushions or engine mounts may make suitable substitutes).

With the cross-member in place, the transfer case can be installed. The NAPCO 4x4 setup includes a different bracket for the muffler, which moves the exhaust system farther outboard and nearer the frame. Other modifications also occur at the rear axle. To mount the springs, a 4 in. spacer is placed between the axle and springs. This spacer requires longer spring U-bolts. Extensions are also welded to the shock absorber bracket, raising the mounting position 4 in. Inside the cab, a hole is cut in the floor for the transfer-case shift lever.

Final steps include installing the driveshafts (with the slip yokes at the transfer case end), bleeding and adjusting the brakes, setting front wheel toe-in to between $^{1}/_{16}$ and $^{1}/_{8}$ in., installing chrome NAPCO plates on the cowl and placing the shift diagram on the glovebox door.

Parts such as the dash decal are available in reproduction form, as are the NAPCO shop and parts manuals. Mechanical parts are less easy to find and NAPCO has long been out of business. Some original NAPCO parts can still be purchased from vintage Chevrolet parts sources (see appendices for listings), and Dodge Power-Wagon authority David Butler says that some of the NAPCO front-drive parts interchange with Power-Wagon items.

Besides the differential in the front axle and higher stance, NAPCO four-wheel-drive-equipped Chevrolet trucks can be identified by the NAPCO hood ornaments and transfer-case shifting plate on the dash. The parts catalog and installation instructions are available in reprinted form.

10

Brake Overhaul

However sound a truck's mechanical systems appear to be, one system that should be inspected and almost always overhauled and rebuilt is the brakes. On a frame-up restoration, the brake system would be rebuilt as a matter of course. Brake

With the brake drums removed, you'll see something like this. Here we have the rear brake assembly on an early 1970s Chevrolet one-ton. The rear brakes on this truck had ceased working, so we knew something was wrong.

systems on older trucks need attention for the simple reason that an original brake system on a twenty-year-old, or older, truck is prone to failure—a dangerous proposition. The primary cause of brake failure is leaking hydraulic fluid, but worn linings, scored drums and improper adjustment can all contribute to poor braking response which can be nearly as dangerous as no brakes at all.

Rebuilding your truck's brake system shouldn't be approached in patchwork fashion. Rather, the entire braking mechanism should be inspected and overhauled, which leads to the question of where to begin. Before addressing this question, let's visualize what happens when we press on the brake pedal. As the foot pedal is depressed, it presses a plunger in the master cylinder, mounted under the floorboard on Chevrolet trucks through the Advance Design series and on the firewall of Task Force and later trucks. This plunger compresses a small amount of hydraulic fluid in the cylinder and in so doing sends a pulse of pressure through the brake lines to the four wheels. Here the pressure expands in the wheel cylinders, forcing the brake shoes out against the brake drums, slowing the vehicle. This is what is *supposed* to happen.

Now let's look at what can go wrong on a worn and out-of-repair brake system. First, the brake pedal can have worn on its shaft so that it binds when pressed, requiring extra pedal pressure. Then, corrosion inside the master cylinder (caused by moisture trapped in the hydraulic fluid) can allow some of the fluid to leak past the plunger, reducing pressure to the lines and causing brake fluid to be lost from the system. As the fluid in the lines receives pressure from the master cylinder, a corroded line could spring a leak, causing the pressure to normalize and preventing brake action.

Assuming the lines are intact and braking pressure is passed to the wheel cylinders, here again corrosion on the cylinder linings can cause fluid to leak past the pistons reducing braking action, or old gummed-up fluid that has collected in the wheel cylinders can result in very little braking movement. If the pedal pressure is transferred through the system, worn linings or grooved, out-of-round brake drums will also hamper braking efficiency. Where a combination of problems occur, as is more likely the case in a deteriorated brake system, braking action will be seriously reduced at each stage between the brake pedal and the wheels.

Overhauling a brake system typically starts by removing the wheels. If this is your first experience with brake overhaul, and you're not doing a frame-up restoration where every part will be stripped, cleaned and refinished, it's a good idea to redo the brakes on one side of the vehicle at a time. This way you can look at the other side for a guide to fitting all the parts back together correctly.

Brake Removal

Loosen the lug nuts with the wheels on the ground, then jack up the truck and support it on professional-quality jack stands, not a makeshift stack of bricks or blocks. With the truck elevated on secure supports, remove the lug nuts and slip the wheels off the brake drums. To remove the brake drums, first loosen the brake adjustment. This is done by popping out the adjusting hole cover in the lower area of the backing plates (in many cases this cover will probably be missing), reaching into the hole with a brake adjusting tool or screwdriver and backing off the star wheel that moves the brake shoes toward the drums. If the star wheel turns, you will know whether you are tightening or loosening the brakes by whether or not you feel the shoes drag as you rotate the drum. In many cases the star wheel will be rust-frozen. Where this is the case, proceed with the steps for removing the brake drum. With luck, the shoes will be worn enough so that the drum will slip off without backing off the shoes.

On the front drums, you will pop off the dust caps that cover the spindle nuts (if these covers are still in place) by inserting a screwdriver between the cap lip and the brake drum hub and prying while working the screwdriver around the hub. Mechanics usually remove these caps by grabbing them with channel-lock pliers and flipping them

On full-size Chevrolet trucks built in 1971 and later, disc brakes are found on the front wheels. This style brake has its own rebuilding procedure which will be described in the shop manual for your truck.

If you see a mess of goop like this on the backing plates when you have removed the brake shoes and retaining hardware, it's a sure sign that the wheel cylinders have been leaking. Hydraulic brake fluid mixes with lining dust to produce this goopy coating.

105

loose, but this leaves the caps with dents that look like the creases in a highway patrolman's hat. With the cap out of the way, you will pull the cotter key from the spindle nut and turn the nut loose with an adjustable wrench, open-end wrench or socket. Don't use pliers to loosen the spindle nut. Their serrated edges will cut into the nut, making it difficult to fit the right tool onto the nut the next time you need to tighten or loosen it.

With the spindle nut removed, the drum should pull toward you easily. If it seems stuck on the brake shoes, grab the edges of the drum and work it back and forth, over the shoes. The difficulty sometimes encountered here is that the brake shoes can wear the drum so that a lip forms at the outer edge of the brake sweep area. If the drums are not turned to cut away this lip when new linings are installed, the lip can become quite deep. Where a lip has been allowed to form, and the brake adjustment star wheel is rust-bound and refuses to turn, the drums may catch on the shoes and refuse to pull loose. When this happens, the

only way to get the drums off may be to cut the ends of anchor pins that hold the shoes to the backing plate with side-cutter pliers or a torch. Cutting the anchor pins will enable you to pull the drums loose, but the shoes will probably pop free of the wheel cylinder which may also cause the wheel cylinder to come apart. This method for freeing the drums should be used only as a last resort.

As you slide a front drum off the spindle shaft, the large washer that sits behind the spindle nut and outer wheel bearing will usually slide off the spindle. The washer and bearing should be picked off the spindle before they fall onto the shop floor, and placed in a container for safe keeping. It is important not to mix bearings from one wheel to another, so it's a good idea to place a container (clean, empty coffee cans work well) at each wheel to hold parts as they are removed. Now you can slide the drum free and place it on the floor in a nearby, but out-of-the-way, location.

Rear wheel drums on Chevrolet half- and three-quarter-ton trucks remove easier than on

On trucks equipped with front disc brakes you'll want to inspect the condition of the cylinder lining on the caliper pistons. Badly pitted cylinders will need to be relined or replaced.

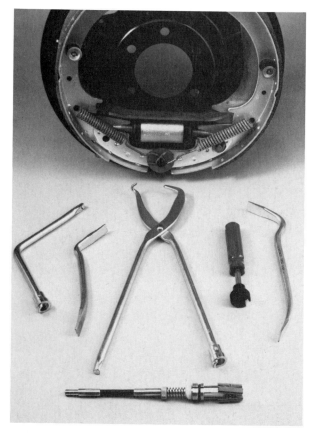

Special brake tools, available from auto parts stores or specialty tool suppliers like The Eastwood Company, simplify the job of disassembling the brake mechanism. If standard tools like slip-joint pliers are used to remove the brake-shoe return springs, the pliers are likely to slip, possibly causing injury or at least frustration. The Eastwood Company

many other makes because they bolt to a flange at the end of the axle rather than being wedge-fit onto the axle shaft. Here, too, the brake adjustor should be loosened as the first step. Then, with the lug nuts removed, the brake drums can be pulled loose. If the drums have rusted to the axle flange and lug bolts, spray penetrating oil around the base of the lugs and hole in the center of the drum. Then tap the drum a couple of times around the flange area (the flat surface beside the lugs) and the drum should pull free. With the drums off, you can now see what's been happening when you mashed down on the stop pedal.

Brake Inspection

Typically, what you'll see as you look at the brake mechanism of an older truck are worn linings (often just a thin layer of friction material will be left over the metal brake shoes), scored drums (with deep scratches in the drum's contact surface), a great deal of dusty material (residue from the worn lining material) coating the backing plates, brake shoes and other internal surfaces, and possibly darker sediment (a mixture of leaking brake fluid and lining dust) around the wheel cylinder. It's possible that you may also see other problem signs such as broken return springs, or cracked linings.

Brake Rebuilding

Since the performance of your truck's brakes is crucial to its safe operation, the overhaul procedure will be essentially the same whether you are restoring or rebuilding. The only difference may be in the thoroughness with which you refinish the brake parts, which will be visible when everything is reassembled.

Fortunately, brake parts for vintage Chevrolet trucks are in good supply. You may even be able to purchase new brake springs, shoes and wheel cylinders from a local auto supply store. The other alternative is a vintage Chevrolet truck parts supplier (see appendices for listings). When rebuilding a brake system, the best policy is to replace all the operational parts. Before any new parts are installed, however, you will remove the brake mechanism and backing plate at each wheel, then clean and refinish the brake drums and backing plates. In a ground-up restoration, brake overhaul usually occurs as the last stage of redoing the chassis. When taking a rebuilding approach, the brakes should be overhauled as the first step to making the truck operational. While the front drums are off, you should also inspect and replace worn king pins (on trucks with straight-axle front ends), as well as refinish other chassis parts such as the front axle and springs.

Disassembling the brake mechanism at the wheels is a simple matter of removing the springs that place tension on the shoes, unhooking the clips and pulling off the shoes. The wheel cylinders attach to the backing plates with bolts that are reached from the back side of the plates. Once these bolts are removed, the brake line has to be disconnected from the wheel cylinder. At the front, the brake line connection is through a rubber flex hose that is usually hardened and cracked. If this is the flex hose's condition on your truck, it can simply be cut and removed later. At the rear, the brake tubing will be connected directly to the wheel cylinder. If the fitting has become rust-frozen to the wheel cylinder, the line will have to be cut.

The backing plates are held in place by four bolts. Loosening these bolts allows you to remove this last part of the brake assembly. The next step is to clean the backing plates and prepare them for refinishing. Next, you will clean and inspect the drums.

Wheel Bearing Removal

The front brake drums ride on two bearings. The outer bearing is held in place by the spindle nut

An air wrench also speeds the brake mechanism disassembly process. Note that the bolts holding the backing plate to the axle flange have been removed. When the brake line to the wheel cylinder is loosened or cut, the backing plate can be removed for cleaning and refinishing.

and washer and comes out when you remove the drum. The inner bearing is located at the rear (inside) of the drum's center opening. These inner bearings can be removed using a special wheel-bearing puller (this is a hook-shaped tool that looks like a miniature crowbar) or by tapping on the perimeter of the inner race with a long punch inserted through the hub. A speedier method for removing the inner bearing, and one commonly used by mechanics, is to replace the nut and washer on the spindle, then slip the brake drum over the nut so that the hub rests on the spindle, and pull the drum toward you in a sharp, downward jerk that forces the bearing cage against the spindle washer. This sharp tug will pop the bearing free nearly every time.

Occasionally it may be necessary to rotate the drum 180 degrees and jerk the drum against the

The brake drums and disc rotors are turned smooth using a brake lathe. Machine shops or brake repair facilities will do this work for a modest cost. Before having the drums or rotors turned, check for cracks and warpage. There is a limit as to how much metal can be cut off these parts. The shop manual for your truck should give minimum brake drum diameter or rotor thickness.

spindle nut again. Although this method usually doesn't damage the seal, on a twenty- to fifty-year-old vehicle these seals are usually dried out and should be replaced.

Brake Drum Refinishing

Rather than assume that the brake drums can simply be cleaned, refinished and reused, the drums need to be inspected for cracks, warpage and adequate wall thickness. If the drum has become cracked from excess heat buildup, the crack will usually show on the lining sweep area. Warpage can be checked by laying the drums, face down, on a flat surface. Drum wall thickness should not be less than twenty percent of the original. On an Advance Design half-ton pickup, this calculates to a maximum inside diameter of 11.1 in., an increase of 0.1 in. over the original 11 in. inside diameter. Measurements this small should be taken with a brake drum gauge. A brake shop will have this measuring tool and will be able to tell you if the drums have enough metal to be turned, or if they will need to be replaced. You should also inspect the drums for cracks or warpage and look for replacements if either of these conditions is present.

Brake drums can be prepared for painting by sandblasting or treating the surface rust with an oxidation neutralizer like Fertan. Acid derusting should never be used on brake drums because dipping the brake drum in an acid bath can make the metal brittle, possibly causing the drum to crack.

Wheel Cylinder Disassembly

Since brake parts for most Chevrolet light trucks are readily available (from auto parts stores and specialty suppliers), it is advisable to rebuild the brake system with new parts. As an alternative to replacing the wheel cylinders with new units, the old cylinders can be rebuilt.

Wheel cylinders fail, that is, they leak fluid or become gummed-up and sluggish, due to contamination of the hydraulic fluid. Unlike newer cars and trucks, the hydraulic brake systems of older trucks are not sealed to outside moisture. This fact can be recognized by looking closely at the cap on the master cylinder. On Chevrolet trucks built prior to the late 1960s, you will be able to spot a small vent hole in the cap. This hole allows air to enter the hydraulic brake system in order to prevent a vacuum from forming as the fluid drops in the brake reservoir. The fluid level drops as the brake linings wear because the wheel cylinders require more fluid to press the linings against the drum.

As air enters the brake system, so does moisture. The standard brake fluid used in cars and trucks is a polyglycol product that carries a DOT 3 designation (brake fluid standards set by the Department of Transportation). This fluid attracts moisture like a sponge. For this reason, service manuals call for flushing and replacing the brake fluid every year or so. In actuality, this is seldom done and the result is moisture-laden brake fluid residing in an older truck's brake system year after year. Eventually, the moisture corrodes the wheel and master cylinder linings and rusts the brake lines from the inside. The moisture also attracts other contaminants which gum up the wheel cylinders. When the wheel cylinders on an older truck are disassembled, they will typically show this damage.

Once the wheel cylinders have been removed from the backing plates, their disassembly is a simple process that begins by peeling the rubber dust boots back from the casting lips. The grooved pins that lock with the brake shoes are inserted through the dust boots and will usually pull out of the wheel cylinders with the boots. Inside the wheel cylinder you will see two small metal cylinders. These are the pistons that move outward in the wheel cylinder to force the brake shoes against the drums when the brake pedal is pressed. If the pistons

move freely, they may be removed from the casting by pushing both pistons out one end of the cylinder. I have seen cases where the internal parts of a wheel cylinder were so encrusted with a mixture of old brake fluid, moisture and rust that they had to be driven out with a punch and hammer.

When you have taken the wheel cylinders apart and cleaned the castings, you can hold them up to the light and inspect the condition of the bores. Quite typically the cylinder lining will be scarred with pits. If the pits are shallow, a smooth lining surface can be restored by honing. In this process, the bore is enlarged a few thousandths of an inch with a grinding stone. Honing isn't something you would do at home, but would be done by a machine shop. On an older truck, pits in the brake cylinder linings are likely to be too deep to be removed by honing. My advice is to forget honing and if any pitting is present, either purchase new wheel cylinders or have the old cylinders relined. This will ensure no fluid leakage at the wheel cylinders.

Wheel cylinders leak or become gummed up because polyglycol-based hydraulic brake fluid attracts moisture. Once the wheel cylinders have been removed from the truck, they will be disassembled by peeling off the dust boots and pressing the pistons out one end of the cylinder. The cylinder bore should be inspected carefully for pits. Badly pitted wheel cylinders should either be relined or replaced. Pits in the cylinder bore allow brake fluid to seep past the pistons, reducing braking effort and causing a loss of fluid.

If the wheel cylinders show only very slight pitting, the cylinder bores can be cleaned with a honing tool. If any pitting is visible, a better approach is to replace or reline the cylinders.

Master Cylinder Disassembling

Typically, if pitting is found in the wheel cylinders, the master cylinder bore will also be corroded. On Chevrolet light trucks through the Advance Design series (up to midyear 1955), the master cylinder is mounted under the floorboard behind the brake pedal on the driver's side. On Task Force (mid 1955) and later trucks, the master cylinder is mounted on the firewall inside the engine compartment.

Once the master cylinder is removed from the truck, its disassembly is a simple process of prying off the piston boot and removing the retaining clip that holds the piston, seals and compression spring inside the casting. While working off the clip, you should press on the piston to prevent the piston and spring from flying out of the housing when the clip is released. Wiping the master cylinder bore with a clean cloth and holding it up to the light will allow you to see whether or not the bore is pitted. If pitting is visible, you should add the master cylinder to your needed parts list.

Rebuild Parts

The brake system parts list will consist of front and rear brake shoes, brake shoe clips, brake shoe retainer springs, flex hoses, wheel cylinder rebuild kits or new wheel cylinders, brake lines, master cylinder (depending on condition) and brake drums (depending on condition).

Many of these parts should be available from a local auto parts store. NAPA auto parts stores have access to an extensive parts inventory for vintage vehicles and are recommended as the place to check first.

Whether or not the cylinder bores of the wheel cylinders are pitted, you will need to renew the seals. This can be done by installing a rebuild kit, a slightly less expensive option than buying new wheel cylinders. If the cylinder bores are pitted, you can have the bores sleeved and install the rebuild kit. This alternative will be at least as costly as buying new wheel cylinders, but has the advantage that the cylinder bore sleeves will be a noncorrosive metal. Wheel cylinder relining services are listed in the appendices. Both stainless-steel and brass sleeves are available. Either metal is noncorrosive, but stainless has the advantage of being very hard and therefore highly resistant to scratching.

On a frame-up restoration, you would replace all brake tubing. Since on trucks built prior to 1968 a rupture anywhere in the lines will cause the loss of all brake action, the only wise approach is to replace old brake tubing whether you are restoring or rebuilding the hydraulic brake system. Instructions for cutting new tubing, bending it to match the original and forming correct double flares on the ends are provided later in this chapter. Brake

Special lubricant is used to coat the wheel cylinder bore before replacing the pistons. Petroleum-based lubricants must never be used on any brake system internal parts.

This device, called a dingleberry hone, is used to polish sound and unpitted cylinder bores to ensure smooth piston movement.

tubing and fittings are available at most auto parts stores.

Wheel Cylinder Rebuilding

If you are installing new wheel cylinders, you can skip this step. The assumption here is that you either have had the wheel cylinders relined or are working with used wheel cylinders that have absolutely clean, smooth bores. Before proceeding to install the rebuild kits, you should refinish the castings. Some relining services will bead blast the castings and send them back in ready-to-paint condition. The castings can also be prepared for painting by wire brushing and treating the metal with a rust neutralizer like Fertan. Aerosol cans work well for painting these small parts. When spraying the casting, be sure to mask off the ends of the cylinder to keep paint out of the cylinder bores.

Wheel cylinder rebuild kits typically consist of new springs, seals and boots, but require that you reuse the old pistons. To make sure that the pistons are smooth and free from scratches, clean them first in solvent, then scrub the outer cylinder area with super-fine #0000 steel wool. Follow this with 240 grit sandpaper to smooth any scratches, then polish the surface with 600 grit automotive sandpaper. After sanding, wash the pistons in soapy water to remove all sanding residue. If the pistons are badly pitted, they will need to be replaced.

The cylinder walls should be lubricated before installing the pistons and seals. Petroleum-based lubricants must *never* be used on any of the hydraulic brake system's internal parts. Wheel cylinder rebuild kits will typically contain small vials of special lubricant to be used for this purpose. If not, special brake system lubricant can be purchased at an auto parts store.

Before reassembling the wheel cylinder, the bore should be wiped clean with a lint-free cloth, then coated with the special lubricant. The spring is inserted into the cylinder next. Then the seals are moistened with lubricant and fitted against the tightly wound coils at each end of the spring. The pistons should also be lubricated before sliding them into the cylinder. You will need to press the pistons against the spring slightly to keep them inside the cylinder while installing the dust boots. A few drops of the special lubricant on the lips of the dust boots will make it easier to slide the boots over the ends of the casting. The last steps are to install new bleeder screws (available from most auto supply stores), and to seal the brake line openings with tape or plug them with a lint-free cloth to prevent dust from entering the cylinders as they are stored before installation.

Brake Line Replacement

You will want to bend the new brake lines to the contours of the old lines to keep the truck looking as original as possible. In order to have a pattern for the new lines, it is important to try to keep the old lines intact as you remove them from the truck. If you spray the connections with penetrating oil and use a wrench with a semi-box end that can get a good grip on the fittings, you should be able to unscrew the connections and have good patterns for the new lines. The long lines to the rear brakes will probably be secured to the frame with clips that will either slide off the frame or need to be unbolted.

With the old lines removed, the next step is to measure each line with a carpenter's tape, making sure the tape follows each bend and curve. Mark down the length of each line and take these measurements to an auto parts store. There you will find new brake line tubing available in a range of pre-cut lengths. If none of the lengths matches those on your list, you can purchase slightly longer lengths, cut them to the measurement for your truck and reflare the ends. Even if the measurements match the pre-cut lengths, it may still be necessary to cut and reflare the ends on the lines to the front brakes in order to fit protective steel coils

Rebuilding the wheel cylinders is a simple process of inserting the inner spring, seals and pistons—then installing the outer dust covers.

over the tubing. At the factory, these coils were placed over the portion of the brake line that passed through the fender shield so as to prevent possible metal-to-metal contact at this point from cutting the line.

The new brake tubing is bent to match the old brake lines with a bending tool, available from most auto parts stores or a specialty tool supplier like The Eastwood Company. This bending tool looks like a large pliers fitted with two round guides and a forming die. To bend brake tubing, a die matching the tubing diameter (¼ in. in this case) is installed on the bender. To make a bend, the tubing is placed between the guides and forming die and the handles of the bending tool are squeezed together. The tighter the handles are squeezed, the sharper the bend. Tubing can be bent at any angle. The only

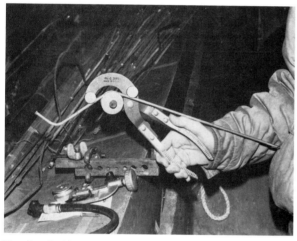

New brake lines are formed to the contours of the originals using a brake bending tool. Note the other tools used in this process lying on the work bench. These include a tubing cutter and flaring tool.

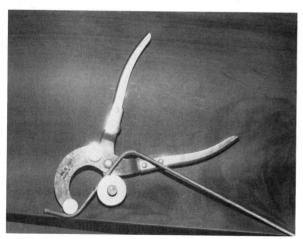

Bends are formed by squeezing the tubing around a larger roller. The roller is grooved to match the diameter of the tube so no kinks occur during bending.

trick to using the bending tool is to place the tubing in the tool so that where you want to bend is directly over the forming die. To get used to using the bending tool, make several practice bends with a spare length of tube.

When all the bends are made in one of the brake lines, place the new line beside the old to make sure you have created an exact match, then mark where the new line is to be cut. You should use a tubing cutter, not a hacksaw, to cut off the excess. On the short lines to the front wheels, slip the protective wire coils over the end where you have made the cut (if your truck used these coils originally). Now you are ready to flare the freshly cut ends.

It is very important that the flaring operation be done correctly. If not, brake fluid will leak from the connections, resulting in brake failure. Putting correct double-wall flares in brake tubing requires a flaring tool, holding bar and crimping die for ¼ in. diameter tubing. These items can be purchased from an auto supply store and sometimes are available from a tool rent-all.

The process for flaring brake tubing consists of four steps: First, clamp the tube tightly in the holding bar so that a length of tube equal to the larger diameter lip of the crimping die sticks out above the bar. Dip the end to be flared in brake fluid. (Lubricating the end helps ensure a proper flare.) Second, place the crimping die over the end of the tube, fit the flaring yoke over the bar and screw the yoke down until the die seats against the bar. Third, loosen the yoke and remove the crimping die. And fourth, tighten the flaring yoke again until the tube is fully flared.

After completing these steps, remove the tubing from the holding bar and carefully examine the

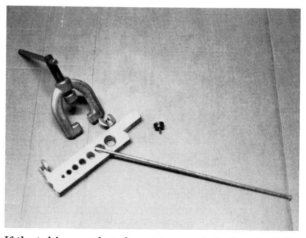

If the tubing needs to be cut to match the length of the original, the ends must be reflared. The flaring tool consists of the items shown here: a clamping bar, flaring die (to right) and the special flaring clamp. Used properly, a double-wall flare is created.

flare for cracks. If you spot a crack in the flare, you will have to cut the tube again and make a new flare. In most cases this will not require bending a new line, since you can usually stretch the line to the needed length by slightly reworking some of the bends and curves. If several reflaring attempts fail, however, it will probably be necessary to cut and bend a new line.

After all the lines are bent and flared, they will be installed on the chassis. Since brake tubing is bare steel, the new lines will rust unless they are treated. To preserve that freshly assembled look (brake lines were not painted when the truck was built), wash the tubing with Metal Prep, then scour the bare steel with #0000 steel wool (tape the ends to prevent steel wool splinters from entering the tubing), and paint the tubing with clear lacquer. This will preserve the bare steel look.

When installing new brake lines it is important that all connections be tight. If you are not hooking the lines up to the wheel cylinders at this point, the ends of the lines should be taped to prevent dust and other contamination.

Brake Assembly

On a frame-up restoration, the front suspension will have been checked and rebuilt, and all components cleaned and painted. The rear-axle assembly will have undergone the same thorough examination and been rebuilt as needed. On repair work, the brakes may be overhauled separately. In either case, the assumption here is that the backing plates are in place on the axles. The next steps are to mount the wheel cylinders, connect the brake tubes to the cylinders and install the brake shoes. Before mounting the brake shoes, it is important to wipe a coating of light lubricant on the anchor pins and to oil the adjusting mechanism. Skipping this step can result in squeaky brakes that become hard to adjust. On the rear brakes you should also lubricate the parking brake cables.

Next, connect one set of shoes to the adjustor by installing the spring at the bottom of the shoes. If one of the linings is shorter, this is the primary shoe and goes toward the front. Note that the star wheel on the adjustor should be near the primary (front) shoe on the left side of the truck and adjacent to the secondary (rear) shoe on right-side brakes. Now attach the shoes to the backing plates with the anchor pins or hold-down springs and position the tops of the shoes in the slots in the wheel cylinder connecting links.

On rear brakes, connect the parking brake cable. Hook the brake return springs through the holes on the shoes, clip the spring from the primary shoe over the anchor pin, then pull the spring from the secondary shoe over this same pin. You will find this job much easier to do if you use a special brake tool than if you attempt to spread the springs with pliers or a screwdriver. Now pull the shoes away

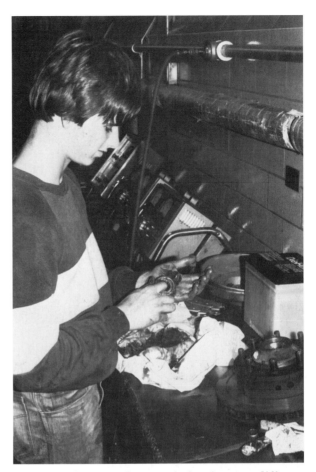

Wheel bearings can be repacked using two different methods. Shown here is the traditional hand-packing approach where grease is scooped into the palm of the hand and pressed around the bearing rollers.

The other packing method uses an aerosol grease container, available at most discount marts. This method is quick and clean.

113

from the backing plates and tap them a couple of times to make sure they are seated on the wheel cylinder and adjustor. Check to make sure the adjustors are turned all the way in, and install the brake drums on the rear wheels.

Wheel Bearing Packing

Before installing the front drums, you will need to repack and replace the wheel bearings. Packing wheel bearings can be like playing in the mud as a kid: when you're finished, your hands are completely gooped and there's likely to be a liberal coating on your clothes as well. The packing method I learned from my father is to scoop up a gob of wheel bearing grease and place it in the palm of one hand, then stroke the bearing (which has been cleaned in solvent and allowed to dry—do not dry bearings with an air gun) through the grease with the other hand. After two or three passes, Dad

If polyglycol brake fluid is used, a length of plastic tubing should be attached to the bleeder nozzle on the wheel cylinder to make sure that the fluid does not run down on the painted backing plates or axle parts. Polyglycol fluid will eat paint. The other end of the tube is placed in a jar partially filled with brake fluid. This prevents air that is purged from the system in the bleeding process from being sucked back into the lines.

would tap the bearing against the heal of his hand to pack the grease, then he would repeat the scooping and tapping steps until grease oozed out around the bearing rollers. This process isn't complicated, but it is messy. Fortunately, there is an easier method.

Aerosol wheel bearing packers that pump grease into the bearing—eliminating the messy hand-packing steps—are available at most auto supply stores and discount marts. To use the aerosol packer, just place the bearing in the funnel-shaped clamp supplied with the packer, insert the aerosol nozzle into the packer and press down on the grease container. In less time than it takes to say "Peter Piper packed a pair of bearings," grease will be oozing out the clamp, and the bearing will be packed and ready for installation.

The inner wheel bearings are installed first and are held in place by a seal ring that presses into the brake drum. (When not available from an auto supply store, replacement seals are available from specialty Chevrolet truck parts suppliers.) The seals are seated by tapping them into the hub with a plastic hammer. Now the front brake drums can be slipped onto the spindle and over the linings. If the drums won't fit, pull them back off, tap the shoes with the heel of your hand to seat them tightly against the wheel cylinder, check the star wheel to make sure the shoes are fully retracted and try again. With new linings, the fit may be snug, but the drums should slide over the shoes, though perhaps with some turning and tapping.

Now the outer wheel bearings can be packed. This done, the bearings are slipped onto the spindle and pushed into the bearing cone in the brake drum hub. A washer fits between the bearing and spindle nut. In tightening the spindle nut, draw up the nut against the bearing until the bearing drags as the drum is turned, then back off the nut until the drum spins freely. Lock the spindle nut in this position with a cotter key and spread the key to hold the nut in place.

Brake Adjustment

Adjustments are made by reaching through the access hole in the bottom of the backing plates and turning the star wheel. While a screwdriver can be used for this operation, a special brake-adjusting tool, shaped like a lazy Z, works best. The brakes should be adjusted by moving the shoes toward the drums until slight drag is felt, then the adjustment is backed off until the drums turn easily. Adjustments at all four wheels need to be as uniform as possible to prevent one or more of the wheels from locking under panic braking and to keep the shoes from dragging.

Bleeding Brake Lines

Although original braking systems used DOT 3 polyglycol fluid, many old-car and truck owners are switching to DOT 5 silicone brake fluid. Unlike polyglycol fluid, silicone brake fluid does not attract moisture. As another benefit, silicone fluid lubricates and helps preserve rubber brake system parts like wheel cylinder seals and flex lines. The disadvantage of silicone fluid is that it has a tendency to destroy hydraulically actuated stop light switches—the type used on Chevrolet trucks with master cylinders mounted under the floor. Since these switches are inexpensive items and installed quite easily, it seems preferable to replace the stop light switch (as required) rather than go through an annual flushing of the brake system to remove contaminated brake fluid—which should be done when polyglycol fluid is used.

Bleeding the Hydraulic Brake System

Whichever fluid you use, before the truck can be driven, trapped air needs to be bled or purged from the brake lines. There are several ways to bleed the brakes, but the simplest calls for two people and takes little more than a half hour—assuming all goes well. The helper will pump the brake pedal to build up pressure while you bleed the air from the lines by loosening the bleeder screws at each of the wheels.

Begin by filling the master cylinder with brake fluid. When the fluid reservoir is full, screw the cap on tight and have the helper pump up the brakes (push down on the brake pedal several times in quick succession until braking action is felt). While the assistant holds his or her foot on the pedal, you will proceed to the wheel farthest from the master cylinder (the right rear) and loosen the bleeder screw to the wheel cylinder. (The bleeder screw inserts into the backside of the wheel cylinder and is accessible on the rear side of the backing plate.) To keep brake fluid from squirting on the chassis and running down the backing plate (polyglycol fluid will eat off paint; silicone fluid is harmless), you should fit one end of a length of plastic or rubber tubing over the tip of the bleeder screw. Place the other end of the tube in a can or jar to catch escaping fluid.

As the bleeder screw is opened, air will escape from the brake lines. As this happens, your assistant will feel the brake pedal sink slowly toward the floor. When the fluid runs clear and free of bubbles, turn the bleeder screw shut. Now ask the assistant to pump up the pedal again and keep pressure on the pedal. Open the same bleeder screw again to make sure fluid from that line runs clear, without

The new brake lines on the front of this Advance Design series pickup have been formed identically to the originals. The fresh, shiny look of the unplated brake lines *can be preserved by scouring the metal with steel wool and applying a clear coat finish. Mike Cavey*

bubbles. Be sure to warn your assistant not to release the brake pedal once it sinks to the floor until you tell him or her to do so. Releasing the brake pedal before the bleeder screw is closed will suck air into the lines, requiring that the bleeding process be done all over again.

Once air is purged from the line to one wheel, refill the master cylinder, then move to the next and repeat the bleeding process. Less than a quart of fluid should be required to fill and bleed a rebuilt brake system. Before finishing, check all line connections to make sure there is no leakage.

Maintenance to a hydraulic brake system consists of checking the fluid level of the master cylinder periodically, watching for leaks at the brake line connections and wheel cylinders (severe wheel cylinder leaks can be seen as streaks on the insides of the tires) and if polyglycol fluid is used, flushing and refilling the brake system on an annual basis. On more modern trucks with self-adjusting brakes, the only other maintenance step would be pulling the brake drums and checking for lining wear at 30,000 mile intervals (or thereabouts). On trucks without self-adjusting brakes, the fall or spring cleanup and maintenance session should include adjusting the brakes.

A properly rebuilt and maintained hydraulic braking system will give your truck more than adequate stopping power and ensure driving safety for you and your passengers.

The rear brake lines on this truck also match the originals. Note the smooth curve around the differential housing. This curve can be somewhat difficult to form.

Also note the flex hose connecting the tubing on the axle with the tubing attached to the frame. In nearly all brake rebuilds, new flex hoses are a must. Mike Cavey

11

Body Sheet Metal Restoration

Unless you own an exceptionally rust-free truck that has led a pampered life, a major phase in the process of restoring or rebuilding your Chevrolet truck will be repairing rusted and dented metal. The first step in this process is stripping off old paint and surface rust. In restoration, the truck is typically disassembled for stripping and derusting. When the rebuilding approach is followed, the fenders and doors may be removed, but the cab is left on the frame.

After the paint has been removed, the extent of the rust and dent damage should be visible. You may also discover old dents that were covered with filler in earlier, amateur repairs. Where rust may have weakened but not eaten through the metal, you will need to determine the seriousness of the rust damage. If you have stripped the body metal by sandblasting, you may see pinholes in the rust-weakened areas. The extent of the rust can easily be determined by jabbing a small-bladed screwdriver into the metal that you suspect to be rust-damaged. On Chevrolet trucks, these areas include the bottoms of doors, cab corners and the cowl panels just past the rear of the front fenders, as well as the bottoms of the pickup box supports. If the screwdriver punctures the metal, you've done no harm. Solid metal would not be penetrated and the fact that you've jabbed a hole only shows that the metal in this area needs to be replaced.

If the rust damage is extensive, you may want to consider finding better parts. For Advance Design series and later Chevrolet trucks, rust-free cabs and doors are still plentiful in states south and west of the Rust Belt. For repairing the common rust areas (bottoms of doors and cab corners) patch panels are available for Advance Design, Task Force and other model Chevrolet trucks. Instructions for installing patch panels are included in this chapter.

Dent Repair

Since trucks are working vehicles, dent damage is common. Although dents can occur anywhere, the most typical places are in the fenders and cab rear panel and roof. Dents can be worked out of fenders most easily if the fenders are taken off the truck. Dents in the cab can usually be

Paint blisters on the lower area of this rear pickup box support are a tell-tale sign of rust damage. The hole in line with the taillight wire has been punched through the spongy metal with a screwdriver. Don't worry about doing damage as you probe for rust. A screwdriver won't penetrate sound metal. If the screwdriver plunges through, the metal needs to be repaired anyway. Mike Cavey

reached from the inside, once the seats and headliner have been removed.

When possible, dents should be worked out with the metal at air temperature. Sometimes, however, extensive dent damage in the heavy-gauge sheet metal of older trucks will require applying heat to straighten the metal. Although warming the dented area with a torch makes the metal easier to straighten, it also increases the

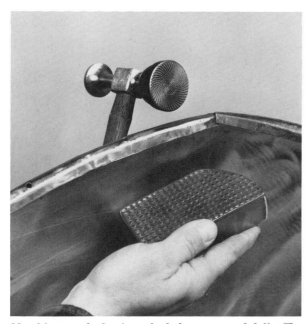

Metal is smoothed using a body hammer and dolly. The dolly is placed on the dent area opposite the hammer so that blows from the hammer actually strike against the dolly. The hammer and dolly shown here have special patterns on the hammer head and dolly face that help to shrink metal that has become stretched by overly aggressive sandblasting or too much heat during welding. The Eastwood Company

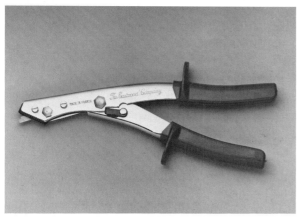

A metal nibbler makes quick work of cutting out rusted areas and shaping replacement metal. This tool is both easier and safer to use than tin snips. The Eastwood Company

chances that the metal will become stretched. The problem is that when you have smoothed the dent, you will have an extra bulge with no recess to fill. This bulge will have to be shrunk in order to finish the dent repair.

The skill of straightening dents comes with developing a feel for the metal, and the best way to acquire this is through practice. Instead of starting out by attempting to smooth the dents on your truck, begin with beat-up panels from a parts truck or buy a fender from a scrap yard with the same gauge metal as that on your truck and pound in some dents, if need be. Then practice working out these dents. After a few sessions of practice "metal bumping," as the skill is called, you will be equipped to start working out the dents on your truck.

Dent repair requires a special set of bumping hammers and dollies. You can buy body hammers and dollies (metal weights that are pressed against the top of the dent to prevent hammer marks and spread the hammer blow over a wide area) from specialty tool suppliers like The Eastwood Company. You won't need all the hammers and dollies shown in the catalog, but you will need an assortment to work various shaped dents.

The first step in straightening a dent is to rough out the depression with a bumping hammer and dolly. Rather than try to force the metal back into shape with a few hard blows, work the dent out gradually, usually beginning at the outside of the depression and working toward the center. Your goal here is not just to straighten the metal, but also to keep from stretching it. When the metal is stretched, you will end up with a bulge that won't

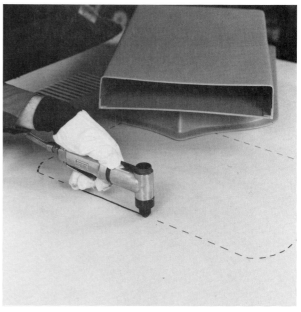

An air nibbler makes the job of cutting metal even easier. This air-powered tool can be operated by a home/shop size air compressor. The Eastwood Company

lie flat no matter how much you work it. There are basically two ways to get rid of these stretch bulges. One is to shrink the metal with a special serrated shrinking hammer and dolly. The other is to heat the bulge with a torch, then quickly cool the metal with water. This heating and quenching method works well on older, heavy-gauge metal body panels, but should not be used on modern, high-strength steel panels.

When the dent is close to the correct contour, you will use a finishing hammer and dolly to smooth the metal as much as possible. The technique is to hold the dolly against the metal on the opposite side that the hammer will be hitting. Dollies have contoured surfaces and it is important to find the contour on the dolly that matches the shape you are trying to bring the dented area back to. It is sometimes possible to smooth the dented area so that only very fine surface imperfections remain. When this is the case, the small hammer marks can be smoothed with a file and any remaining blemishes covered with primer. More likely, however, a skim coat of body filler will be needed to cover hammer marks and other traces of dent repair.

Rust Repair

Mending rusted metal requires welding skills and some additional specialized tools in addition to a welding outfit. While the rusted area can be cut out using tin snips or a hacksaw, a metal nibbler or cut-off tool makes the job much easier. The patch panel will need to be cut to fit the rusted area, and a panel nibbler also makes this job easier. Other tools that are highly useful to the metal repair process include:

• Panel flangers—used to form an offset flange so that replacement panels can be flush-fit

• Crimping pliers—used to pinch replacement skins to the door frame

• Carbide burr—used to grind weld beads

• Panel holding clamps—used to secure panels for welding

• Heat-sink putty—used to prevent heat warpage

Panels can be welded in place using both gas and arc welding methods, but as the next section will explain, wire welding (a form of arc welding) is the superior method for attaching patch panels with the least risk of heat damage to the surrounding metal.

Wire Welding

Both gas welding and standard arc welding that uses a flux-coated rod for the electrode present problems as methods for welding in patch panels. Gas welding creates intense heat that will almost invariably warp the panel. Fusing body metal with the standard type of arc welding is

difficult for the amateur to do. But these problems do not mean that the hobbyist can't do his or her own body repair. Quite recently, wire welding equipment, designed with the handyman and hobbyist in mind, has become available at prices that are little higher than a standard arc or gas welding outfit. The advantage of wire welding is that with a

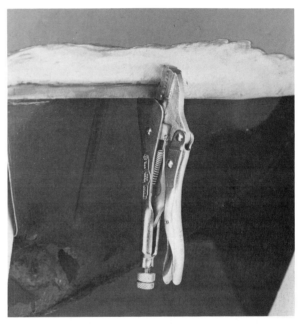

Panel-flanging pliers are used to form a lip on the edge of the patch area or patch panel. This lip allows a lap joint that is easier to weld than a butt joint. The Eastwood Company

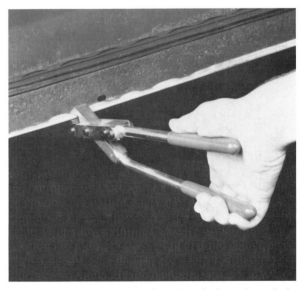

Crimping pliers are used to bend the edge of the replacement panel over metal to which it attaches. The most common use of this tool is in attaching door skins. The Eastwood Company

little practice you'll be laying down professional-looking welds, and the localized heat of this welding method means that it can be used with minimal risk of warping the surrounding metal.

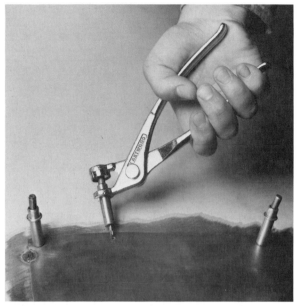

Panel holders are extremely helpful in clamping a patch in place for welding. These holding devices work where clamps cannot reach. The Eastwood Company

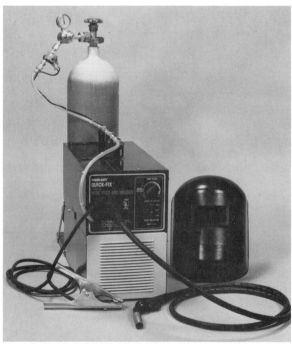

A MIG welding outfit consists of an arc welder, shielding gas and a wire-feed gun. This professional welding equipment is now available in the hobbyist restorer's price range. The Eastwood Company

The basic difference between wire welding and "stick" arc welding (stick refers to the use of a filler rod that also serves as an electrode in standard arc welding operations) is that with wire welding, the filler material is very thin (0.030 in.) and is fed automatically into the weld area. The thin filler material of wire welding is ideally suited to sheet-metal repair, and the fact that the filler wire is fed out automatically means that the operator needs to concentrate only on moving the electrode holder along the work surface. With standard stick arc welding, the operator also needs to concentrate on maintaining the correct gap between the electrode and work surface, a somewhat complicated matter since the electrode is continually being consumed in the weld.

Welding Equipment

Two types of wire welding equipment are available to the hobbyist. One uses wire with a flux

A good way to learn wire welding is to practice attaching patches to a scrap of metal (an old car hood that has been cleaned of paint works well). Note that the patch is first attached with short beads of weld in the corners. Then short welds are laid down along each side. Finally, the welds are connected. This approach prevents heat build-up, hopefully preventing panel warpage.

core as the electrode and filler metal. The flux core shields the weld in the same way as the flux coating does on an arc stick welder. The advantage of this wire welder is its relatively low cost. The disadvantage is a generally thicker wire due to the flux core. Thicker wire increases the possibility of burn-through on thin body metal.

The other type of wire welder uses an inert gas to shield the weld. This MIG (short for Metal Inert Gas) welder has the advantage of using wire as thin as 0.024 in. and because the weld is shielded with gas rather than flux, the welding process creates little smoke and splatter. Professionals definitely prefer MIG to flux core wire welders, and the difference in price between the two types is not so one-sided as to necessarily make the lower cost equipment the hobbyist's choice.

Because of its ease of use, wire welding equipment allows a hobbyist to become a proficient welder in a short time. Further, wire welding works equally well in horizontal or vertical positions. This means that welding patch panels in place on the truck body requires no special skills beyond familiarity with the wire welder. Once the equipment is set up, the procedure for wire welding is to attach the ground clamp to the truck body near the work area, turn on the welder, set the wire speed control and heat dial, then strike the electrode to the work surface and proceed across the seam that you are joining with the weld.

Welding Technique

To get used to the rate at which the wire feeds out of the gun and lays down a smooth bead, you should practice on automotive-gauge metal. A common practice exercise used in welding classes is to weld rectangular patches to a piece of auto body metal. If scrap metal, like an old hood, is used, the areas where the patches will be attached need to be sanded or stripped to bare metal. The patches are first tack welded in place at the corners, then finish welded along the sides. This pattern of joining a series of short welds is also used when attaching patch panels to the truck itself. When welding in patch panels, you will work the bead a couple of inches across a seam, then release the feed button on the gun and move to another point on the seam or to the opposite end of the seam you are welding and lay down another two or so inches of weld. Then you can go back and continue the first weld for a short distance, skip back to the other weld and so forth. This way, you will keep heat from building up in one area and warping the metal. On large, flat panels, such as doors, heat can also be contained by using a heat dam made of asbestos putty sold through specialty suppliers like The Eastwood Company.

Typically, the biggest problem novice welders experience when first practicing with wire welding is having several inches of wire feed out of the gun

An inexpensive alternative to a wire welder is this stitch welder gun which can be used in conjunction with any AC arc welder. The stitch welder is faster and easier to use than standard arc welding, providing a budget alternative to wire welding. The Eastwood Company

before finding the starting location on the seam, and striking an arc. The extra wire will melt once the arc is struck, but will become a glob of metal at the start of the weld. A technique for easily striking the arc without the problem of excess wire feeding out of the gun is to touch the electrode to the seam where you intend to begin welding, with your helmet lifted and the welder turned off. Then when you lower the helmet over your face and press the feed button on the gun, you can begin to move the gun along the seam as soon as the arc appears. A steady cracking and hissing sound is a sign that you are holding the gun the correct distance from the work surface and moving the gun at the proper rate.

On thicker metal, multiple passes may be needed to build up the weld to the full depth of the metal. With flux-core wire welders, the slag that forms on the weld will have to be chipped off between passes in order to get a sound weld. With MIG welding there is no slag, so you can simply apply additional beads as needed for thicker metal. The special feature of MIG welding is that a shielding gas, usually carbon dioxide, is blown around the arc to keep oxygen away from the weld. With flux-core wire welding, the slag serves to shield the weld. The purpose for keeping oxygen from the weld is to prevent oxidation (rusting) from occurring as the weld is formed.

After the patch is welded in place, the seam should be ground smooth. Since these welds are hard, this is best done with a carbide grinder. If the patch was joined in a butt joint, grinding the weld may be the only finishing step required before priming and painting. More commonly, however, some filler, either lead or plastic, will be needed to smooth the seam.

Wire welders designed for light-duty auto bodywork are available from specialty tool suppliers (see appendices for listings). Someone with a basic background in arc welding should be comfortably proficient with wire welding after a little practice. Instructions with the welder will provide a guide to setting the wire feed and heat controls on the welder. If you are a newcomer to welding, the best way to learn is to enroll in an evening welding class at a skill center vo-tech college. These classes typically cover gas, stick arc and wire-feed welding and will give you practice on all three methods. In addition, you will learn and practice good safety rules—the most important of which is to wear proper eye protection. Always be sure to wear a welding helmet when doing wire welding. The bright flashes from the weld, looked at with the naked eye, can burn the retina. This condition is not correctable and can lead to blindness. Also, if you are welding in the presence of others, be sure to caution them not to look at the weld. This is particularly important when children are in the work area. Their natural curiosity will draw their eyes to the bright arc flashes. It's best to make sure that children are out of the area before starting to weld.

Cab Repair

Just as cars have their rust-prone areas, so do trucks. Spots most susceptible to metal rot include the rear cab corners, bottoms of the doors, front cowl section (behind the front fenders), pickup box supports, fender eyebrows on mid to late 1950s Task Force series and box sides on later Fleetside trucks. In the section that follows, you will be taken through the process of repairing rust damage using patch panels. For the more common rust-out areas, like cab corners, repair panels are available to fit most any year Chevrolet truck.

The repair sequence described here is not uncommon on a truck that has been driven extensively in road salt. For a southern or western truck, rust damage to the extent shown in the photos would be extreme, but even on these trucks some repair in the moisture-catching lower cab areas is likely.

On an Advance Design pickup, the most rust-prone areas are the lower cowl, floor and adjoining

This Advance Design series cab shows extensive metal rot that is typical on trucks that have been run for years in road salt. Damage is typically worse on the passenger side. Although the rust looks severe, the cab can be repaired like new with patch panels. Dick Matott

Before cutting out the rusted metal, be sure to brace the cab. Otherwise, after the new metal has been welded in place you may discover that the cab has become twisted or tilted in an odd angle and difficult to straighten. Dick Matott

Extensive rust damage on the passenger side and a brace that has been welded across the repair area. Note that the repair will extend all the way to the top of the cowl. Dick Matott

firewall. Repair panels, which are die stamped to the correct contours and made of original-gauge metal, are now available to repair the rust shown in the photos. But at the time of this truck's restoration, repair panels for these areas weren't available and had to be fabricated.

Assessing Damage

The first step in any metal repair process is to assess the extent of the damage. Quite typically, a badly rusted section will look more solid than it is. The only signs of rust may be blisters in the paint. As mentioned earlier, jabbing a thin-bladed screwdriver into a paint blister is a quick way of checking the condition of the metal. Don't worry about doing damage. If the metal is sound, the screwdriver won't penetrate. If the screwdriver protrudes through, you can proceed with the steps described here. The rust may also manifest itself in gaping holes. Whether the rust is hidden or evident, the next step is to find where sound metal begins, because you can't weld the patch to rust.

Once you've established the limits of the rust, you can draw a line to show where the rusted metal is to be cut away. A pencil line will show up well enough—what's important is to make the line as straight as possible (use a ruler or some sort of straightedge). The cut-away area doesn't need to match the size and shape of the patch (which should be larger than the rust-out). In most cases you'll cut the patch to fit the hole.

Cutting Out Rusted Metal

Before cutting away any of the metal, it's important to brace the cab, as shown. The cab becomes very flexible when the step board, lower door pillar and parts of the floor are removed. If the repairs are made with the cab in a distorted position, it will be difficult to bend back to the proper shape. An air-driven cutter wheel is the best tool to use for cutting away the rusted metal. The cutter can be guided along easily by the pencil line, and will slice out the damaged area in seconds. Be sure to wear safety glasses or goggles to protect

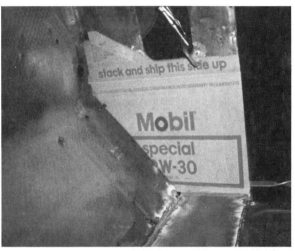

The way to cut a patch to fit the repair area is to first make a template. A sheet of cardboard works well for this. The outline of the template is then scribed onto a sheet of metal from which the patches will be cut. Dick Matott

Rust in the cowl section is usually accompanied by rusted floor and rocker panels. These floor and rocker panels have been patched first to restore the cab's structural integrity. Dick Matott

A saber saw with a metal cutting blade is used to cut out the cowl patch. If the patch is being joined with a lap joint, the outline should be drawn ½ in. larger than the hole the patch will be used to fill. Dick Matott

123

your eyes against flying sparks and metal chips. If you don't own a cutter wheel, a hacksaw or tin snips can be used, but these leave jagged edges which will have to be smoothed before installing the patch.

In some areas, such as the cowl section, you will need to cut the tack welds that hold this section of the cab together. An easy way to remove the tack welds is with a spot weld cutter. Now that you have opened up the areas needing to be repaired, you will either fabricate a patch or cut a preformed patch to fit the hole. A sheet of cardboard can be used to make a template from which a patch can be cut. If you are using repair panels, the panel can be held up to the hole and marked for cutting.

Welding in Patch Panels

Two methods can be used for attaching the patch to the existing metal. One is called a lap joint. Using this approach, you will form a lip along the edges of the patch where it joins the body metal. When the patch is installed, this lip will fit behind the sound body metal and the panel will be welded along this seam. The other approach is to cut the patch so that it fits perfectly to the contours of the hole, and weld the seams between the patch and surrounding body metal. A butt weld, as this smooth seam is called, reflects superior workmanship, but is harder to do since the fit has to be nearly perfect.

To form a lap joint you will cut the panel about ½ in. larger than the hole. Then you will bend the edges of the patch with a special lip-forming tool. Next you will fit the patch in place. For welding, the patch has to be clamped tightly to the body metal. This can be done with pop rivets, which can be drilled out and the hole filled later, or with panel holders. Various welding methods can be used to fuse the patch to the body metal, but wire welding is preferred because as previously discussed, this method creates less heat—thereby lessening the risk of warping the body panel. As an alternative, a stick welder can be used—if care is taken to avoid heat buildup. Oxyacetylene welding is almost sure to produce warpage unless a heat dam is constructed around the joint.

To weld a butt joint, the patch is fitted precisely in place and tacked in several locations. Again, this is best done with a wire welding apparatus. If the joint is a tight fit, the patch can be welded into the hole so cleanly that it may be possible to grind the weld, prime and paint. If you achieve this quality seam, you are indeed doing professional work. More likely, the seam will need some filler.

Cardboard templates can be used to cut patches to virtually any shape. The patches shown here will form a splash shield between the inner and outer cowl panels. Dick Matott

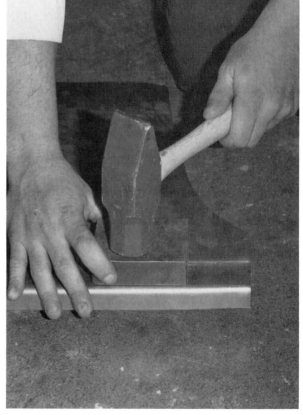

Repair panels can be formed to certain shapes using homemade die blocks.

124

Before welding, the cab corner patch also needs to be fitted around the edge of the door pillar. This fit is made by tapping along the edge of the patch with a body hammer until a tiny lip curls around the edge of the pillar. You will also see this lip in the original metal. Advance Design cabs were not the one-piece welded construction seen on light trucks today. Instead they were formed from numerous panels, some with unfinished seams—as is the case at the door pillars.

On the cowl patch, it is also necessary to re-create the track welds that were made at the factory to attach the cab's rear panel to the door pillars. This can be done in two ways. One is to drill a series of holes in the patch at the approximate locations of the spot welds, then weld the two layers of metal together through the holes. The other is to drill holes through both layers of metal and weld the holes closed. Either method will ensure that the weld penetrates both layers. When the welds are ground smooth, they will look like the original factory spot welds.

With the patch welded in place, attention can now be given to smoothing the seam. As mentioned earlier, if the patch has been butt welded, the only finishing work may be to grind the seam, prime and fill remaining blemishes with NitroStan, then wet sand, add another primer layer and finish paint. More likely, whether the patch is attached by the lap or butt weld method, some filler will be needed

to smooth the seam. Since no moisture should be able to penetrate the seam, plastic filler can be used. Some purists feel that only body lead should be used as filler, but this material can present paint blistering problems. If the solder flux becomes trapped under the metal it may work to the sur-

The inner cowl panel has been brazed in place. Amateur restorers often prefer brazing to welding because the brazing process requires less heat. Brazing, however, also has disadvantages. The bond is not as strong as a weld, and flux from the brazing process can bleed out of the joint, causing the paint to lift. Dick Matott

The repaired cab is now ready for final metal finishing and painting. Note that patch panels have also been installed in the rear cab corners. What once looked like it was ready for the discard pile is now restored to like-new condition. Dick Matott

This method would be used when repair panels were not available.

face, blistering the paint. When this occurs, the only remedy may be to remove the paint, melt out the lead filler, clean the metal and rework the seam.

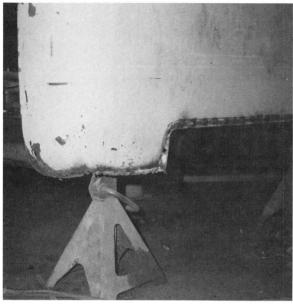

Rear cab corners are a rust collector on most any pickup. The rust problem typically results from moisture and dirt collecting against the metal on the inside of the cab. Although no visible rust-out is seen here, paint blisters indicate weakened metal. Ric Hall

If the patch was installed using the lap joint method, it is advisable to weld or caulk the lap joint on the inside of the cab. If this seam is left open, moisture may collect and blister the paint or rerust the metal. After the inside seam has been filled or caulked, and the outside seam smoothed by grinding and applying a skim coat of filler as needed, the repair should be invisible.

Repairing Lower Cab Pillars
By Ric Hall

Cabs on 1955–1959 Chevrolet and GMC trucks are prone to lower cab pillar rust. Repairing this damage is relatively easy with a lower-door-pillar repair panel available from Mar-K Specialized Manufacturing Company (see appendices for address). This patch panel repair is made as described earlier by cutting out the rusted metal, and fitting and welding the patch panel in place. The lower-door-pillar repair panels are made from 16 gauge electrogalvanized steel, and have adjustable cage nuts welded to the backside as on the original.

First, hold the patch over the area to be replaced and scribe around it. Next, cut out the rusty section using a die-grinder with a stone wheel, a pneumatic hammer and/or tin snips. If you leave ¼ to ½ in. overlap, your weld warpage will be less and the edge can be crimped for a flush fit. Vice grip hand crimpers or pneumatic crimpers can be used to form this lip. Then grind all burrs, paint and surface rust from the weld area.

To determine where to cut the cab, the repair panel has been held against the cab corner and a line scribed around it. The cut is being made with a die-grinder. This tool makes speedy work of cutting out the rusted metal. Ric Hall

Before welding the patch in place, the cut needs to be cleaned up to remove burrs, paint and surface rust from the weld area. A wire brush mounted in a drill chuck is being used to scour the edge of the cut to ensure a strong weld. Ric Hall

Before welding, use a coating to prevent rust from forming under the splice and on the back of the patch. A recommended product is The Eastwood Company's Cold Galvanizing compound.

Now tack weld the patch about every inch, then go back and fill between the welds ½ in. at a time. Alternate from one area of the patch to another to reduce warpage. A wire-feed welder is used here, but gas welding can also be used if you form a heat dam with heat-sink putty.

Hammer welding is a technique well worth trying when using a gas welder. It involves using a hammer and dolly to flatten and control warpage. As you finish each ½ in. of weld, set down the torch and quickly hammer and dolly the weld before it has a chance to cool. This technique requires that you can get access to the back of the weld.

Regardless of the welding method, little filler should be required. The results are a permanent repair—much better than filling over rust, only to watch the filler bubble or fall off soon afterward.

Replacing Floor Panels

It's not uncommon for an otherwise rust-free truck to have rusted floors. Road salt isn't the only rust culprit. Dirt, sand and debris that is tracked in to the cab and builds up on the floor is an ideal moisture collector—with the wetness settling against the metal at the bottom of the grime. If the truck has been driven in a climate where salt is used to melt ice and snow off the roads in winter, then the floors are also attacked with rust from the underside. In either condition, the result is rusted floor panels that need to be replaced.

Determine the extent of the rust. Is the damage just on the floors, or do the cab mounts also need to be repaired? This done, order repair panels. These are available from parts vendors specializing in your year truck.

Cut out the floor panel to remove rusted metal. It is wise to leave as much of the sound metal as possible and cut the replacement panel to fit. If the cab support braces are also rusted, provide support for the cab and cut these away also. These braces can be replaced more easily if the cab is off the truck. Replace the cab support braces. These supports are typically welded in place.

Fit and weld the replacement floor panels. Grind the welds and finish the seams as needed.

Fire-Window Cab Conversion
By Ric Hall

Metal work on an older truck sometimes goes beyond welding in patch panels or putting on a door skin. An example would be when entire side panels on a Fleetside box are replaced because the existing panels are rusted beyond repair. Another example is in the conversion of a three-window Advance Design pickup cab to a deluxe five-window. To many collectors, the nearly panoramic view of the five-window cab makes it a much more desirable truck. So if your truck has the more common three windows (the three windows consist of the two door windows and back light; the five-window also has corner windows), you may want to follow this relatively simple procedure to convert to five windows.

When installing the patch panel, begin by making a tack weld every inch or so, then go back and fill between the welds a half inch at a time. To prevent panel warpage, you should alternate from one area of the patch to another. A wire welder is being used to make the welds on this panel. Ric Hall

Typical door pillar rust on a 1955–1959 Chevrolet pickup. The rusted area at the corner of the floor can be repaired with sheet steel, but the hinge support at the bottom of the pillar poses more of a problem. The solution is to install a patch panel in this area. Mar-K Specialized Mfg. Co.

If you are interested in making a five-window conversion on an Advance Design Chevrolet or GMC truck, the instructions given here will guide you through the process step by step. Although the specifics will vary, the instructions are similar to those followed when replacing any large panel. Tack welds will need to be cut, seams cut and opened, the panel positioned correctly, then the panel is welded in place and metal finished.

The three-window cab shown here goes with a rare two-ton cab-over-engine (COE) truck. Using a five-window cab off the more plentiful half-ton model, it is possible to combine the two, creating a COE with the deluxe panoramic cab. This process can be used with any Advance Design series cab and is accomplished with little body and fender skills.

Why would you want to cut up your perfectly good three-window cab? One reason is you need not remove your truck's cab from the frame, which is a monumental labor savings over the time required to remove all the front sheet metal, electricals and other steps involved in swapping cabs. If the cab is rust-free in the floor and front lower corners but the five-window you have found is not, then you have another reason for using this method to give your truck a deluxe cab. Door gaps can also be greatly improved when joining the two cabs—and this is a *big* bonus. In the process of this conversion, you will improve the door fit and gaps that have deteriorated over the years, or were never very good from the factory in the first place. Doors adjust only so much, but now the door openings can be made to fit the doors.

The method shown requires a minimum amount of metal finishing. The only body filler needed will be at the windshield posts and only a very thin coat is used even there. Some have considered cutting the corner windows out of one cab and welding them into the other. This method would require a huge amount of metal finishing on the outside, not to mention on the interior panels as well.

To make this conversion, first remove the front and rear glass and remove or mask the door windows and gauges with heavy paper to prevent pitting during grinding and welding operations. The only other things to remove are the seats, weather-

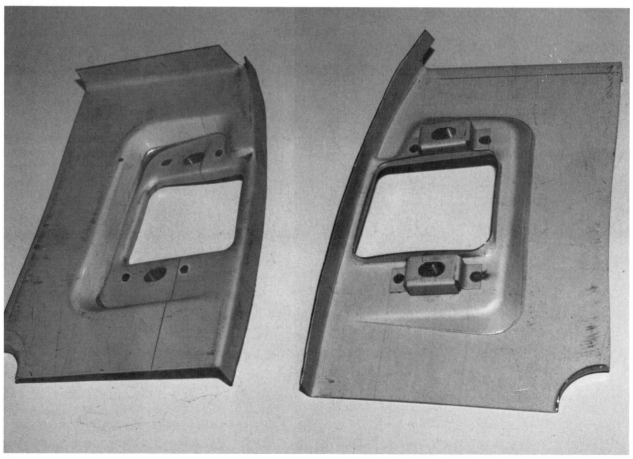

The door-hinge patch panel is shown in both a front and back view. In the back view (left), note the adjustable *cage nuts as found in the original door-hinge mount.* Mar-K Specialized Mfg. Co.

stripping and most importantly, the gas tank. Adjust the doors next for fit at the cowl and top. Don't worry too much about the back edge, since this is where the new cab can be fitted to the door later.

The door striker should be unbolted from the cab doorjamb to prevent any preload from a poorly adjusted striker. Most of the door adjustment on this model truck is obtained where the hinges bolt to the door. More likely than not, you will have to remove the doors and hinges to free them up from rust so they can be adjusted. Reinstall the hinges and doors, adjusting one hinge at a time until you are happy with the door gap. A block of wood and a floor jack are invaluable in this process. It may take some time; several hours per door is not uncommon.

Cutting Out Posts and Spot Welds

Carefully measure a midway point on the windshield posts for cutting. The window opening has too many curves to get a good measurement, so a template works well. I used an old plastic for-sale sign cut to fit the window opening as a template. This enabled me to mark each cab at exactly the same spot. Double-check your work here; this is the most critical part of the conversion. Then go ahead and cut through the posts using a hacksaw. The center support can be drilled or twisted out easily since it is barely attached with spot welds.

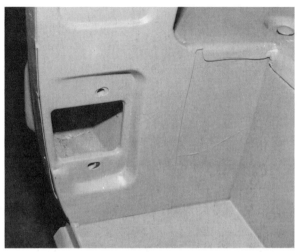

The completed repair can't be detected from original metal. Note that the patch panel preserves the stamped recess of the original hinge box perfectly. Mar-K Specialized Mfg. Co.

With the rusted area cut out and the patch panels welded in place, the cab is now restored to solid metal. After grinding the weld bead smooth and sandblasting the cab floor to remove surface rust, the cab will be ready for refinishing. Mar-K Specialized Mfg. Co.

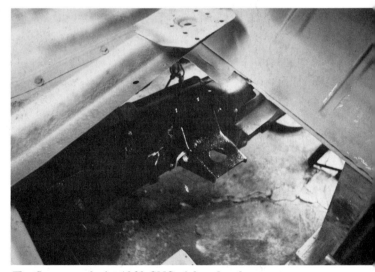

The floor panel of a 1969 GMC pickup has been cut out for repair with a replacement panel. As much of the original floor has been left as possible. The new floor panel will be cut to fit. Note that the outrigger pad for the cab support bracket (top center). The small holes show where this piece was welded at the factory to the front support. This pad must be removed if you are replacing the front and rear supports with original equipment types. Jon Bagley

The rear of the cab has spot welds along the lower edge. Drill these out on both cabs. A couple types of spot weld cutters are available at auto paint supply stores or specialty suppliers. Be careful to drill only through the rear panel since the other cab's spot welds are in the same place. If you also drill out the spot welds in the floor, there will be little to weld the new cab onto.

The most secure welds to contend with are in the doorjamb area: one down low and another at the seat support. Use a cutting torch here to cut as close to the weld as possible, being careful not to cut into the part you want to save. Once the cab is apart, the remaining metal and weld can be ground

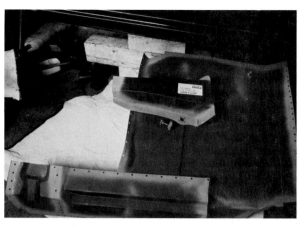

The new floor pieces and cab support. Note the hole in the main floor panel. A nut for the seatbelt bolt will be welded over this hole on the underside. The new panels will be welded in place to existing floor metal through the small holes to give the effect of factory-style spot welds. Jon Bagley

The rear cab mount with much of the support brace removed. The new support will be lapped over the old 1½ in. and welded in place. Jon Bagley

The front cab support has been replaced and the outrigger pad welded in place. Jon Bagley

The new floor panels are put in place and checked and double-checked for fit. If the rocker panel is also being replaced, as is the case here, it will be clamped for fitting only and be the last piece welded. In this sequence, the door is reinstalled for fit, but will be removed before welding starts. Jon Bagley

off. Inside the cab are five braces to be cut, three behind where the gas tank mounts and two down inside the corners. Cut the braces in each cab so that they will overlap. A flush splice is not needed here.

The part of the three-window cab that is not being saved can most easily be removed by pushing it onto its back. This should pop loose any spot welds not fully drilled out. Be more careful with the five-window cab, prying it loose and lifting it off to prevent bending the cab back. When it is removed, lay it down onto some padded sawhorses. Use a stone grinding wheel on a body grinder to remove remaining metal and weld.

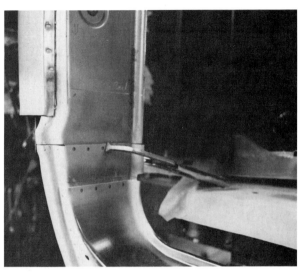

If the floors have rusted due to road salt, it is also likely that adjoining metal, the rockers and cab pillars, will also need to be replaced. Patch panels are also used to make these repairs. Jon Bagley

With the windshield, back light and gas tank removed, the roof of both cabs is cut off beginning at the windshield posts. It is important to cut both cabs at exactly the same spot. A template is used to make sure the location of the cuts is the same. Ric Hall

Here's the three-window cab that we're going to make into a five-window. Many restorers prefer the deluxe cab with its panoramic windows. The conversion method described here is much simpler than replacing the entire cab. The arch in the front of this cab indicates that it is from a cab-over-engine (COE) truck. Ric Hall

The rear of the cab has spot welds along the lower edge. These welds are best removed with a spot weld cutter. It is important to drill only through the outer metal skin, since new welds will be made in this spot when you join the five-window roof to the three-window cab base. Ric Hall

Cleaning Weld Areas

Remove all burrs, rust and paint from areas to be welded. If you want to clean the metal with sandblasting or use a chemical stripping method,

A spot weld cutter inserts into the chuck of a drill and cuts around the weld. The Eastwood Company

The back of the cab is cut loose from the doorjamb and seat support with a torch. Inside the cab there are five braces that also need to be cut. Three are located behind where the gas tank mounts. The other two are down inside the corners. Ric Hall

there is no better time to work on the inside of the cab than now. Before welding, seal blind areas against rust by using a cold galvanizing compound like that sold by The Eastwood Company. Unlike paint, this product has weld-through capabilities.

Welding New Posts and Spot Welds

After positioning the five-window cab piece by lifting it onto your truck's cab platform, you can hold the two cab parts together with vise grips. Now adjust the position of the back panel to give the doors a proper fit—not too tight, not too loose. Then weld the windshield posts, rain gutter and all. To make the strongest possible splice, the metal on the inside of the post should also be welded together. To accomplish this, cut and remove about a 2x3 in. section on the doorjamb for access. This section can be welded back into place after making the inside post welds.

A wire-feed welder is best suited for making this cab conversion because it creates less heat and warpage, but a gas welder can also be used. Take it

The five-window cab roof and back has been cut at the windshield posts and front of the seat support. The seat support area will need to be cut away before this cab portion can be jointed to the former three-window cab cowl and base. Ric Hall

The two cab portions are joined first at the windshield posts. To make the strongest possible splice, the inside of the posts should also be welded. A benefit of converting a standard three-window cab to a deluxe five-window by this method is perfect door fit. Ric Hall

This reproduction of the 1958–1959 Chevrolet truck battery tray matches the original in all respects. Battery trays are often badly corroded or have been replaced with something cobbled up by an earlier owner. This tray is available from Mar-K Specialized Manufacturing Co. Mark Sharp

This side tire mount looks original (even though Chevrolet didn't offer this tire carrier option in these years) and saves having to crawl under the truck to get at the spare. David Bush

easy no matter what welding method you use, especially when making the spot welds on the back panel. If you are doing gas welding, use a heat sink putty to prevent warpage of the surrounding metal.

After welding the windshield posts, replace the spot welds. Leave the lower rear doorjamb until last to ensure proper door alignment. The door-jamb should be welded in the same place as the factory welds. The five braces inside the cab can be welded or bolted together since they will not show once the gas tank is in place. Now with very little metal finishing, nobody should be able to suspect that the cab didn't come from the factory as a five-window—unless you tell them why the doors fit so well!

Fabricating a Spare Tire Mount

by David Bush

For some reason, it seems, lots of people who originally had 1941–46 Chevrolet pickups removed the under-bed spare tire carrier and lost it. This was the case with my 1946. All of the hardware was missing. After some research I decided that Chevrolet didn't offer a side-mount tire carrier for these trucks.

Since I couldn't find the hardware for the original carrier, and also because I really wanted the side-mount, I decided to design one myself. I took measurements, built a scale model from cardboard, drew up the plans on graph paper to scale and took them to a local welding fab shop. One week later I got my side-mount. Although the rear fender is not welled (fitted with a cutout for the tire), I think the result looks reasonably original. The mount is made of five pieces of sheet steel, the basic frame being built of ⅛ in. plate, and the tire mounting flange being ¼ in. plate. It attaches by five stainless-steel ⅜ in. bolts to the bed side and the forward stake pocket. I've done some preliminary testing for strength (it's strong enough for me to stand on and hasn't fallen off when I've driven down some bumpy dirt roads), and now it's at the powder coater's getting a gloss-black finish.

12

Priming and Painting

Almost every older pickup will need repainting. If your truck is undergoing restoration, its various components and assemblies will go through the painting process at different times. If you are overhauling the truck, chances are you will repaint the entire truck at one time. Whichever approach you take, the steps in the painting process are essentially the same.

Repainting your truck starts with researching original colors and selecting a color from this list. Here you probably have two concerns: what was the truck's original color, and what other colors were available? If your truck has been repainted, and odds are that it has, you can determine the original color quite easily by checking locations

that aren't likely to be repainted—like the firewall. The colors Chevrolet made available on your make and model truck can be found on a paint sheet, available from suppliers like Jim Carter's Vintage Chevrolet Parts (see appendices for address). The paint sheets cover Chevrolet trucks from 1936-1959 and GMC trucks from 1938-1959. These are only paint listings; paint chips are not included. You can get a sense of what these colors looked like from original Chevrolet sales brochures. These brochures can be purchased from antique car literature dealers at large flea markets. However, the brochures give only an *idea* of what the color looked like because, in most cases, the colors shown on the brochures are likenesses, not exact matches.

As you pick the color, keep your truck's interior color scheme in mind. Until 1954, Chevrolet

If the truck's original finish is still in good condition (no surface rust or cracking) you may use it as a base for the new finish. However, the old paint will need to be scuffed up with a D/A sander and any dent or rust areas repaired. This 1969 C–20 Longhorn Camper Special has spent most of its life in California and has a rust-free body. However, minor dent work was required as can be seen on the rear panels.

As the front view shows, scuffing up this truck's finish involved nearly as much effort as would have been required to remove the old paint. When weighing the alternatives—to paint over the original finish or bare metal—it is advisable to strip the finish and work from bare metal.

offered basically one interior color which they more or less matched with a limited range of exterior colors. In 1951, for example, the interior color was a deep maroon on the seat upholstery and door panels with a silver dash. Whatever the exterior color, this was the interior scheme. On more modern Chevrolet trucks, particularly those from the mid-sixties and later when choices in seat covering material became available, you should select the exterior color to harmonize with the interior. For example, let's say that your truck's original seat covering is blue and the upholstery looks fresh enough to keep as is, you would not want to select a conflicting exterior color (such as green). In the event that you decide to change the interior to match an exterior color that catches your fancy, you should be aware that original-looking fabrics may not be available in a harmonizing color. So like it or not, the interior color scheme needs to be taken into consideration.

Once the color has been selected, the next question is where to buy the paint. If you are planning to use a modern paint (acrylic urethane or acrylic enamel), your local automotive paint supply store may be able to mix the paint for you. The other alternative is to order the paint from a vintage Chevrolet truck supplier. The original colors are available. Unless you are dead set to paint your truck a certain nonoriginal color, it is advisable to stick with the original color schemes and this includes not coating the chassis in wet-look paints like DuPont's Imron. Not only do nonoriginal colors detract from your truck's value, but the wet-look paints chip easily and are difficult to touch up.

Before starting the painting process you need to decide what type of paint will be used for the final finish. This is essential because the type of finish paint determines what type of primer will be used. Enamel finishes can be sprayed over a lacquer or enamel primer base, but a lacquer finish should not be applied over an enamel primer. If this is done, the lacquer solvents will penetrate and lift the primer coat. Modern urethane paints are designed as a system. This means that if you decide on a urethane finish, you should select compatible polyurethane base coats. In modern paints, particularly the urethanes, selecting compatible primer and finish products is important to get strong paint adhesion and to prevent the top coat color from sinking into the primer.

The alternative to scuffing up the old finish is to strip off the old paint using paint remover. If the truck has been repainted, the old finish should probably be removed.

This Advance Design pickup has been disassembled for a ground-up restoration. Mike Cavey

Paint Preparation

The success of the final finish lies in the attention given to the primer coat. Arriving at a smooth primer finish involves a multi-step process that begins by making sure the surface to be painted is clean and rust-free. If you will be painting over an older finish, make sure that rust isn't bleeding through from underneath and that the paint isn't cracked. The best assurance of a smooth new finish is to remove the old paint layers. However, if the existing finish is sound and limited to the factory coating, you may decide to paint over it. If so, the old paint must first be sanded to ensure a good primer bond.

Sanding

To scuff up the old finish for repainting you should use a D/A (dual action) sander. A rotary sander will leave circular marks and gouges that will show up in the finish, and trying to sand the old finish by hand is not only extremely tedious and time consuming, but will also result in an uneven base. A dual-action sander is an air-powered tool

that operates in slow motion and is ideal for surface preparation. Before approaching the old finish with the D/A sander, be sure to wipe down the truck's exterior with a wax remover solvent available at the automotive paint supply store. If you used paint remover to strip off the old finish, you will still probably use the D/A sander to clean off paint and primer residue.

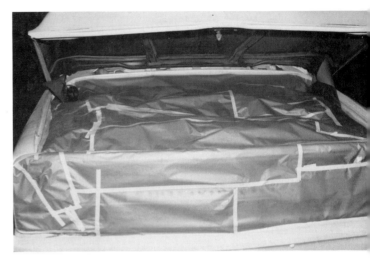

Note that the engine compartment has also been masked. This is important to keep painting dust and overspray from coating the radiator, wiring, engine and other mechanical assemblies under the hood.

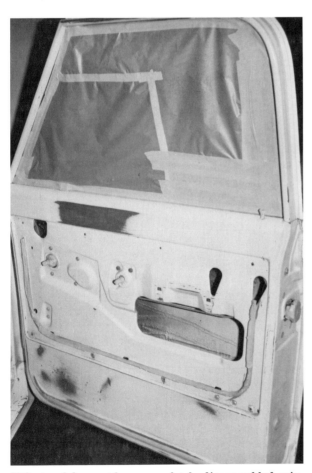

If the truck has not been completely disassembled, windows and trim will have to be masked before priming and painting. It is also advisable to remove trim and weather-stripping prior to painting.

From the rear, little masking is required—in this case only the taillights, step-and-tow rear bumper and rear window have been covered. The side-marker lights have also been removed, along with trim.

Metal Preparation

If you are applying the new paint coating to a bare metal finish, you'll get better paint adhesion if you wipe down the fresh metal with dilute phosphoric acid, sold in automotive paint supply stores under trade names such as Metal Etch or Metal Prep. Instructions for applying the acid to etch the metal are shown on the container. When the acid coating dries it will leave a dull grayish yellow coating on the bare metal surface. The phosphoric acid treatment improves paint adhesion by etching the surface of the metal—in effect, turning the smooth metal into a landscape of hills and valleys. The acid coating also protects the bare metal from rapid rusting. Untreated metal will quickly develop a rust coating even when stored inside, if any humidity is present.

Primer and Paint Sequence

• Over bare metal:
Treat metal with dilute phosphoric acid (Metal Prep or comparable product) to retard rust and help paint adhesion.

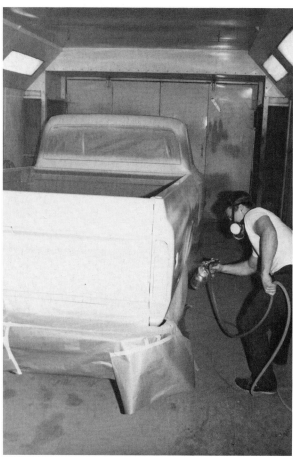

The ideal condition for priming and painting is a spray booth that allows only filtered air into the painting area. Note that the painter is holding the air hose so that it will not rub against a freshly primed surface.

Coat areas prone to rusting (inside of doors, lower areas of the cab) with a zinc-rich primer such as Zinc Chromate.

• Over bare metal or prior finish:
Apply epoxy or traditional lacquer or enamel primer (gray, red oxide or black). Apply dust coat with contrasting color for block sanding.

• Over base primer to fill surface imperfections:
Apply buildup of primer surfacer.

• Over primer layer as preparation for finish coat:
Use primer sealer or sealer.

• Over sealed primer coating:
Finish paint in acrylic lacquer or enamel or modern catalyzed acrylic urethane.

• Over finish coating (optional with urethane system paints):
Apply acrylic urethane clear topcoat for extra high-gloss and wet look.

Primer Coat

The primer coating is applied with a pressurized spray gun in the same manner as the final finish. Its purpose is to provide adhesion and a

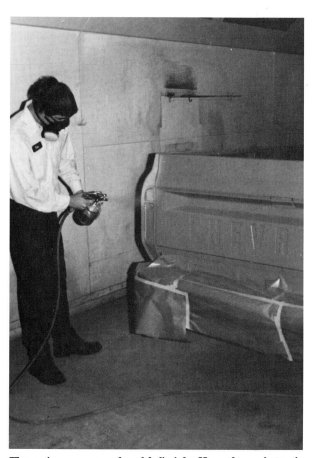

The primer covers the old finish. Here the painter is wearing an effective respirator. This is a health safety must.

base coat for the finish paint. The primer layer is also used to smooth any minor irregularities in the metal's surface. The priming process actually consists of building up a series of primer coats and sanding this primer buildup until the base layer is completely smooth. Although you will hear talk of restorers who achieved a final finish on their trucks that had the depth and gloss of a Marine's spit-shined boots by applying numerous final finish coats, in reality the success of the final finish lies in the smoothness and absence of flaws in the primer layer.

Successful painting lies as much in knowing what products to use in what sequence as in knowing the technique. Strictly speaking, the primer coat is a bond coating used to adhere subsequent base and finish coats to a metal or previous coatings. Some primers also contain corrosion-resistant properties. These are used on inner body panels and chassis parts where moisture condensation can cause rust problems. Examples of corrosion-resistant primers are Zinc Chromate, available from most paint suppliers, and The Eastwood Company's Cold Galvanizing Compound. These primers are not sanded.

On visible surfaces, primer surfacer is typically applied over the primer layer. Primer surfacers give fast buildup for filling minor surface imperfections. This coating is sanded and often several primer surfacer coatings are applied, with sanding between each. Rough surface areas where rust has been removed by sandblasting will require an extra-thick primer buildup that can best be achieved by filler products like NitroStan or a sprayable filler like Sandy, also available from The Eastwood Company. When a smooth surface has been achieved, a primer sealer coating is applied. The sealer layer prevents sand scratches from opening up underneath the final finish and enhances the color in the finish coat.

Spraying Primer

For spraying, both lacquer and enamel primers need to be diluted with solvent. Catalyzed primers are mixed with an equal proportion of catalyst. The thinning proportion for lacquer primer, which is mixed with lacquer thinner, is 125 to 150 percent. This means that you will add somewhat more than an equal amount of thinner to lacquer primer. The solvent used with enamel primer is called a reducer and the reduction mix is thirty-three percent reducer to primer. This means you will add approximately one third the amount of reducer to enamel primer.

You will find that there are various grades and types of thinners and reducers. The primer coating does not require as high a grade of solvent as does the finish coating. Other variations are for the temperature in which you will be doing the painting. If you are applying the primer or finish coating

in warm temperatures (above 75 degrees Fahrenheit), you will use a less volatile (slower evaporating) solvent than if you are spray painting at a

The painter is being careful to hold the spray gun perpendicular to the work surface. Each pass in this area will sweep the truck's forward section.

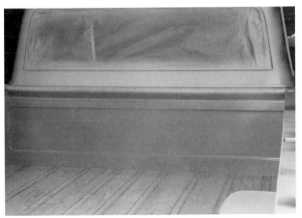

The front box panel also receives a primer coating. On later-model Chevrolet trucks the bed floor, whether wood or metal, was painted body color. In this case, the bed floor will be primed and painted later.

Powder Coating

by David Bush

Powder paint is not really paint, but a dry, granular material. Since it's dry, there is no way to tint it at all. The color of the powder is the color you get. The selection of colors is broad, however, so this generally isn't a problem unless you are trying to match a color exactly for authenticity's sake. Parts to be powder painted must be sandblasted completely to bare metal. All rubber or plastic parts (or anything that would be damaged by high heat) must be removed. The parts are then hung on a metal frame and enclosed in a large cabinet. The parts are negatively charged electrically and the powder is sprayed into the cabinet where it is attracted to the charged metal. This is then baked for several hours at around 500 degrees or so. The resulting finish is much tougher than paint.

Because of the baking process, you can't do bodywork and then powder paint. It is also a fairly expensive process. Occasionally the finish doesn't come out right and the part has to be redone, which means starting over completely with sandblasting. A reputable powder painter should be willing to do this without charge, as mine did.

cooler temperature (65 degrees, say). The counter clerk at your automotive paint supply store can advise you on the correct solvent for the type of primer and temperature conditions.

It's important to be precise in mixing primer with the correct solvent or catalyst. A good way to do this is to cut the top of a solvent can, pour in the primer (or finish paint), then add the solvent or catalyst—whichever the painting product requires. Use a graded measuring stick available from the paint supply store to determine when the correct mixture has been reached. Stir to mix in the sol-

When the truck is disassembled, each major assembly is primed and painted separately. Disassembly saves masking at this stage. In this shop, the restorers have set up a makeshift paint booth by sectioning off the painting area with plastic sheeting. When this is done, air ventilation needs to be provided by placing intake and exhaust fans in windows or holes cut in the wall. Furnace filters work well to keep the incoming air dust-free. Mike Cavey

vent or catalyst. Be sure to pour the primer through a paint strainer (cone-shaped paper strainers specially made for this purpose are available from automotive paint supply stores) as you fill the spray gun cup.

Spraying primer coating does not require an especially high level of painting skill. If the primer mix is right, the air-line pressure is within the accepted range (35-45 psi for lacquer; 55-60 psi for enamel; 40-50 psi for catalyzed primers), the spray gun is adjusted correctly, the temperature is workable (70 to 85 degrees Fahrenheit) and the gun is held an appropriate distance from the work (8 to 10 in.), virtually anybody can apply the primer coating.

Unlike finish coats where buildup should be consistent, with the primer coating it may be desirable to build up a thicker layer in repair areas. This is done by applying several coats, allowing drying time between each. While runs in the primer surface are not desirable, if they occur there's no loss except the time required to sand them out and reprime for a smooth surface. The main purpose here is getting the primer on the vehicle.

Areas you don't want to receive a primer coating need to be masked. Newspaper works well for this, but be sure to overlap the perforations at the edges of the sheets. Unless you overlap these perforations or lay a strip of masking tape over the perforations, dots of primer will appear on the underlying surface. Also, if you are priming an assembled truck, you will need to loosen the box from the frame and slide it back, or take it off the chassis to paint the rear of the cab and front of the box.

Sanding Primer

Before sanding, the primer coat needs to cure. Curing times and temperatures will be listed on the container. If you attempt to sand the primer coat-

ing before it has dried sufficiently, it may roll up in little balls on the sandpaper. Not all primer coatings should be wet sanded (a technique where automotive-type wet-dry sandpaper is dipped in water periodically while sanding). Most of the traditional lacquer and enamel primers are water-porous, which means that wet sanding may allow water to penetrate to the metal surface causing rust to form—which may eventually blister and lift the paint. For this reason, primed metal should not be stored outside where dew or rain can settle on the primer finish. Traditional lacquer and enamel primers should be dry sanded. This is a dusty job for which you should wear a dust mask or painting respirator.

Most of the catalyzed primers have a moisture barrier, which means these products can be wet

The guide coat is used with a technique called block sanding to ensure a perfectly smooth base coat for the final finish. After the guide coat has been sanded off, the surface is wiped with water. This cleans off the sanding residue. Now the area that has been sanded can be examined for high or low spots. Slight depressions can be filled with NitroStan. More minor surface imperfections are filled with subsequent primer or primer surfacer coatings.

After the primer coat, a light dust coating of contrasting color is applied to serve as a guide in sanding. Notice that no attempt has been made to keep this guide coat uniform.

sanded. This approach eliminates the dust, prolongs sandpaper life and gives a smoother finish. Wet sanding is simple. Automotive sandpaper has a water-resistant backing, which allows the sandpaper to be dipped in water (just fill a gallon pail and set it near the work) to provide a lubricant for the sandpaper grit. With wet sanding, the finish can be washed periodically to check on the sanding progress while the sandpaper is washed clean by dipping it in the water bucket as often as the grit begins to become plugged.

With the primer layer, a coarser sandpaper grit is used on the filler coats and finer grit for the coating that will form the base for the final finish. The relatively coarse 220 grit used for cutting down the filler coats will leave scratch marks that need to be filled by additional primer coatings which are sanded with 360, 400 and fine 600 grit papers.

To get the longest life from a sheet of automotive sandpaper, fold the fresh sheet in half (the long way), then rip the paper at the fold. Now fold the half sheet in thirds (as you would a business letter). Doing this, you have created three sanding surfaces. If you are dry sanding, you can tap the sandpaper against a board or other hard object periodically to clean the grit of sanding dust. When one surface becomes clogged, you can continue sanding with one of the other fresh surfaces until the entire sheet is used up.

For newcomers to automotive painting, one of the most difficult parts of the priming process is knowing when the primer layer is smooth. Since primer has a dull surface, it is very difficult to tell visually whether the primer is criss-crossed by scratches that will show up in the finish coat, and if the primer surface is smooth or rippley. To keep scratches from showing up in the final coat, use the

Block sanding is a time-consuming, tedious process but is necessary to ensure a perfectly smooth base for the final finish. Note that a dish detergent bottle is used to spray water onto the sanding area.

After block sanding, low spots will be visible as dark areas on the primer surface while the underlying finish or bare metal will show through in high spots. The priming, block sanding process may need to be repeated two or three times to smooth the high and low areas.

graduated sanding scheme described earlier, and apply a sealer before the final finish. There are several ways to avoid a rippley surface. One is to use a sanding block rather than hold the sandpaper in your hand. The sanding block cuts the primer in smooth sweeps. Hand-held sandpaper rubs harder against the primer at the base of the knuckles and palm, cutting deeper in spots rubbed by these surfaces. Another method for ensuring a smooth surface is to lay down a guide coating of contrasting colored primer; use gray primer over red or vice versa. As you sand, the guide coating will be quickly sanded away. Any remaining spots of contrasting color will show low areas that need to be filled and resanded.

Putty-like fillers (NitroStan with traditional lacquer and enamel primers, or Poly Putty with catalyzed epoxy primers) are used to build up nicks and other small surface imperfections. NitroStan comes in a tube (like toothpaste) and is applied by squeezing a small amount from the tube onto a rubber applicator. Poly Putty is packaged in a metal container and is mixed with hardener. Only a very thin coat of filler is applied. When dry, the filler can be sanded using the block sanding technique.

Primer Sealer

Although the finish coat can be applied directly over primer (providing compatible base and finish paints have been selected), for best results it is advisable to apply a sealer coating before the final finish. Sealer is available as a clear coating that serves only to prevent moisture and painting solvents from penetrating the primer layer or as a combination primer sealer that can be sanded, but forms a hard coating as it cures. The advantage of primer sealer is that this product consolidates two steps into one. The only drawback to using any sealer product is that if you seal the finish and wait

an extended amount of time to do the finish painting, the sealer coating becomes very hard. This makes it difficult to sand out any scratches that may occur from carelessness. The hard coating

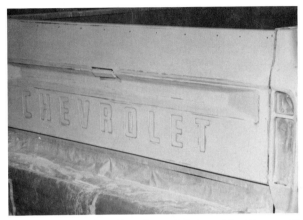

When sanding the primer layer it is important to smooth recesses such as the letters on the tailgate.

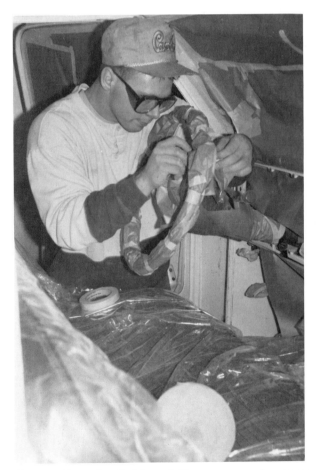

Preparations for finish painting may require more extensive masking. The interior of this 1969 Longhorn is being masked to allow repainting.

The entire truck receives the block-sanding treatment. Note that high and low spots are visible in many areas.

also makes a poorer surface for the final finish to bond to than does the softer surface of fresh sealer.

Top Coat Preparation

Amateur painters have preferred lacquer finishes over enamel because lacquer is faster drying and therefore easier to apply. With slower-drying paints, runs are more likely to develop and it is harder to get a wet finish coat which is important for a high gloss. A major reason for the popularity of modern acrylic enamels is that these paints are as easy to spray and dry as rapidly as lacquer. This fast-drying quality can be a disadvantage when spray painting in hot weather. Above 80 degrees Fahrenheit, the solvents in fast-drying paints are likely to evaporate so quickly that the surface will have a rough, gritty texture. This can be true both

of primer and finish paints. Retardants can be added to slow drying time, but if the temperature is sufficiently warm, these will have little effect.

If it is essential to spray paint in very warm temperatures, slower-drying enamel may be the only way to achieve a smooth, glossy finish. I learned this the hard way one summer when I was attempting to refinish the inside of my pickup's cab in the midst of a heat wave. The local paint store was able to mix my truck's color only in a lacquer paint. Each time I applied the paint the finish looked like I'd taken a mouthful of paint and sprayed it out through my teeth. Experienced painters told me I had three options: do the painting very early in the morning before the air warmed up, wait for a break in the heat wave or use enamel

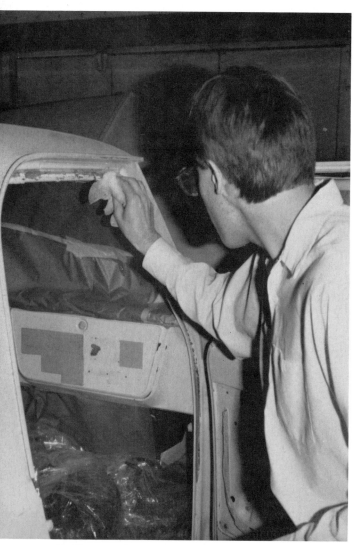

Rubber weatherstripping is typically removed as part of the priming/repainting process. Traces of glue or old weatherstripping that stick to the metal can be removed with a cloth soaked in wax-remover solvent.

Modern urethane paints are mixed with both reducer and a catalyst. These paints contain toxic isocyanates and should be applied only if you are wearing a proper respirator and in properly ventilated conditions. As the product label on the paint container states, urethane paints are intended for use by trained professionals wearing proper equipment. Although as a hobbyist you can purchase these paints from your local auto paint supply store, you should not use them unless you are equipped with proper safety equipment.

144

paint. I chose to combine the first and third options, and sprayed the cab with enamel primer and finish coats during the early morning hours.

It is imperative that the surface be completely free of dust before painting. To remove sanding dust, first blow off the areas to be painted with an air nozzle. Be sure to blow into seams and crevices on the vehicle, as well as into seams and folds on the masking paper that might hold trapped dust. Then wipe down the entire surface with tack cloths, available wherever paint supplies are sold.

If you are doing a ground-up restoration, the painting process will occur in stages. Typically the chassis is painted first, then the cab interior, fol-

lowed by the insides of the fenders and hood, the cab assembly with front fenders and hood attached, and finally the box. The problem with this approach is that unless you are careful, preparing the next unit for painting can mess up those already refinished. One way to solve this problem is to cover the chassis with a large sheet of plastic (available from building and farm-supply stores), then mount the cab and front-end assembly on top of the plastic. This approach allows you to sand and finish paint the truck's sheet metal while keeping sanding dust, paint overspray and wet-sanding drippings from collecting on the chassis. After the finish painting process is completed, the plastic

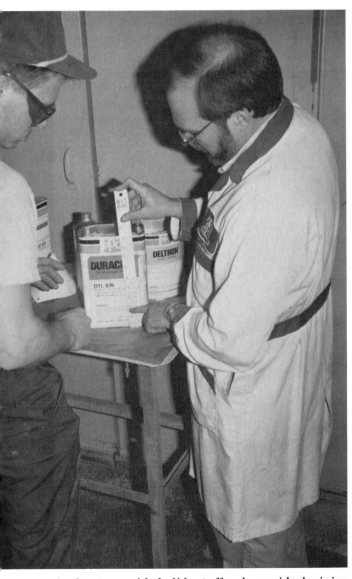

A solvent can with the lid cut off makes an ideal mixing container. Automotive finishes are mixed by volume using a marking stick. After mixing, the paint is stirred thoroughly before being poured through a strainer into the painting cup.

The interior is painted first. Note that the instrument panel and heater controls have been removed. All other non-painted interior surfaces have been masked. If the interior roof panel is metal it too receives a fresh finish coat.

145

can be torn off and discarded and everything it covered will be spotless.

When painting an assembled truck, you should cover the engine to prevent sanding dust and painting overspray from settling on vital parts. Tires are protected from paint overspray by covering them with garbage bags or jacking up the truck, supporting it on jack stands, and then removing the wheels. The new finish will look much more professional if you have taken the time to remove model markings and other trim.

Before starting a painting job it is important to buy enough paint to do the whole truck. When mixing the paint, pour some paint from different cans. This helps prevent subtle (or sometimes visible) changes in the color caused by the paint mix.

Even with paint of a consistent color, shading variations can appear in areas of the finish that are applied on different days under different temperature and humidity conditions. The recommended approach is to spray all areas receiving one color at one time.

Top Coat Painting

Whereas priming can be done in the open shop, finish painting requires a dust-free environment—preferably a painting booth. Just because your home shop doesn't have this expensive facility doesn't mean you can't do quality finish painting. A spray booth can be fabricated by sectioning off a portion of the shop with large sheets of plastic. You will need to install an exhaust fan in a window or opening cut into the side wall to draw painting overspray and solvent fumes out of the spraying area. You will also need to construct a ventilation system to bring in fresh air. The ventilation opening, which can be another window or hole cut in the plastic, should filter the incoming air. Furnace filters can be used for this.

Other interior surfaces receiving a fresh finish include the rocker and door panels. Note that the door upholstery panel has been removed, along with the handles.

Before the exterior receives its finish coat, all surfaces are wiped down with tack cloth and an air gun is used to blow dust out of seams and crevices.

146

Along with doing the spray painting in a well-ventilated area, you also need to wear a professional-quality respirator. An appropriate respirator should be available wherever paint supplies are sold. Respirators with charcoal-activated, rather than paper filters, are needed to protect you from the toxic chemicals, most notably the isocyanates, found in many of today's paints. A better respirator for these paints is the type that draws the air supply from outside the painting area. This fresh-air style respirator is described later in this chapter. Paint products containing isocyanates are very dangerous and if sprayed without adequate ventilation and proper air filtration can induce a condition called ARDS (Acute Respiratory Distress Syndrome), which has the symptoms of a heart attack. ARDS is nothing to be taken lightly because it can cause death! Toxic paint chemicals are not to be fooled around with.

In applying the final finish you should follow a pattern which starts at the top, then works around the truck from front to back or back to front. Before starting to paint, be sure that the air vent on

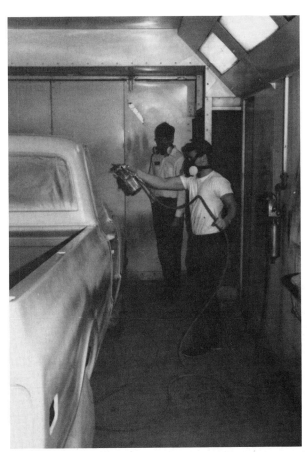

Once the first coat has flashed (dried sufficiently to hold the second coating), the painter continues around the vehicle. The final finish typically consists of four coats.

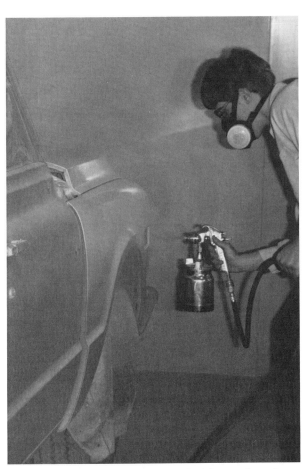

Finish painting begins at one end of the truck and proceeds top to bottom around the vehicle. Note that the painter is pointing the spray gun directly at the work surface.

The 1969 Chevy now has its new white finish, but the marking lights and trim still need to be reinstalled. Before this is done, the tailgate will be masked to repaint the lettering. On 1955 First Series and earlier trucks, the Chevrolet name on the tailgate was not painted a contrasting color.

Painting Tips for Chevrolet Trucks

• Cast-iron parts on Advance Design and earlier models were sometimes painted, sometimes not, depending on the production pace. In restoration, these parts can be painted with a "cast blast" coating which gives the look of fresh-cast metal.

• To paint the letters on the hood nameplates, rather than trying to mask the individual letters, paint the lettering and compound the excess off the plate using a piece of leather to work the compound.

• The division point between interior and exterior colors is where the exterior skin ends.

• When painting the engine, don't put too much paint on the block. Paint hinders heat transfer.

• Paint the top primer layer for the undercarriage black and chips in the final finish won't show a drastic color change.

• When painting trim and other smaller parts, hang up the parts on wire strung between two stepladders.

• When fitting painted parts during reassembly, tape off the edges with 2 in. masking tape and pull off the tape after the parts have been fitted, just before bolting up.

• Tailgate lettering 1955 and earlier was painted the same color as the tailgate, not contrasting.

• On 1947–1948 Advance Design series trucks, the grille bars and backsplash bars were painted body color. The leading edge of each outer bar had a horizontal stripe matching the cab stripe.

• From 1947–1953, cabs and fenders were the same color. Two-tone cabs were first available in 1954. Then the top was white as an option only on deluxe five-window models.

• On 1949–1953 Advance Design trucks with the painted grille, the backsplash was painted light gray or white. On chrome grilles, the outer bar was plated and the backsplash was Waldorf White.

• On 1952 and 1953 Advance Design trucks, many formerly chrome-plated items were painted. These included hubcaps, bumpers, grille, radio speaker trim and glovebox door.

• Dark green was the standard exterior paint prior to 1955 Second Series.

• A Juniper Green body with Cream Medium striping and Black wheels was the standard finish for all 1954–1955 First Series models, with twelve other colors available at no extra cost. On deluxe models with single or two-tone paint combinations, the wheels were painted lower body color. The only color available for the roof (called upper body color) was Shell White, and the belt line was striped with the lower body color except on trucks painted Pure White, Cream Medium or Omaha Orange, where the body stripe is Black. Exterior colors for First Series trucks were unchanged except that the upper body color on deluxe two-tones was now Bombay Ivory.

• The grille on 1954 trucks was painted body color with lettering in Waldorf White. On First Series models the grille was painted Bombay Ivory with Black inner bars and Chevrolet lettering on header bar also in Black.

• On Advance Design series trucks, the pinstriping consisted of two stripes on the wheel rims and one stripe around the cab. The stripes were ⅛ in. wide. The cab stripe was located right in the middle of the two creases which formed what is referred to as the cab belt. Standard wheel color on the Advance Design series was black. Deluxe wheels were painted body color and pinstriped. The stripes are ¼ in. wide and the outer stripe is located dead center on the valve stem hole. There is a 3½ in. space between the inner and outer stripes. The inner stripe is not covered by the hubcap, but is near the hubcap's outer edge.

the paint cup lid is opposite the spray nozzle. Otherwise, paint will drip out of the gun onto the hood or top when you spray these horizontal surfaces. Most novice painters sweep the spray gun in an arc over the work surface. This approach applies more paint in the center of the pass than at the entry or exit. To keep the paint layer even, pass the spray gun at an even distance (8-10 in.) from the work surface and always point the painting nozzle directly at the work area. After making a pass, move the gun down the panel so that approximately one third of the paint sweep area overlaps. On this pass, move the gun across the panel in the opposite direction. Continue overlapping the bottom third of the previous sweep and reversing the direction of the pass until an entire panel is painted. Then

move to the next panel and repeat the same approach.

The technique for achieving a gleaming show finish is to build several coats of paint, wait until the paint cures, then micro sand the finish using very fine 1000 to 1500 grit sandpaper, and finally compound the finish to a mirror sheen. In building up a multiple coat finish, the first coat has to set up (become tacky) before the next can be applied. Otherwise, runs will develop. If you are spraying a fast-drying finish (lacquer, or a modern acrylic or catalyzed enamel), by the time you have worked your way around the truck, the paint will have dried enough to begin applying the next coat. Don't get the paint too thick as heavy coatings are likely to crack in time, but you'll need enough paint on the truck to micro sand and compound. Typically four coats (that's four passes around the vehicle) are sufficient. Be sure to get good paint coverage on lower panels and stamping ridges.

Before sanding, the finish needs to cure. Instructions on the container will give the recommended curing time. As mentioned, micro sanding is done with very fine 1000 or 1500 grit sandpaper

With the rear of the truck thoroughly masked and careful masking around the letters, the Chevrolet name is ready to be painted. On lighter colored trucks, the name is painted black.

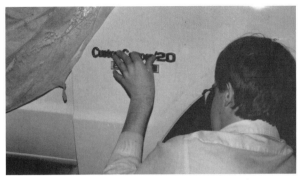

The trim markings are replaced as one of the last steps. Usually these are held on with clips that are attached from the inner side of the fender panels. The Longhorn marking is unique to Camper Special trucks built from 1969–1971 that added a 6 in. "stretch" panel to the 8 ft. pickup box and lengthened the wheelbase the same amount.

Where the truck is undergoing a ground-up restoration, the frame and chassis are refinished first, then covered by a sheet of plastic to protect this assembly from sanding dust and paint overspray. The firewall, underside and interior of the cab are finish painted before mounting on the chassis. Then the remaining exterior surfaces are given a finish coating. Mike Cavey

using the block sanding method. Be careful to stay away from sharp curves or ridges—like the reveals on the tailgate. These edges have less paint buildup and if you sand these spots, you will expose the primer very quickly. To prevent accidentally sanding into a low-paint-buildup area, place masking tape over any sharp edges (like the ridge around the hood on 1967–72 Chevrolet and GMC trucks) and any sharp curves (as on the tailgate letters). These will be carefully hand-compounded later.

Micro sanding will leave the finish somewhat dull, so to restore the gloss the paint needs to be buffed with polishing compound. It is difficult and time consuming to polish a finish effectively by hand, so a power buffer should be used. To protect the finish and to heighten the gloss, many restorers cover the final color layer with a clear coating. This clear coating gives the finish the appearance of a deeper depth and eliminates the need for frequent waxing to prevent the color coat from oxidizing. The drawback to clear coating occurs when spot repair is needed to touch up a chip or other flaw in the finish.

A quality finish has two key ingredients: thorough preparation, and micro sanding and polishing the final coating. If you use compatible painting products in the correct sequence following the exact mixing formulas and apply these paints according to the guidelines given, you will achieve a high-quality paint job.

High-Tech Painting Tools

Modern, high-tech painting products are extremely toxic—to the point of being life-threatening if used carelessly. The fact that these products can be purchased conveniently from any automotive paint supply store, with no warnings other than those on the product label, presents a real danger given the typical hobbyist's easy-going attitude about personal safety. The reality, however, is that you shouldn't use today's professional painting products unless you are willing to learn about and follow the safety and environmental precautions that modern paints require.

Respirators

Even though some shade-tree restorers still think they can paint a car in their garage wearing no more protection than a disposable dust mask, the days of painting without a respirator are gone. In selecting a respirator it's important to know that even a professional-grade painting respirator

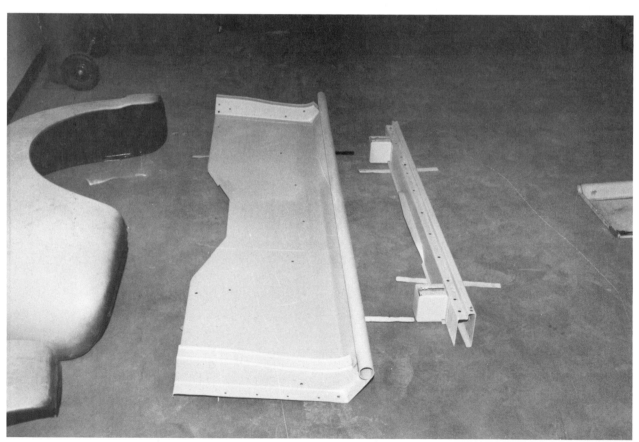

On a ground-up restoration each part is painted separately. Note that the underside of the fender has been *painted first. The outer side will also be painted before hanging the fender on the truck. Mike Cavey*

The cab has been finish painted, the doors painted and hung and the front fenders installed. At this point the hood is being fitted. Note the padding around the edges of the hood to prevent marring adjoining panels while the hood is being attached and adjusted. Mike Cavey

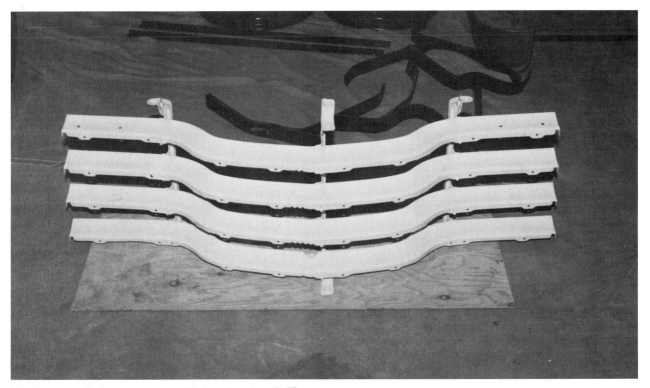

The inner grille bars are assembled and painted. The outer grille bars are chromed and will be attached once this assembly has been installed in the truck. Mike Cavey

doesn't give adequate protection against today's catalytic paints with their toxic isocyanates.

To avoid taking serious health risks when painting with modern refinishing products, a respirator should be worn that supplies air from an external source. This style of respirator consists of a face mask and air hose which is attached to a compressor that is located outside the painting area. It is important that the compressor be one that provides oil-free air. Although a respirator with external air source gives the painter somewhat less freedom of movement than a face mask alone (the air hose to the mask has to be contended with as well as the spray gun hose), the assurance of personal safety makes this equipment a must when applying today's high-tech paints. To ignore safety measures is to invite a condition known as ARDS, as previously mentioned, which closely resembles a heart attack. Without prompt emergency medical care, ARDS can lead to death. Modern paints are not to be fooled with and if the expense of the necesssary safety equipment is outside your budget, you should either avoid using the modern two-part painting products or have your truck painted by a professional.

High Volume, Low Pressure System

Besides paints, paint spraying technology is also changing. Traditionally, automotive finishes have been applied with high-pressure (35 to 80 psi) spray outfits. Although this high-pressure paint spraying method produces a fine-quality finish, only twenty-five to thirty percent of the paint and solvent actually ends up on the vehicle. The other two thirds blasted off the vehicle's surface as overspray and is either exhausted into the atmosphere or settles on nearby objects (including the painter). If the painter is not wearing a proper respirator, large amounts of this overspray and solvents are inhaled. The hobbyist concerned with painting only one vehicle may not consider the paint and solvents lost in overspray a significant waste, but to the professional painter, losing seventy to seventy-five percent of the painting product amounts to a sizeable financial waste as you may already have discovered. Modern painting products are by no means inexpensive.

The other problem presented by painting overspray is the damage refinishing solvents are doing to the air we breath. Volatile organic compounds in painting solvents are a major contribu-

In a ground-up restoration, the wheels and other small parts such as the bumper brackets shown here are also refinished off the truck. Mike Cavey

At this stage the bed has also been refinished, assembled and mounted back on the chassis. Note the stunning gloss that reflects the bed strips in the front bed panel. This truck's restorer worried that he might get marked down in show competition for what looked like rivet marks on the back of the cab. In fact, the cab's finish is flawless, but the paint is so mirror smooth that it picks up the reflection of the assembly rivets on the pickup box. Mike Cavey

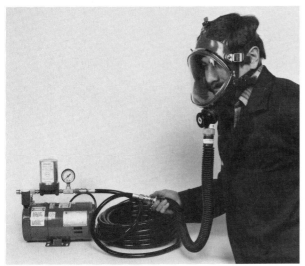

When applying two-part catalyzed paints safely, a respirator should be worn that supplies air from a source outside the spraying area. A painter wearing this external air source respirator has to contend with two air hoses (one to the spray gun and the other to the face mask), but the respirator hose can be slung over a shoulder to keep it from brushing against the vehicle. The Eastwood Company

New High Volume Low Pressure (HVLP) painting technology greatly diminishes wasteful overspray. The result is significant savings in the cost of paint and solvents as well as greater protection for our fragile environment. Legislation in several states is moving toward mandating that HVLP paint-spraying systems be adopted for all refinishing work. The Eastwood Company

tor to the formation of dangerous ground-level ozone (not to be confused with the earth's beneficial high-atmospheric ozone layer). Clean air legislation in several states restricts the use of automotive painting solvents and requires that automotive finishes be applied using less wasteful methods.

In response to both the wasteful nature of high-pressure paint spraying and the health and environmental hazards this older technology presents, the automotive refinishing industry has developed a new technology for applying automotive finishes. The new technology, called High Volume, Low Pressure (HVLP), results in almost no overspray and applies up to ninety percent of the paint to the vehicle. Besides significant savings in paint and solvents, HVLP paint spraying systems reduce the amount of toxic chemicals going into the air while also significantly cutting down on paint overspray. Although the cost of an HVLP paint spraying system is more than a good-quality gun purchased alone (this assumes that you already own the compressor), savings in paint and solvent, lowered health risk and environmental benefits, plus the fact that this technology is likely to be mandated by

law in the near future, make an HVLP paint spraying setup an investment definitely to be considered.

The heart of an HVLP painting system is a turbine compressor that is capable of producing a very high volume of air. The portable air compressors typically used by hobbyists have an air supply capacity of seven or eight cubic feet per minute. The turbine compressor in the HVLP system will deliver from 60 to 90 cubic feet of air per minute. Because air becomes hotter when compressed and because heat tends to dry up moisture, the turbine compressor supplies air that is both warm and dry—which is ideal for automotive refinishing. Also, a turbine compressor does not contaminate its air supply with oil, as can be the case with piston compressors.

The HVLP spray gun is handled identically to a traditional paint spraying gun. Adjusting knobs on the gun control fluid flow and spray pattern. The distance the painter holds the gun from the work surface is the same (6 to 8 in.) as with high-pressure spraying, and the gun is kept parallel to the painting surface. The only difference is in what happens to the paint after it leaves the gun. In

This is what the dash looked like before powder painting. In a word, its finish was a mess—the result of previous amateur work. David Bush

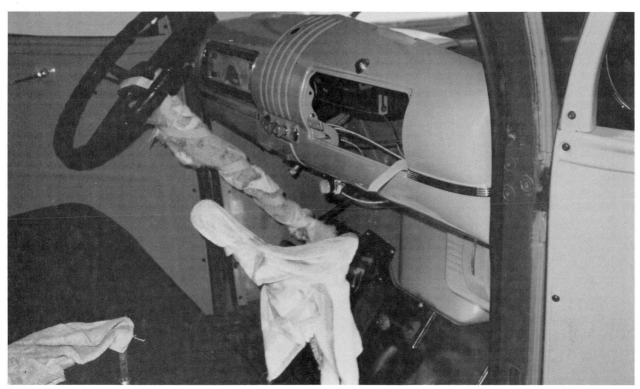

The dash has now been powder painted and is being replaced in the truck. Note the wrapping around the shift and brake levers and steering column. This is done to prevent scratches on the dash as well as on the column and levers. It was necessary to suspend the dash like this to reconnect wiring and cables. David Bush

The powder-painted dash back in place. The baked-on finish is very tough and scratch resistant. David Bush

high-pressure spraying, the paint is blasted onto the work surface with such force that only a small portion actually sticks and stays there. The rest is blown off in a turbulence that sends it billowing about the painting area. With HVLP the paint blows onto the work surface with just enough force to adhere and flow so almost no overspray results. Unless a metallic is used, finish coats applied with HVLP have nearly the same smoothness and appearance as a high-pressure paint job.

If you are just developing your skills in automotive refinishing, learning to use an HVLP system will present no special problems. If you have experience with high-pressure painting, switching to HVLP will present no more difficulty than getting used to a new spray gun. Besides the environmental and health benefits, as well as savings in painting products, another plus for HLVP is the fact that systems are marketed to hobbyist restorers that are within the average person's budget.

Because the tehnology is new, there are some disadvantages, the most notable being a problem getting metallic paints to diffuse properly and sometimes providing a rougher finish than would result from high-pressure painting. If you plan to apply non-metallic paint and will be micro sanding and polishing the finish coat, neither of these drawbacks need cause you concern.

Just as high-tech painting products are more expensive than traditional lacquers or enamels, so too the high-tech painting tools require a somewhat larger investment than a simple filter-style respirator and high-pressure paint gun. However, the cost difference does not factor simply to a higher quality, more durable finish. Your tool investment is also ensuring your personal safety when working with the potentially lethal high-tech painting products, and helps protect the environment—which should be everyone's concern.

13

Wiring Harness Installation

If you're wondering whether or not your truck's wiring needs replacing, the simplest way to make that decision is to take a close look at the condition of the wiring. If the insulation is cracked or maybe even missing in places, or new wiring has been spliced in and old wires wrapped with electrical tape, a new harness is definitely in order. Failure to replace deteriorated wiring invites problems on the road, burned-out electrical equipment or an electrical fire that can destroy the vehicle and the truck as well as the building in which it is stored. If you have any doubt about your truck's wiring, replace it. As you will discover in this chapter, the procedure is not difficult and does not require electrical expertise. On a frame-up restoration, you will install a new wiring harness as a matter of course.

On a frame-up restoration, the harness will be removed when the truck is disassembled so a wiring diagram plus the instructions provided with the harness will be used to show the correct connections. For a guide as to where to route the harness, you will need to refer to photos you took of your truck before disassembly, the factory assembly manual or other original or correctly restored trucks.

Tools and Supplies

Regardless of the truck you are rewiring, you will need essentially the same tools and supplies, including a new wiring harness, a shop manual with wiring diagram, pliers, wire stripper, butt connectors, assorted screwdrivers—regular and Philips—a socket set, vise grips, test light (a VOM meter is also desirable) and in some cases a steering wheel puller.

Be sure to order the harness only from a reputable vintage Chevy parts dealer or harness manufacturer. I've had Chevy truck owners tell me that the "bargain" harness they ordered from a discount mail-order auto parts outfit was so far from original standards in color coding, wire size and lengths

Problems with original wiring are easy to spot. Here the metal conduit that originally surrounded the taillight wiring has rusted so extensively that only a small section remains. The portion of conduit that remains is able to slide back and forth on the wires, chafing the fabric insulation and causing a short.

Here's another tell-tale sign of faulty wiring. A poor ground to the taillight on this truck has necessitated running a separate ground wire to the frame. Patchwork connections of this sort may appear in abundance on an older, unrestored truck.

that they had to discard it and order another from a quality wiring harness supplier. The harness described in this chapter is made by Y n Z's Yesterday Parts in Redlands, California (see appendices for address). It is constructed of the correct-gauge wire and covering and has the original color coding. Its installation presented no difficulties whatsoever.

Preparation

With their harnesses, Y n Z's provides a clearly written and illustrated instruction sheet showing hookup connections. Even so, you should also have a service manual with a wiring diagram for your year and model truck to refer to as you install the harness. (Wiring diagrams can also be purchased separately.) The wiring diagram will help you understand your truck's electrical system and will be used to troubleshoot any problem circuits. Before replacing the wiring, spend enough time studying the diagram so that you are comfortable with the major circuits and understand the color-coding scheme. The schematic will identify each wire by its color (and sometimes by gauge as well). You should practice tracing various color wires

from a component, the taillight for example, to their power source or ground. This way, if you have questions about which wire from the harness attaches to which terminal on a component, you can find the answer in the diagram. As you study the wiring diagram you will also realize why it is so important to have a correctly color-coded harness.

Wiring diagrams for trucks built before the mid to late 1950s won't show signal lights due to the fact that until this point, signal lights were considered an aftermarket add-on, installed either by the dealer or owner. Lights used for signaling during this period were typically mounted on the front fenders and at the corners of the box, and were turned on or off by a switch that clamped to the steering column. If you are restoring your truck for show competition, you will probably choose to omit signal lights on trucks where they were aftermarket items, but if you plan to drive your truck, signal lights are important for safety in today's traffic where other drivers will probably mistake hand signals as gestures.

It is possible to convert the parking and taillights on a truck to function as signal lights. For most, this is the preferred approach, as few owners

The most obvious sign that the wiring harness needs replacing is a mixture of patched-in wires and original wiring with frayed insulation. The electrical system may still function, but operating a truck with wiring in

this condition is very risky. Not only could electrical circuits fail suddenly, but the bare wires could short, burning out the harness and starting a fire.

are satisfied with the look of the large, aftermarket signal lights that mount on top of the fenders. You will find the signal light conversion especially easy if you specify the signal light option (on earlier trucks without standard signal lights) when you order the wiring harness. It will still be necessary to convert the parking and taillights to double-filament bulbs and add the signal light switch (if your truck doesn't already have one), but you won't botch up the new wiring by running odd-colored wires to the signal lights.

You should look at other options that may be available with the harness as well. Y n Z harnesses can be ordered in original-style cotton-covered wire or with modern plastic-coated wiring. The cotton wrapping makes sense for originality; if you are restoring or rebuilding your truck to drive, plastic-coated wire will be more durable.

During Chevrolet's Advance Design styling period, two different fuel-tank sending units were used: one with a separate ground wire and one where the sending unit grounded to the tank. You'll need to check your truck's original wiring or a wiring diagram to order the right harness. If you plan to equip your truck with an original heater, and this accessory also ties into the electrical system, you will also need a heater harness. Accesso-

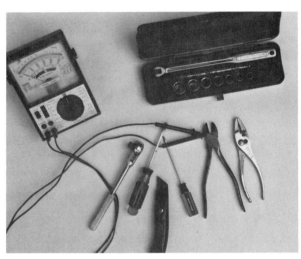

Tools needed for replacing a wiring harness include pliers, wire cutter, assorted screwdrivers, socket set plus test light or VOM meter. You should also have access to a wiring diagram for your truck, found in the Chevrolet shop manual.

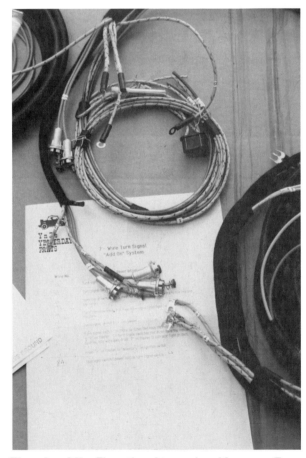

We ordered Y n Z's optional turn-signal harness. Turn signals were available as an accessory on trucks of the later forties and early fifties and make a wise safety addition on any truck that will be driven in today's traffic. The Y n Z turn-signal harness will convert the taillights (two rear lights will be needed) and parking lights into turn signals. Note that light sockets are provided as part of the harness. Detailed installation instructions come with the harness.

A quality wiring harness is made from correct-gauge wire, color coded to match the original, with original-style connectors. Harnesses for older trucks where fabric-covered wiring was used originally are available with either fabric or modern plastic-coated wire. The fabric covering is used on trucks that will be restored for show purposes. The plastic-coated harness will have a longer life and is desirable on trucks that will be driven. Pictured is a high-quality wiring harness from Y n Z's Yesterday Parts for an Advance Design pickup.

ries such as overdrive (not available on Chevrolet trucks until the mid 1950s) also required a separate harness, as does the optional tachometer on late 1960s and 1970s trucks.

Besides making sure that the wires on the new harness are connected to the correct terminals on the gauges and other electrical components, it is also important that the contacts be clean, and circuits like the lights that ground through the body sheet metal are making a good grounding connection. Electrical systems in older cars and trucks used a rather primitive grounding method whereby most circuits ground through the body metal and frame. On original vehicles, this ground path is easily broken by rust buildup and on restored trucks a heavy coating of paint can also break the ground path. You can help ensure a good ground by using new or derusted and replated bolts to attach the electrical components (like the lights, for example), and to scrape away paint or surface rust at some of the mounting points to make sure that a ground path occurs.

Buy new grommets and junction blocks before installing the new harness. On Advance Design pickups, the junction blocks are mounted on the front inner fender and are made from fiberboard. The grommets are used to plug holes where the wiring passes through the firewall and other locations in the sheet metal. (Both junction blocks and grommets are available from most of the parts suppliers listen in the appendices.)

Replacing the Old Harness

The first step in installing the new wiring is to lay out the new harness on the ground along the driver's side of the truck. The portion of the harness that runs under the hood and to the lights can be installed by disconnecting the old wires and replacing them with the new, one terminal at a time. This process is easy and straightforward, providing the wiring has not been modified greatly. It also works, obviously, only when the original wiring is still in the truck. With a frame-up restoration, the old wiring will have been removed long

On most trucks, hooking up the connections behind the dash is the most difficult part of installing the new harness. Not only is there little room to work, but you're practically standing on your head. Removing the seat cushions makes this job slightly easier, and banging your head on the clutch or brake pedal is something

you'll want to do only once. On later trucks, hooking up the dash wiring is a snap. As can be seen on the back of this 1967–1972 instrument panel, the instruments receive current from a printed circuit board and a single connector links the circuit board to the main wiring harness.

ago. In these cases, you will have to rely on a wiring diagram (found in a service manual for your year and model truck) and the harness manufacturer's instructions.

Wiring the Dashboard

As you lay out the new harness alongside the old, you may find that the hole through the firewall is not large enough to accommodate both harnesses. You can cut the old harness at the firewall and then disconnect the entire dash wiring as a unit. When doing this, either make a note of the connections or make sure your shop manual is clear on the connections for the headlight switch and gauges. If you plan to repair or replace the gauges or headlight switch, it's a good idea to do this before taking the trouble to hook up the new wiring.

You'll find that removing the seat cushions and sliding the seat all the way back make the job of lying on your back and working above your head underneath the dash slightly more pleasant. Banging your head on the clutch or brake pedal is something you will not want to do more than once or twice. You will find that it's necessary to have the cushions out to connect the gas tank wires, so you might as well take them out before working on the cab wiring.

With the old harness out of the way, you can feed the new harness through the firewall. The original-style wiring harness from Y n Z's Yesterday Parts used a system of numbering the wires and combined with the excellent instructions plus the Chevrolet shop manual, it makes the task of hooking up the complex dash wiring as simple as a paint-by-number set. The main problem is the cramped work space and the contortionist position needed to reach most everything under the dash.

Wiring the Cab

If you are installing new wiring in a well-preserved or original truck, you may have to remove the headliner in order to run the domelight wire. In a frame-up restoration, the wiring would be installed before the headliner is installed, so in this setting the headliner would not be a problem. In running the domelight wire up through the windshield pillar, simply tie the new wire to the end of the old wire and pull it through.

Wiring the Engine Compartment

With the dash and cab wiring out of the way, turn to the engine compartment. All connections here are easy to make; it's simply a matter of disconnecting one wire and connecting its replacement on the new harness. If you plan on painting or detailing under the hood, this should be done before installing the new wiring. When you come to the connections at the junction blocks (on the front fenders) you will probably also find that the

blocks have deteriorated and should be replaced. You will also need a set of grommets to plug the holes where the harness passes through sheet metal. This gives the new wiring a finished look and prevents chafing, which can eventually cut through the harness wrapping and create a short circuit or

Running the wire to the dome light proved to be an easy job on this original Arizona truck from which the headliner had been removed. On a restoration, new wiring will be installed before replacing the interior. On a well-preserved original truck, it may be necessary to remove the headliner in order to replace this wire. Jim Hinckley

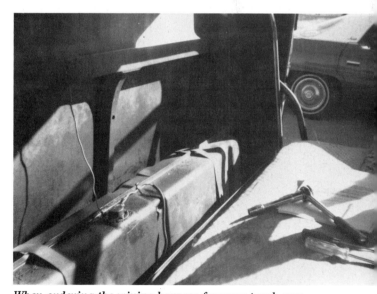

When ordering the wiring harness for your truck, you should note whether the fuel-tank sending unit has a one-wire or a two-wire circuit. If the original wiring is in place you can tell which is used just by looking at the old wiring. If the wiring has been removed, you will have to check the number of connections on the sending unit. Jim Hinckley

burn out the electrical system. Most vintage Chevrolet truck parts suppliers also carry replacement rubber boots to cover the hole where the wiring enters the back of the headlight buckets. In most cases, these boots will be deteriorated and should be replaced.

Wiring the Headlights and Parking Lights

With the driver's side wired to its junction block, move on to the lights. First, though, remove the headlights and inspect the condition of the buckets. This is a common rust area and in some cases you may have to replace the buckets along with the light sockets.

You may choose to convert the parking lights to serve both as parking lights and turn signals. The first step in this procedure is to run the parking light wire from the junction block through two clips mounted on the front of the fender behind the grille. The second step is to remove the parking light housings. Since you will need to change these lights from single- to double-filament bulbs, you will also need to remove the light sockets. Removing the parking lights is easy; on a 1947-1953 Advance Design series, just two bolts secure each light housing. Another plus is the fact that the light socket is screwed to the housing, not riveted.

To add a larger, double-filament socket to the light housing, lay the housings on a work bench, backside down. Then, using a small chisel, star the edges of the original hole and bend the new tabs back, install the larger light socket and bend the tabs tight against it. To make sure the sockets do not work loose, drop a bead of solder or braze at several points where the tabs and socket contact. With the new sockets installed, replace the parking light housings in the grille. The parking light and turn-signal conversion is recommended for several reasons, as it preserves the truck's original look and is an improvement in appearance over large, add-on turn-signal lights.

Wiring the Coil and Starter

If the old harness has been left in place this is a simple matter of disconnecting one wire and connecting another. If the harness has been removed, carefully follow the instructions with the harness and a wiring diagram. If you plan to replace the ignition switch, now is the time. You will find that making the connections to the ignition switch is easier if attempted from the passenger side.

The wiring harness should be secured in place by metal clips. Replacements for these clips are available from vintage Chevy truck parts suppliers. If you can't determine the routing of the wiring from the old harness, drawings and diagrams in a factory assembly manual will show the harness's original path. Note the neatly routed wiring in the engine compartment of this restored Advance Design series truck. The clips holding the wire to the firewall are plated, not painted. Mike Cavey

Electrical troubleshooting requires a test device to check the integrity of the circuit. Three alternative test devices are shown here. They are the VOM meter, the commercial test light (with pointed probe) and homemade test light (consisting of an automotive bulb to which two leads have been soldered.)

Wiring the Dimmer and Brakelight Switches

Now it's down and under to wire the dimmer switch, which is an easy hookup. The brake light switch is a simple connection, but if you plan to replace the switch, now is the time. Besides vintage Chevrolet parts vendors, these switches can be obtained through a local NAPA store.

If the original harness clips are still in place and in good condition, you can reuse them. Otherwise, you can order replacements from one of the vintage Chevrolet truck parts suppliers. These clips hold the harness in place as it runs along the frame.

Wiring the Gas Tank

Next hook up the new wiring to the gas tank. When both single-wire and two-wire fuel-sending unit harnesses were used, as is the case in the Advance Design series, the new harness manufacturer will ask you to specify which is correct for your truck. If the old wiring is in place, you can tell easily just by looking at the old harness. If the wiring has been removed, you will have to check the number of connections at the sending unit. Replacing the wiring at the fuel tank is simple, thanks to the fact that only the sending unit wire comes from the main loom at this point.

Wiring the Rear Lights

Hooking up the rear lights is not complicated. Two taillights were an option in 1950, but it seems that over the years most of these trucks have acquired the second light. If the taillights on your truck have been replaced by aftermarket units and you want to return to the original-style light, Jim Carter's Vintage Chevrolet Parts has correct replacement lights, as well as mounting brackets.

For running the harness to the rear lights, Y n Z provides an extra foot or so of wire to enable you to route the harness in the direction that best suits your needs. Run the harness to the driver's-side light as original, and cross to the passenger-side light inside the last frame rail. Two connections are made per light.

If you are also using the rear lights as turn signals, at this point install the turn-signal switch.

Wiring the Horn

Finally, you can hook up the horn. This is a single-wire connection, but the steering wheel

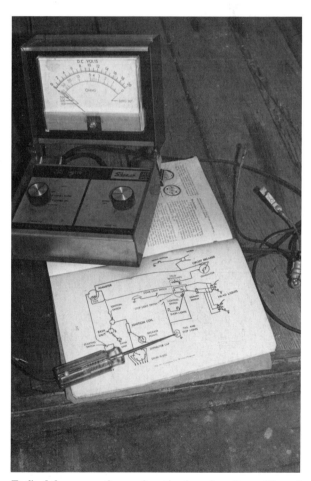

To find the cause of a nonfunctioning circuit, you'll need a diagram of the truck's wiring. Once you have traced the circuit, you can check current flow with a test light or VOM meter. Electrical circuits on older trucks tend to be relatively simple. This diagram is for a 1938 Chevrolet half-ton pickup.

Electrical Shutoff

Replacing frayed and decayed wiring certainly gives great peace of mind, but even so it's wise to disconnect the truck's battery from the electrical system during storage, or even when days or weeks will pass without the truck's being driven. If your truck has an original electric clock, it is imperative to disconnect the battery because the clock will run down the battery in a relatively short period and burn itself out in the process. Even on trucks without clocks it's wise to disconnect the battery because of the possibility of an unnoticed trickle discharge somewhere in the system that will not only discharge the battery but could produce a fire.

Rather than loosen and remove a battery terminal each time you store the truck, the easier method is to install a quick-disconnect switch on the battery terminal. if you plan to enter your truck in shows, this switch can easily be removed at showtime.

All that remains is to get in the habit of using the disocnnect switch each time you park your truck. You will also find that the switch provides a small measure of anti-theft protection, since would-be thieves may not notice or want to take time to by-pass the switch.

must be pulled. There are several ways to remove the steering wheel, but the best route with the least chance of damage is to use a steering wheel puller. This tool is available from specialty tool suppliers like The Eastwood Company, Sears and NAPA stores. The new horn wire is pulled up through the steering column by tying it to the old wire.

Troubleshooting Electrical Problems

It's not uncommon after installing new wiring that some electrical component will fail to function properly. For potential electrical problems, it's helpful to know some electrical troubleshooting techniques and have an understanding of how an electrical circuit operates.

Check for a Faulty Circuit

First, let's start with the circuit. If the lights, horn, heater or some other electrical component won't work, there are three potential causes for the problem. Power is not getting to the component, the circuit from the component is open due to a

poor ground, or the component itself has failed. Let's use the example of a nonfunctioning taillight to see how the three potential electrical problems come into play and what troubleshooting approaches are used to solve the problem. We'll assume that when the headlight switch is turned on, the headlights illuminate but the taillights don't. If we were dealing with an original wiring system, we would probably suspect a break in the wiring to the taillights. With a new harness, we have every reason to believe that the wiring is intact. Therefore, if the circuit is broken, the break has occurred either through an incorrect or poor connection, or is the result of a poor ground. It is also possible that the taillight bulb is burned out, although this is not too likely if both lights are out.

Test for Current flow

The first step when electrical troubleshooting is knowing that the problem has a logical cause. To find the cause, you would begin by removing the taillight lens and bulb. This done, you will check to see if current is flowing to the taillight socket. Two devices can be used to check current flow. One is a simple test light that you can buy for a few dollars in the automotive section of a discount mart or an auto parts store, or make yourself from an automotive light socket and two short sections of wire (one to bring current to the light and another for ground). The other test device is a VOM meter. A VOM meter is preferred to the test light because it also tells you how much current the circuit is receiving. These meters are available from discount marts and electronics stores for about $25.

Whether you are using a test light or VOM meter, the connections will be the same. Place the hot lead (the red wire on the meter or commercial

Often the cause of a nonfunctioning taillight is a poor ground connection. To test for power to the light socket, ground the test light on the truck body or bumper.

Decayed wiring can be another cause of a failed electrical component. A new wiring harness should eliminate this problem, but poor or incorrect connections can also disrupt current flow.

test light) on the contact point in the light socket. Now hold the other lead (which will be black) against the side of the socket. If the test light illuminates, or the meter hand swings into the appropriate current range on its dial (6 volts for a 6 volt electrical system or 12 for a 12 volt system), you know that the problem with the light is a burned out or improperly installed bulb. More likely, the test light or meter will not show current flow. If this is the case, keep the hot lead on the contact point and touch the ground wire to a location on the body or chassis where you are sure to have a good ground. You need to touch the lead to an unpainted surface, a spot of clean bare metal or a plated bolt to give it a good ground. If the light or meter now shows current flow, you know the problem is an improperly grounded taillight.

You can correct for a poor ground in two ways. The first is to remove the light housing, clean the mating surfaces so that some bare metal is exposed and reattach the housing. If the light socket is dirty or corroded, you will also clean the socket using mild steel wool or emery cloth. Now test the circuit again, this time grounding to the socket. If the test device works, the problem is corrected.

Sometimes it is difficult to create a good ground through sheet metal. When this happens, you may have to run a ground wire from the component to some point on the chassis. This approach should not be taken when doing a show restoration because the ground lead will be nonoriginal and will cause your truck to lose points. But on a truck that is being overhauled so that it can be enjoyed and driven, running a ground wire is an easy way to ensure a properly functioning circuit. You can attach one end of the ground lead to the component, in this case to the light socket, and the other end to a bolt on the frame.

Test for a Broken Circuit

If current flow didn't result with a good ground, the circuit is broken somewhere ahead of this component. What needs to be done now is to determine the location of the break. You will do this by tracing back along the circuit, following the harness and then referring to a wiring diagram, until you find a switch, junction or other accessory powered by the same circuit. At this point, you will again test for continuity (power flowing to that point).

With a taillight, tracing back the circuit would take you to the light switch on the dashboard (or brake light switch if the problem was with the brake lights). Now you will check to see if the circuit is live to the switch. You will do this by placing the red lead of the test light or VOM meter on the hot lead to the switch (the wiring diagram will show which lead supplies power to the switch). If current is flowing to the switch, the problems may be a

corroded or misplaced connection or a faulty switch.

Check first for a poor connection by removing the wire going to the portion of the circuit that is dead (the taillight wire in this case) and cleaning the end of this wire, plus its contact on the switch with a piece of emery cloth. Now replace the wire, turn on the switch and check the circuit. If the component works, you have solved the problem. If it doesn't, chances are the problem is with the switch. You can test the switch by removing the wire to the component (the taillight in this case) and press it against the hot lead to the switch. The component should work. If this happens, you will need to replace the switch.

This troubleshooting example applies quite commonly to hydraulically operated brake light switches on 1950s and earlier trucks that attach to the back of the master cylinder. Replacements for

A battery disconnect switch is a wise investment to prevent the risk of electrical fire. This switch is a must if your truck has the original electric clock. The disconnect switch attaches to a battery post; the cable to that post then attaches to a lug on the switch. Removing the knob on the top of the switch has the same effect as removing the battery cable. The switch also provides a small measure of anti-theft protection. Bathurst, Inc.

A solar charger will preserve your truck's battery through a slow-trickle charge. The battery cannot become overcharged, and the solar charger will produce its trickle of current even on cloudy days.

these switches are readily available through NAPA auto parts stores.

Following this step-by-step troubleshooting process, you will be able to trace the source of any electrical problems and make the necessary repairs until all your truck's electrical components are functioning properly. Keep in mind that it's

entirely likely that electrical accessories like the horn, clock, heater motor, fuel-sending unit or radio may well have quit working long ago and will have to be rebuilt or replaced. Repair services that specialize in rebuilding electrical accessories for older vehicles are listed in the appendices.

14

Interior Restoration

Although truck interiors are designed for utility, ruggedness and durability, a vintage Chevrolet truck would have to be extremely well cared for not to show signs of wear and perhaps some tears on the seat, a sagging headliner and other signs that the interior needs to be upgraded or replaced. Fortunately, redoing a truck interior is a much simpler and less expensive process than replacing the upholstery in a car. Until the mid 1950s, Chevrolet truck seat coverings consisted of plain, durable Naugahyde or vinyl, headliners were simple cardboard strips, door panels (when not steel) were vinyl-covered cardboard and the cowl kick panels were simply painted steel from the Advance Design series onward (the kick panels are cardboard covered on pre 1947 models). Through the mid-forties, even the color of the interior was durable. On the Art Deco series (1941–1946) and earlier Chevrolet trucks, seats and cardboard interior trim were a sort of moose brown that withstood soiling because dirt and grease blended right in. But that's not to say that a worn, soiled interior will look good in a refinished truck. One of the most dramatic improvements you can make is to recover the seats, refinish the interior and install new headliner, door and cowl panels on trucks with these bland interiors.

Thanks to seat covering, headliner and door panel kits, which are available for most Chevrolet light trucks between the years of 1937 to 1972, redoing your truck's upholstery can be a highly satisfying do-it-yourself undertaking. If you'd rather have an upholstery shop redo your truck's interior instead of tackling the job yourself, it still pays to work from a kit for two reasons. First, with a quality interior kit from a reputable Chevrolet light truck parts supplier (see appendices), you'll come as close as possible to matching the original color and materials. Second, besides keeping your truck as close to original as possible, a kit enables a professional upholsterer to replace the seat coverings and install the interior panels in a small fraction of the time that would be required to fabricate

these items. If your upholsterer has had a bad experience with an automotive interior kit, he or she will be understandably leery of the kit concept. You can assure him or her that shoddy materials and workmanship will not be the case with a Chevrolet truck interior kit purchased from a reputable supplier.

A complete pickup interior consists of several items that are typically sold separately. These include the seat coverings, new coils with which to rebuild the spring sets, the headliner, door panels (for trucks that used fabric panels), kick panel (where used), sun visors, armrests and related hardware. When ordering a seat covering kit, make sure the supplier includes padding and all other material and hardware needed for this job. If you plan to do the installation yourself, ask if the kit contains instructions. However, recovering seat cushions is not complicated, as you will see.

The truck's interior should be painted before replacing the seats or installing the headliner, door and kick panels.

Interior Finishing

Year	Interior coverings	Material
1936–1938	Door panels	Steel, painted
	Headliner	Cardboard
	Kick panels	Cardboard
1939–1940	Door panels	Steel, painted
	Headliner	Cardboard
	Kick panels	Cardboard
1941–1946	Door panels	Steel, painted
	Headliner	Cardboard
	Kick panels	Cardboard
1947–1955	Door panels	Vinyl-covered cardboard
	Headliner	Cardboard
	Kick panels	Steel
1955–1959	Door panels	Steel
	Headliner	Cardboard on deluxe models and Cameo
	Kick panels	Steel, painted
1960–1966	Door panels	Steel
	Headliner	Cardboard on deluxe models
	Kick panels	Steel, painted
1967–1972	Door panels	Vinyl-covered cardboard
	Headliner	Vinyl-covered cardboard on Cheyenne
	Kick panels	Steel

Interior Painting

The interior should be repainted before the seats are replaced or the headliner, door and kick panels (on trucks where these items were used) are installed. The typical sequence is to paint the truck's interior before the exterior. If the truck has not been completely disassembled, extensive masking will be required to protect the windshield, steering column and wheel, and the dash assembly (if it has not been removed) from overspray. If the cab has been completely stripped and removed from the frame, the advised procedure is to paint the bottom and firewall first, then drape plastic sheet-

The interior is typically painted before the exterior.
Mike Cavey

ing over the frame and mount the cab. Now you can paint the interior, and hook up the mechanicals, run wiring to the dash and so forth. The plastic sheeting will protect the frame from overspray when you paint the cab exterior and do the follow-up wet-sanding process that leads to a mirror finish.

When repainting the cab interior you will need to pay special attention to detail. In late 1930s Chevrolet trucks, the dash has a special cackle finish. When detailing the cab of Advance Design series trucks, the recesses between the ribs on the stainless-steel dash plate are painted the interior cab color. On 1952 models, where this dash plate is plain steel, the recesses are painted interior color and the ribs are painted silver. On Task Force and 1960s models, the top of the dash is covered with a nonreflective finish. On whatever year and model truck you are restoring, you should note the interior paint scheme and finish details of this sort before stripping/sandblasting or other preparation steps.

After the cab is painted, you can install the interior coverings—just be very careful not to nick or scratch the paint.

Recovering Seat Cushions

As with other phases of your truck's restoration, interior work calls for a few special tools. These include heavy-duty scissors, hog-ring pliers, a utility or Xacto knife and a heavy-duty wire cutter. The seats are usually removed from the truck during body repair and painting, so they can be recovered anytime. Installing the headliner and door panels will wait until after exterior and interior painting. If your truck still has the original cardboard headliner and door panels (refer to the chart to see if your truck had steel or upholstered panels), you should take detailed photos or make sketches of exactly how these pieces fit. It's also a good idea to keep the original pieces to use in checking the authenticity and fit of the new panels. The original headliner can also serve as a guide when bending the replacement to fit the roof contours.

Several preparation steps need to be done before actually recovering the seats. First, the cushions will be removed from the truck and stripped of whatever remains of the old covering, padding and spring wrapping. When the old covering has been removed, you can inspect the spring set for soundness. It's not uncommon to find breaks in the seat frame as well as broken or badly sagging coils, and a light to heavy coating of surface rust. If the springs are badly worn you have two alternatives: find a better set, or rebuild the set you have.

Even though no one will see the seat from this angle, before recovering, the springs should be cleaned and refinished. In this case the spring sets were sandblasted and repaired as needed with new coils. Mike Cavey

On Advance Design and newer series Chevrolet trucks, it should not be difficult to locate a set of sound, recoverable seats at a scrap yard or through want ads placed in a club newsletter. On earlier trucks, finding replacement seat springs may not be as easy. Spring sets can be rebuilt by welding cracks or breaks in the frame and replacing the broken or sagging coils. New seat spring coils are available from some of the parts suppliers listed in the appendices. Where the spring frames are rusted, you should clean the metal by sandblasting or with a wire brush, then spray on a protective coating of rust-resistant paint. If you haven't already done so, this is the time to order the seat covering kit.

Seat springs can be recovered by one person but an extra pair of hands makes the job much easier, especially when stretching the new covering over the repadded springs. Starting with the seat frame, the first step is to replace any weak or broken coils. Once the frame is sound, the seat frame will be wrapped with the burlap covering supplied with the kit. The burlap attaches to the seat and backrest frames with hog rings that are also supplied with the kit. The purpose of the burlap covering is to keep the padding from settling into the coils.

Next you will place cotton padding over the top and around the sides of the springs (here you will work one spring set at a time). In most cases, kits provide the exact amount of padding, so don't cut any excess until you are sure everything is installed right. If the kit includes foam rubber, as well as cotton padding, the foam is placed over the cotton padding on the top of the cushion. If the kit

Seat covering kits are available for Chevrolet trucks from the mid thirties to late fifties. With a kit, recovering your truck's seats is a job you can do yourself. Truck seat upholstery is much simpler than that used on cars, and the job requires only a few specialized tools. You should have an assistant to help you with this job. Mike Cavey

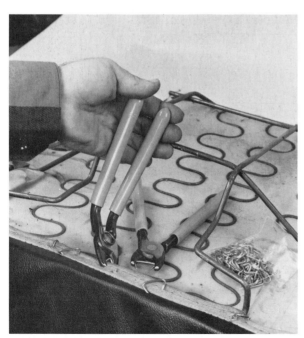

A stretching tool enables you to pull the covering tight over the springs without tearing the fabric. Hog-ring pliers (seen here lying on the springs) are used to attach the fabric to the seat frame. The Eastwood Company

does not include foam padding, you will probably want to purchase a sheet of 1 in. thick foam rubber to place over the cotton padding. Otherwise, as the truck is driven, the cotton will compress, lowering the cushion height and giving the seat a less comfortable feel. Foam rubber is resilient so it will preserve the seat's cushiony feel, and maintains the right cushion height for many years. The padding and foam are held in place by the cover which will be fitted over the cushions next.

As you pull the cover over the padded spring set, your three goals are to align the seam around the edge of the cushion, work out all wrinkles in the covering and pull the fabric tightly enough so that it won't sag when you sit on the cushion, but not so tight that the cushion has no give. Once you have worked the cover over the springs, with the seam forming an even outline for the spring set, smooth out any wrinkles, then turn the cushion over and pull the fabric tight. Now you can begin to attach the covering to the spring frame using hog rings. (If these wire clips are not supplied with the kit they can be purchased from most any upholstery shop, auto dealer, hardware store or ordered through a restoration supplier such as The Eastwood Company.) The hog rings have sharp ends that allow

170

them to be pressed easily through the cover fabric. The rings are then squeezed around the seat frame using hog-ring pliers.

The sequence for attaching the seat covering begins at the front. Here you will clip the covering to the seat frame with a few hog rings along the front edge. Next you will pull the fabric snug and attach a few hog rings at the rear. If the covering has too much give, or not enough, you can remove the clips at the rear of the frame and allow a little more slack or pull the covering tighter. By adjusting the tension from the back of the seat, any holes left from refitting the hog rings won't be noticed. When the covering has the desired snugness, it should be pulled slightly tighter to allow for future stretching, then secured to the frame with hog rings spaced about two to three inches apart. Repeating this process on the other spring set (cushion or backrest) finishes the seat upholstering job. Recovering a truck's seat cushions is easy enough so that after one set you'll feel like a pro and can give advice or assistance to friends who are restoring their trucks.

Installing Interior Coverings

As the interior descriptions chart shows, in some years, Chevrolet finished its truck interiors with a cardboard headliner and door panels. In other years the cab interior surfaces were simply painted. From 1936 to 1946, and some earlier years, the interior finishings included kick panels made of cardboard. These interior coverings are available for Chevrolet trucks through the late 1950s in easy-to-install kit form. Unlike car interiors where blind tacking and other tricks of the upholsterer's trade are used to conceal door panel and other trim fasteners, trim panels on trucks are held in place in straightforward manner with sheet-metal screws. In the 1941–1946 Art Deco series and earlier models, metal strips along the edges of the headliner and kick panels are used to secure these coverings. Metal strips also position the windlace around the doors on Chevrolet trucks through midyear 1949.

Although Chevrolet did not use a full headliner in its pickups, as did some of the other manufacturers, the interior roof covering is still somewhat

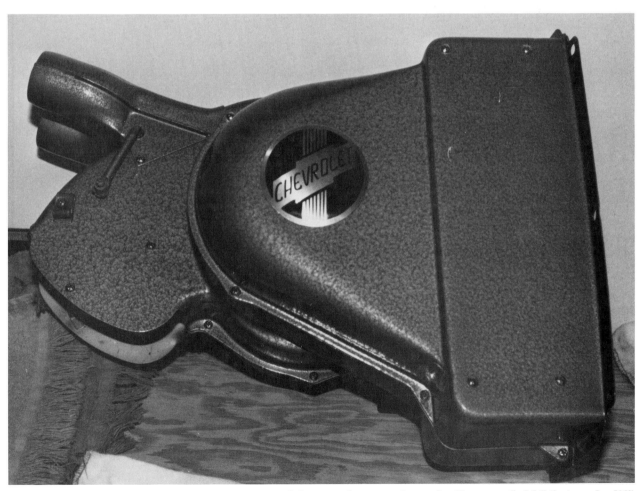

When repainting the cab, it is important to pay special attention to detail. The heater on Advance Design trucks, *for example, used a "hammer finish" that can be difficult to duplicate.* Mike Cavey

tricky to install—particularly when forming the bends for the roof contour. If you try to bend the headliner dry, you will probably crease the cardboard in attempting to make the bends. The correct procedure is to moisten the backside of the cardboard in the areas where the bends will occur with a mixture of eighty percent household ammonia and twenty percent water. This mixture can be placed in a Windex bottle and sprayed onto the cardboard (remember to spray the backside so that stains will not show on the good side). The cardboard should not be soaked, just moistened. The ammonia may smell for a day or so until it dries. You will find that the moistened cardboard will bend easily without crinkling. You'll find also

that installing a headliner is definitely a two-person job, so plan to have a helper on hand when you tackle this project.

Pickup door coverings will also fit Suburbans and Panels. Seat coverings and headliners are also available for early 1940s to mid 1950s models of these trucks in kit form. Other interior coverings for these specialty models will need to be fabricated by a trim shop.

Trim items completing an interior restoration include armrests, sun visors, glovebox liner and windlace for the door opening. Quality reproduction armrests are available for Advance Design through early sixties models. During most of this period, Chevrolet installed only one armrest—on the driver's side—but the passenger-side armrest was an option. Likewise, reproduction sun visors are available for Advance Design and Task Force trucks. Here, too, Chevrolet installed just the driver's-side sun visor, making the passenger visor an accessory. Since reproductions of the right-hand bracket are available for the most popular models, many restorers choose to install both visors. The original cardboard glovebox liners are often torn or missing. Replacement liners are also available for most years.

Through the Advance Design series, Chevrolet sealed its pickup cabs against air drafts with wind-

An authentically restored 1958 Cameo. Another example of cab interior detail, the top of the dash on Task Force trucks is covered with a nonreflective finish. Trent Stephan

Firewall Cover Preservation

by Russell Emond

After removing an inner firewall cover that is good enough to use again from a 1947–1953 Chevrolet, do not store the cover on the floor. To keep the cover from changing its shape and becoming difficult to reuse, hang it on the wall or stand it in a corner. I failed to do this to a firewall cover on one of my trucks and it was so out of shape when I went to reuse it that I had to junk it. Here is the best way to preserve the cover's shape. Do this the same day the cover is removed.

Cut a piece of 3/8 or 1/2 in. plywood to the dimensions 24x58 in. Cut ten 3x3 in. squares from 1/8 in. Masonite (or plywood). Gather ten 1 1/4 in. screws (drywall screws work well). Lay the firewall cover on the plywood backing, and using the 3x3 in. squares, secure the cover to the plywood through the same holes that it fastened to the firewall. Do not disturb the padding on the back and do not overtighten the screws. Place wadded-up newspaper under the hump. Do not pack the hump tight. Hang the cover on the wall upside down.

When I followed this procedure, I took the cover down twenty months later, blew it off, brushed it, wiped it down with paint thinner, gave it three coats of flat-black and installed it. It looks like new.

lace that installed on the inside of the door frame. This windlace, which looks like oversize fender welting, is placed against the door outline with the round section projecting into the door opening and the flat tacking strip against the door outline. Most commonly, windlace is held in place by tacks or staples which go into a tack strip. The tack area is then dressed out with metal retainer strips. From midyear 1949 to the end of the Advance Design series, this door windlace slides into a metal track.

Instrument Cluster Restoration

On most older trucks, the instrument panel will be faded, some of the gauges may have quit working and the gauge faces will be faded and the markings obscured. As part of either a cosmetic upgrade or a complete restoration, you will want to refinish the dash. Services are available that do this work and can guarantee quality results. But you can also redo your truck's instrument cluster yourself.

The job of cosmetically refinishing an instrument cluster begins with disconnecting the wiring and removing the gauge set from the truck, but if some of the gauges are not working you will want to do some electrical troubleshooting first to determine if the problem is faulty wiring, a bad sending unit or the gauge itself. How to troubleshoot a nonworking electrical component is described in the wiring chapter. Once you have determined whether or not the gauges are functioning and have the instrument panel out of the truck, you can disassemble the instrument cluster and remove the gauges. Refacing kits that you can apply yourself to give your truck's gauges a like-new look are available for Chevrolet trucks from 1936 to 1966 from the major vintage parts suppliers like Jim Carter. Where the gauge lettering is applied to the dash face, as is the case with the 1940–46 models

Although Chevrolet did not use a full headliner in its pickups, the interior roof covering is still somewhat tricky to install. You'll find it to be definitely a two-person job. Note the metal edging that holds the headliner in place.

Door trim panels on trucks are much simpler and easier to install than door upholstery on cars. Here the door trim panel has been removed from this Advance Design pickup. Taking off the old trim panel is a simple job of removing the window crank and door handle, plus the armrest, then loosening the screws that secure the trim covering the door's inner panel.

As an alternative to sending your truck's gauges to a specialty restoration service, you may decide to redo the gauge faces yourself. Decal kits make this job relatively easy. For Advance Design series gauges, pictured here, new chrome trim bezels are also available.

The 1967–1972 deluxe gauge unit after it has been separated from the plastic bezel. This instrument panel does not have the optional tachometer (which would be located in the top center).

and the plastic instrument faces used on the 1955–59 Task Force series, show-quality replacements are available.

The instrument panel face will need to be repainted a flat (nonglossy) finish. Flattening agents are available from automotive paint suppliers. In many cases, the chrome bezel around the instrument cluster (found on Advance Design and earlier series) will also need to be rechromed or replaced. Professionally rebuilt speedometers are available from vintage Chevrolet suppliers for most years, or you can send your truck's speedometer to a specialty speedometer rebuilder (see appendices for listings). Typically, the speedometer rebuilder will ask if you want the odometer to show the

existing mileage or set back to zero.

Redoing your truck's instrument cluster makes an ideal winter project. The process requires more patience than skill, and an advantage of making this an off-season project is that any time delays such as sending the speedometer off to the rebuilder won't interfere with driving your truck.

1967–1972 Instrument Panel Restoration
by Alvin Shier

The instrument panel on this series of trucks differs in two important ways from the earlier gauge layouts. First, the gauge housing is plastic with a chrome-plated appearance (this is also true of the 1966 dash facing). Second, rather than being individually connected to the wiring harness, the instruments in this series and later Chevrolet and GMC trucks are wired to a printed circuit that in turn connects to the wiring harness. While these differences do not make an instrument cluster from this series more difficult to restore than an earlier-gauge set, a few special instructions do apply. Much of the procedure described for restoring this more modern instrument cluster also applies for the earlier units.

The instrument panel used in 1967–1972 Chevrolet and GMC trucks is both practical and good looking. On standard models, the cluster consists of two gauge displays with the speedometer on the left and a combination fuel gauge, warning lights for oil and alternator output, plus temperature gauge in the large, circular opening on the right. A center circular opening can be filled with an optional tachometer. The deluxe version of this instrument panel, installed as standard equipment on CST (Custom Sport Truck) and Cheyenne trucks and available as an option on the Custom models, added four small gauge openings along the bottom of the dash panel. Inserted in these openings were the amp, engine temperature and oil pressure gauges. The fourth opening could house an optional vacuum gauge or clock. On this deluxe instrument panel, the large opening on the right housed only the fuel gauge.

When new, the attraction of this instrument panel came not just from the easy-to-read gauge layout, but also from the appealing combination of the panel's chrome edging (including gauge insets) and black matte finish. On Cheyenne trucks the panel's face had a woodgrain covering. With age, these instrument panels become drab and dull looking. The bright chrome wears off and fades away, the plastic gauge coverings scratch and become cloudy, even the instrument needles take on a dull appearance. What was once a highlight of the truck's interior now calls attention to itself by its shabby look. As a result, renewing the instrument panel can be considered a must-do step whether you are restoring or upgrading a 1967–1972 truck.

If yours is a standard truck, your first step will probably be to locate a deluxe instrument panel—that is, unless you want to keep the truck factory original. The deluxe instrument clusters with their row of smaller individual gauges along the bottom of the panel have a much higher quality appearance than the standard panels. The deluxe instrument panels are still relatively easy to find in swap

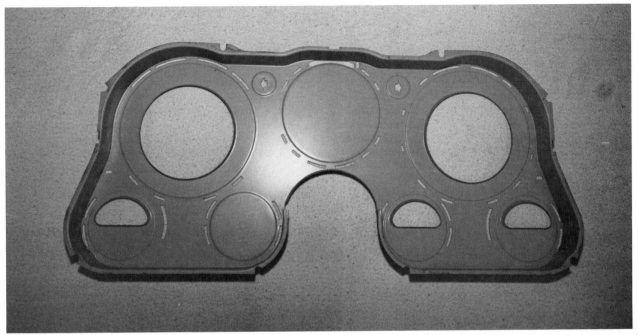

The instruments mount as a unit into this inner casing. This inside surface is painted green. Unless the truck is badly weathered, the inner casing surface should not need refinishing. Note that this casing does not have the cutout for the tachometer.

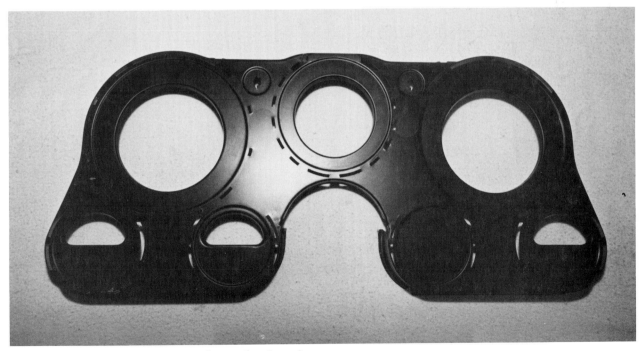

Outer surface of the instrument casing, painted semi-gloss black. This casing has the optional hole for the tachometer.

meets or scrap yards. Many collectors feel that the deluxe panel isn't complete without a tachometer. This desirable accessory is also relatively plentiful, with used examples showing up at swap meets and new units still available from specialty suppliers.

Panel Removal

Whether you are renewing your truck's gauge set, or installing one you purchased, you will need to remove the instrument panel from the truck. This job is much easier than you might think because of the printed circuit and its single connector to the main wiring harness. Now that you know the wiring is not a hassle, you might assume that the instrument panel can be removed simply by loosening the screws at the top and sides of the plastic housing. However, the job is not quite that simple. It's really not all that complicated, either.

Before starting the actual removal process, disconnect the battery. Then, back inside the cab you will loosen the steering column at the base of the dash (remove two ⁵/₁₆ in. screws which hold the steering column tight to the dash). This allows the steering column to drop down slightly. Next you will remove the screws holding the panel to the dash. You'll find the panel is still held in place by the light switch and wiper knobs. The wiper knob removes easily by loosening the small set screw. With the knob off the shaft you can unscrew the bezel. The light switch knob is a bit trickier. This knob attaches to a long shaft that inserts into the switch box. The knob doesn't come loose until you reach under the dash and push in a button on the top of the switch box housing. As you hold down on this button, the light switch knob and shaft will slide out easily. Now you can unthread the nut holding the light switch box to the instrument panel.

Before removing the gauge cluster, you will need to reach up from underneath the dash and loosen the speedometer cable and oil gauge tube (if your truck is so-equipped—some aren't). The oil line connector takes a ⁵/₁₆ in. wrench. Some oil may drip from the line. To prevent the oil from dripping onto the floor mat or carpet, tie a plastic bag around the open end of the line. Now you can pull the instrument panel four to six inches away from the dash. This space will enable you to reach behind the panel and disconnect the large electrical connector that inserts into the back. Squeezing the lock tabs on the sides releases the connector. The instrument panel can now be lifted free of the truck and is ready for the restoration process.

Note: Some trucks may also have throttle and/or choke controls. These controls would also have to be removed before the cluster can be lifted out of the dash.

Panel Disassembly

To prepare the instrument panel for restoration, you will remove the nuts and bolts holding the circuit board to the outer case. All of the twist-turn light sockets are also removed. Then the circuit board lifts free. It is worth noting that most printed

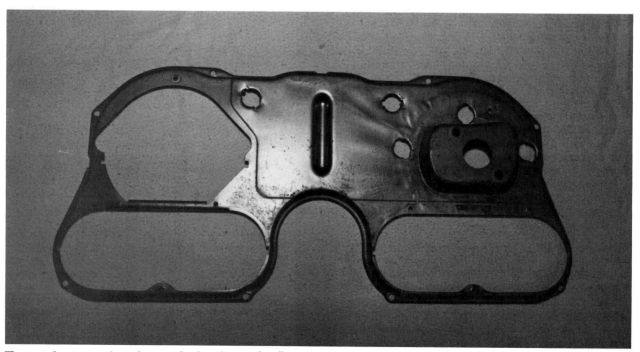

The metal outer casing often needs cleaning and refinishing. This casing is for the deluxe gauge unit without tachometer.

Refinished instrument panel with nearly all the desirable accessories. Note the optional speed minder in the speedometer (white needle pointing to 50 mph), the hard-to-find vacuum gauge (to the left of the oil pressure gauge), and tachometer. The speed minder was not available as an option in 1971 or 1972.

This deluxe instrument panel has the woodgrain finish that was used on the GMC Sierra Grande and Chevrolet Cheyenne trucks in 1971 and 1972. The plastic-plating service will apply either the woodgrain finish or the semi-gloss black finish on the front of the instrument bezel at the customer's request. This unit has the optional tachometer but not the vacuum gauge.

circuits I have dealt with in twenty or more years are very easy to break. Sometimes the break is not even visible, so my advice is to replace the printed circuit. This can solve a lot of electrical trouble-shooting later on.

Now remove the instruments by loosening the screws that hold the metal instrument housing to the plastic housing. Be careful to observe where everything goes so that you will have no trouble at reassembly time. As you lift the metal gauge assembly off the panel facing, you will find the clear plastic gauge covering as well as several small, black spacers. Put the spacers with the screws in a container so that you don't have to hunt for these easily misplaced items when reassembly time comes.

Refurbishing the Gauges and Faces

The next step is to send the plastic gauge housing out for replating (see the appendices for a plastic-plating service). For a small additional charge, you can have the plating service repaint the face of the panel (or replace the woodgrain finish if the panel is for a Cheyenne model). While the dash cluster is apart, you may want to touch up the gauge needles and send out the speedometer for cleaning and reconditioning.

Brightening up the gauge needles is an easy process. Use a common fluorescent paint; you can obtain spray bombs of fluorescent paint in almost any hobby store. The technique here is to spray some paint into the spray can lid or other suitable container. Allow the paint to "flash off," allowing enough time for the paint to become thicker and brushable. Using a small good-quality brush, practice on a toothpick until you can complete the painting operation in one stroke. For success in this, you will discover that it is important that the paint be the right viscosity. If you have to stop and start again along the needle, you will break the flow and this break will be visible. After you have mastered painting the toothpick, you can graduate to painting the gauge needles. Be careful not to drop any paint on the gauge face, as this will permanently mark the gauge and spoil its appearance.

The black face of the instrument cluster can be cleaned quite nicely with soft tissue and warm water (go gently, as too much pressure on the face will mark the semi-flat black surface). After cleaning the instrument face of dust, dampen a Kleenex with Armor All and lightly reclean the surface. Then gently polish the surface with another tissue or soft cloth. This process is a little tedious, but if you do a good job the results are well worth the

A restored deluxe gauge unit ready to go back into the truck.

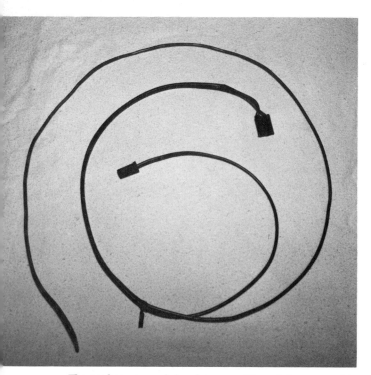

The tachometer wiring harness. The wiring assembly shown here is homemade, but appears exactly like the harness once available from Chevrolet.

time spent. After finishing with the instruments, you can set them aside in a safe place.

Cleaning the Lenses

The next steps are to clean up the inner and outer cases and polish the lens. If the green paint on the cases needs to be refinished, most well-equipped hobby stores can supply the color you need. Failing this, you can ask nearly any auto parts store that sells paint products to mix up the paint and package it in a spray can. The black inner case is sprayed a semi-gloss.

The instrument lens is still available for these trucks under part number 6458264 (full instrumentation but no tach) and 6458266 (with tachometer). Purchasing a new lens is no guarantee of a clear face for the instruments, some come smudged or otherwise imperfect from the factory. Reject these and reorder until you get a lens that's perfect—after all, why pay a new-part price for a substandard part? The day will come soon, however, when new parts will no longer be available. If you choose to reuse your original lens and it is not too badly marked up, you can restore it to like-new appearance. Here's what to do.

When attempting to refinish the plastic instrument lens, it is important that the scratches be very superficial—otherwise you will not end up with a clear face. Begin by sanding the front of the lens (this is the side without the numbers) using micro fine 2000 grit wet-dry sandpaper until all the scratches are gone. Now you can either power polish the surface or apply a coat of clear paint to the sanded surface. Either will produce a crystal clear lens—though of the two methods, clear coating is the easiest. Apply the same clear coat that is used over final finishes. For those desiring a bit of a custom look, you can add a few drops of black paint to tint the clear. This will give the panel facing a slightly cloudy appearance. Don't add too much black or you will make the instruments hard to read. If you don't have access to spray painting equipment, you can polish the face using a very fine grit polishing compound and end with 3M's Imperial Machine Glaze or Hand Glaze.

Tachometer Installation

If you plan to install a tachometer, adding this option is still relatively easy because three of the accessory parts that make up the tachometer package are still available from GM. These are the tachometer head (part number 6468228), the tachometer lens (part number 6458266) and the tachometer printed circuit band (part number 6290459). Unfortunately, the inner and outer cases for the tachometer are no longer available. One way out of this is to find a large truck (one-ton and up) in a salvage yard and buy the instrument panel. Most of these trucks had tachometers and many

The factory-installed radio in this 1969 Chevrolet pickup was an AM unit. Not only was the sound tinny, but reception was limited. For long drives, a modern AM-FM stereo cassette seemed desirable.

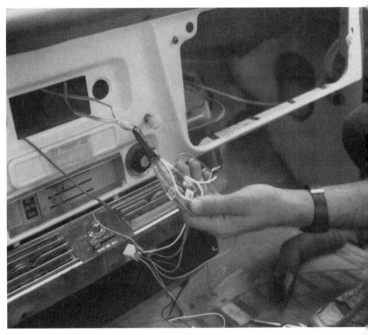

Instructions for installing the new radio called for dropping the air conditioning unit and heater controls to open access to the radio from below. We decided to see if the radio could be reached from the side simply by removing the glovebox door and liner. This proved to be an easy job and gave us plenty of room to remove the old radio and install the new. Reaching the radio through the glovebox opening easily shaved a couple of hours off the job. The new radio came with connectors for auxiliary speakers which could be mounted under the seats. The radio was supplied with dual high-powered speakers on a special mounting that allowed them to be installed in the original speaker location, so the decision was made not to go with a four-speaker setup.

also had the desirable vacuum gauges and super-rare clocks.

Panel Assembly

Now you're ready to reassemble the panel. Start by placing the rechromed gauge housing face down on a soft, clean surface. A section of blanket or old towel makes a soft surface that will protect the new chrome on the gauge housing from becoming scratched while you assemble the gauge cluster. Next, replace the small, soft rubber tubes that act as a buffer between the lens and gauge housing. Now lay the lens in place in the housing, making sure that the locator pin lines up properly. The inner case goes on next followed by the outer case and gauges. Screw these parts together.

The circuit band installs last. Be sure to handle this part carefully because it is delicate. The circuit band is held to the metal instrument case with cap

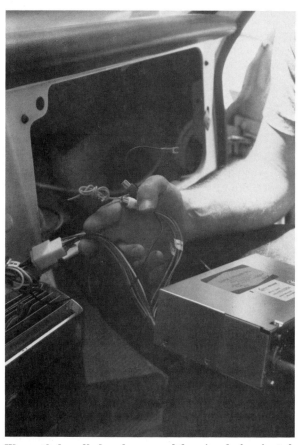

We neatly bundled and wrapped the wires before installing the new radio. This way, the wires wouldn't drape down and become tangled with controls or cables. The instruction sheet advised testing the radio before installing it in the dash. We did this by mounting the speakers, plugging in the antenna and hooking up the radio to its harness. The radio worked perfectly and the original AM antenna provided a good FM, as well as AM, signal. During this testing step we put the radio through its paces, trying out the cassette as well as tuning in stations on AM and FM frequencies.

screws. If you have purchased a tach unit and circuit band at a flea market, beware that it is possible for the printed circuit board to have a short. This will show up if the gauges fail to work properly or if the fusible link at the battery burns out. To test for a short in the circuit board, you must check each circuit for continuity. If any of the circuits fail, you will have to replace the printed circuit. As mentioned above, circuit bands for this series Chevrolet and GMC trucks are still available through your Chevrolet dealer.

If you installed the tachometer, you will have to make up a wiring harness as this item is no longer available from GM. This harness is very simple to make. It consists of a brown 12 gauge pink wire 65 in. long which connects the tachometer to the coil, and a pink 12 gauge wire 35 in. long to connect the tach to the ignition side of the fuse block. The tachometer head is marked "coil" and "battery" to guide you in attaching these wires. You will need to attach clips to one end of both wires to mate to the tabs on the back of the tachometer. The other end of the brown wire will need an eye or U connector. The pink wire attaches to the tab on the tachometer marked "battery" (or sometimes "12 Volt") and to a hot location in the fuse block (located under the dash above the driver's left foot). To prevent the tachometer from draining the battery when the truck is in storage, this hot lead should attach to a location that is dead when the ignition switch is turned off. The brown wire attaches to the coil lead on the tachometer and the negative pole on the coil.

The correct place to route the tachometer harness through the firewall is slightly down from the fuse block connector and to the right (as viewed from underneath the hood). You will need to drill a hole in this location. To complete the factory look, and to protect the wire from abrasion, you can first place a rubber grommet in the hole and run the wire through it. Grommets are available from auto parts stores.

The rebuilt panel goes back in the truck by reversing the order of steps that you followed to remove it. A restored instrument cluster goes a long way to upgrade a truck's interior.

Radio Installation

Chevrolet first made a radio available in its trucks in 1947. While original radios are available, unless you are preparing your truck for show competition you'll be better served by installing a modern radio than by locating an original. Not only is the quality of the sound far superior in the modern radio, but you also gain FM and tape-playing capability. Specially designed radios are made by Custom Autosound, in Anaheim, California (see appendices for address), for installation in Chevrolet trucks from the Advance Design series and later.

This AM/FM stereo radio and auto-reverse tape player has all the features one would expect from a modern sound system and is designed to fit the Chevrolet truck dash, and even has the Chevrolet bow-tie emblem on the tape cassette door.

The installation shown is in a 1969 C–20 Longhorn pickup. The truck's original radio, a basic AM player, had an annoyingly raspy tone and limited reception. Since this truck travels extended distances to shows where it is used to promote the Light Commercial Vehicle Association, there was no question that a modern radio would be an improvement. The unit selected is Custom Autosound's Model USA–01. The high-quality stereophonic speakers that are supplied with this radio are mounted in a compact assembly that installs in the same location under the dash as the original single speaker.

Radio and Speaker Removal

The first steps to installing the new radio are to remove the old radio and speaker, or if the truck is not fitted with a radio, to gain access to the area behind the dash where the radio will be mounted. On most Chevrolet trucks, access to the place where the radio mounts in the center of the dash is gained most easily by removing the glovebox door and liner. On this 1969 model, taking out the glovebox liner (a simple matter of removing eight sheetmetal screws and two bolts) is far easier than reaching the radio from underneath—which on this truck would have meant unhooking an aftermarket air conditioning unit, dropping the heater controls and taking out the ashtray assembly. With the glovebox liner out of the way, the speaker could be reached easily to loosen it from its mounting. A mounting bolt in the back and lock nuts on the radio controls were all that held the original radio in place.

Radio and Speaker Installation

After taking the old radio and speaker out of the truck, preparations for installing the new radio began by splicing the new sound system's wiring harness into appropriate power sources. This step looks more complicated than it really is because the wiring harness supplied for the radio contains outlets for a power booster as well as speaker wiring. Actually, only two wiring splices need to be made and these are for the power supplies (modern radios require two power supply sources). One power supply needs to be to a constant current source. The other should be wired to a source that will be dead when the ignition switch is turned off. For the constant power source, we tapped into the hot wire to the cigarette lighter. For a power source that turns off with the ignition switch, we used the wire that supplied current to the original radio.

Installing the new double speaker unit was a breeze. The speaker assembly was designed so that

Smaller than the original radio, this new radio slipped easily through the glovebox opening and aligned perfectly with the original openings. As my helper observed, "The guy who designed this radio did a heck of a job. A+ to him." It should be noted that the radio we installed, marketed by Custom Autosound, is specially built for installation in Chevrolet trucks. It was not an off-the-shelf product from an electronics outlet.

it attached to the original speaker bracket. The wooden speaker mount could be seen through the speaker grille in the dash, so we covered the speakers with black cheesecloth from a fabric store. The cheesecloth won't distort the sound nor muffle the speakers, but it does camouflage the speaker mount. With the speakers in place and wiring hooked up, we bench tested the radio—that is, we attached the antenna lead and tried out the radio and tape assembly before fitting the sound machine in the dash. The instructions call for this bench-testing step, and it's a wise one. Should the radio be defective, or if the wiring has been hooked up wrong, you'll want to know this before putting in the time to fit the radio in the dash.

Our radio tested out fine, so the next step was to disconnect the radio from the wiring harness and tie up the harness so that it wouldn't drape down on the heater controls. Before positioning the radio, we slipped on the plastic face plate. A brightmetal plate to line the dash opening is also supplied, but we decided not to use it. The radio fit into place easily with the control knobs lining up perfectly in the holes. Support for the radio comes from the control knob shafts in the front and a bracket which attaches to the speaker mount in the rear. To get the proper support from the control knob shafts, you will need to thread a set of nuts onto the shafts and adjust their position so

The completed installation—note the Chevrolet bow-tie on the cassette opening cover. Painting the washers on the control knob shafts would add a finished touch, but Custom Autosound promises to release a bezel that will enclose the control knob shafts, which we will install when available.

that they press-fit against the dash when the radio and its face plate are fit tightly into the hole. A set of washers fits over the control knob shafts from the outside, and another set of nuts is threaded onto the shafts and turned finger tight. You'll find that the radio will have a more original look if you paint these washers to match the dash. A set of spacers is now cut to the correct depth and fitted over the control shafts, then the knobs are pressed in place. With the ignition switch turned on, the radio can be taken through its functions. You'll want to set the digital clock and pre-set stations, adjust the base/treble control and become familiar with the radio's many features.

The Custom Autosound radio is made to fit a vintage Chevy pickup. Everything went in place as it should with no modification. The only improvement you may want to make would be the addition of a carpet to help reduce the tinny sound created by the metallic box, otherwise known as a cab. If you want all-around sound, under-the-seat speakers are preferable to making the sheet-metal alterations required by door mount, armrest or overhead console speakers. You will find that many car stereo companies offer box speakers specifically designed for use in pickups.

Other Interior Upgrades

With its CST (Custom Sport Truck) and Cheyenne models which appeared in the 1967-72 series, Chevrolet began to dress up its pickup interiors with carpeting and high-fashion seat coverings. Bucket seats and center console were also offered as an option. Buckets give a superior ride over a bench seat, but the tradeoff is loss of the third passenger seat space. Trucks from this series are plentiful enough in scrap yards that it's not difficult to find the dressier Cheyenne door panels and headliner. Fabric for a 1969 Camaro matches the Cheyenne seat covering and is available from Camaro specialists. Bucket seats were installed in Blazers and so they, too, are fairly plentiful. Typically the vinyl covering will be torn, but new, correctly embossed coverings are available.

15

Rubber and Glass Replacement

In making plans for upgrading your truck's appearance, it's easy to overlook the need to replace the rubber parts. Window and door seal, the rubber donut around the gas filler pipe and other rubber items on the truck deteriorate at roughly the same rate as the rest of the vehicle, so the rubber's condition doesn't stand out (unless the truck has spent time in the southwestern United States where the hot sun and dryness seem almost to fossilize the rubber). If you're doing a ground-up restoration where all the rubber items will be removed, the need to replace these items will quickly become obvious because most will be destroyed as you take

the vehicle apart. Where rubber parts sometimes get neglected is in the rebuilding approach. Here, deteriorated window rubber or door weather seal may not be noticed until after the truck is painted. The smarter approach is to take inventory of the truck's rubber parts and begin ordering replacements early on in the restoration or rebuilding process. In most cases, your shopping list will soon grow to a respectable order.

Checking Rubber Parts for Wear

Dryness, cracking and chunks of missing rubber are not the only reasons for replacing a truck's rubber parts. The 1969 Chevrolet Longhorn pickup pictured in chapter 11 had sound-looking door

In the process of disassembling the truck, be sure to take an inventory of weatherstripping and rubber parts that will need to be replaced when the truck is reassembled. Since this truck will be undergoing a complete restoration, all rubber parts will be replaced. On the cab, these include the hood anti-squeak strip, the windshield and back light rubber weather seal, the cowl vent seal, rubber donut around the gas-tank filler pipe, and numerous other parts. Mike Cavey

Replacing rubber weather seal is not just a matter of gluing the new rubber onto the truck, but knowing where the weather seal is supposed to go. Note that the door rubber on this Advance Design truck wraps up at the bottom where it is held in place by a metal strip.

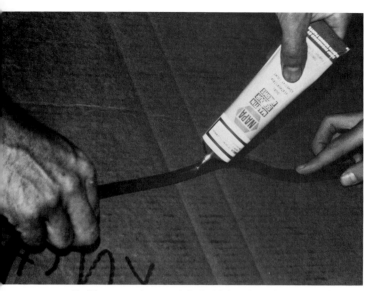

Rubber weather seal is held in place by a special glue available from auto parts stores. Let the glue become tacky before pressing the seal in place. Any excess can be cleaned up with wax remover.

weather seal, yet air could be heard hissing in around the door openings. As door weather seal ages, the rubber loses its elasticity. It appears to be resilient enough to make good contact with the door, but instead collapses when the door is shut. Windshield rubber deteriorates by drying out and cracking, causing water to seep past the glass and drip onto the dashboard and into the cab. If you are disassembling your truck for a major restoration, you will want to replace all possible rubber parts so this job doesn't have to be done later, and so that everything will have a consistent, like-new appearance. Even where a full-scale restoration isn't planned, you will still have plenty of reason to replace door weather seal and many other rubber parts.

Trucks that have been partially or completely disassembled, or have received an amateur restoration, often lack many of the original rubber items. The problem this presents is figuring out what's missing. One way to determine what rubber items belong on the truck, and their locations, is to order a vintage truck supplier's catalog or buy a copy of the factory assembly manual and compare the rubber items shown in the catalog or assembly sequences with those on hand (if your truck is disassembled for restoration) or those still on the truck. Likely to be missing are draft seals for the clutch, brake, starter pedal, floor shift lever, hood bumpers and corner pads, grommets and other small parts.

A convenient place to start taking inventory of needed rubber parts is at the cab. If the door weather seal is original, it's probably cracked and large chunks may be missing. On newer trucks, this weather seal may be intact, but should still be replaced. While you're checking off the rubber items visible on the outside of the cab, notice the condition of the large rubber grommet (often called a donut) around the gas tank filler pipe. Chances are the rubber has hardened, cracked, torn or is missing altogether. The rubber moldings around the windshield, back light and vent windows are also likely to be cracked and hardened.

Inside the cab you'll add brake and clutch pedal pads, boots for the accelerator, floor shift lever and hand brake (on trucks where this brake is floor mounted) to the rubber parts inventory. Even though they're likely to be missing, don't overlook the clutch and brake draft seals that fit over the pedal shafts and rest against the floorboards (on trucks where the clutch and brake pedals depress through the floorboard). On Task Force and 1960-1966 models, the kick-panel air-vent door seals may also need replacing. Also add the steering post pad and check for missing firewall grommets.

You should also check the condition (and presence or absence) of the hood and cowl lacing, door window channels and glass sweepers. If your truck has experienced a lot of use and abuse, the lacing that forms a pad for the hood at the cowl and radiator may have been torn off and discarded. To check the condition of the lacing, just open the hood and look for a thin strip of woven fabric running up the sides and over the top of the cowl and nose assembly. If the original lacing is still in place, most likely it will be worn, compressed and generally look its age.

Window channels (the U-shaped, whisker-lined grooves in which the window glass slides) may also be missing. Since these channels prevent drafts and keep the window glass from rattling against the door, replacements should be installed if the originals are missing or worn. In most cases, the sweepers at the bottom of the window openings will also need to be replaced. These sweepers attach to the door at the base of the window frame and keep water from dripping down inside the door. They also clean the window as it is rolled up and down.

Checking the condition of the rubber parts on the outside of the truck, you may notice previously unseen rubber gaskets sandwiched between the headlight buckets and front fenders. From 1947-1957, Chevrolet placed rubber gaskets between the headlight buckets and the front fenders. These are likely to be cracked and should be added to the rubber parts list. As you're walking around the front of a 1947-1955 First Series, note the cowl vent and add its seal to the rubber parts inventory. On early Advance Design series (1947-1950) you should also add the rubber seal for the side cowl vent. On 1955 First Series and older pickups, fender welt is often used to seal the seam between the rear fenders and the box. Welting is also used on the front fenders through the Advance Design models. On 1955 Second Series and later Stepside pickups, there should be a weather seal between the short "step" and the box. If this seal is missing, moisture can collect in this crevice and cause rust-out.

At the truck's business end, you may notice that two important rubber parts are missing—the tailgate chain covers. These will join the wanted list. If you trace the path of the wiring harness, you'll probably discover that grommets intended to protect the wiring harness as it passes through holes in the body have also disappeared. Replacement grommets are not supplied with new wiring harnesses, so these, too, need to be added to the list.

The rubber parts inventory is growing longer, but probably isn't complete yet. Have you inspected the shock absorber bushings? If the truck predates airplane-style telescoping shocks, the lever shocks will probably be removed for cleaning,

refilling and possibly repair. When they're replaced, you'll also want to install new rubber bushings on the shock arms. Did you notice the condition of the door bumpers (on trucks so-equipped) when you looked inside the cab? And on 1930s through 1941–1946 Art Deco series trucks, have you checked the condition of the hood pads, or are they missing altogether? Rubber parts differ with the various model trucks. You may notice other items not mentioned here. In any event, make as complete a list as possible of the rubber and other weather seal parts that need replacing. Then you can go shopping.

Sources for Rubber Parts

For more recent models (mid-sixties and up), the place to start is your Chevrolet dealer. Many collectors overlook the dealer as a parts source thinking either that new car and truck dealers

That glossy black look of new rubber parts is preserved by periodic coatings with Armor All. This rubber rejuvenator also moistens the weather seal to prevent cracking.

New rubber parts show themselves off in a quiet, inconspicuous way. Inside the cab, rubber parts include the floor mat, brake and clutch pedal pads and accelerator rod grommet, to name a few.

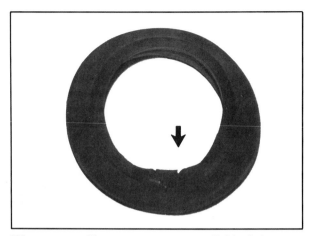

Where new rubber parts are not available, it is sometimes possible to repair the original. The rubber gas-tank filler donut shown here is cracked from age. These cracks will be filled to illustrate the rubber repair process.

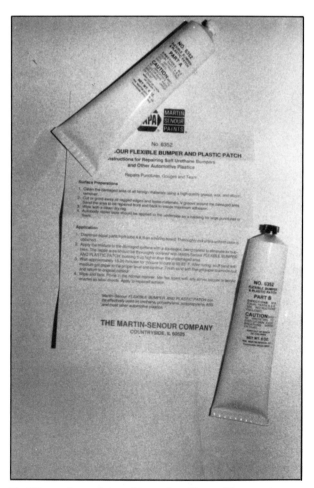

To fill cracks and mend tears in older rubber parts you will use NAPA's Martin-Senour Flexible Bumper and Plastic Patch kit or a comparable product from another refinishing supplier. This two-part epoxy material is designed to repair plastic facia and fender flares on modern cars.

carry parts only for the latest models, or that manufacturer's prices will be higher than alternative parts sources. Most often neither is the case. Dealership parts departments usually list parts in their computer inventory for models built within the last decade, often earlier. It's also possible that a well-established dealer who has been on the same site for several decades may have accumulated a sizeable cache of parts for older models. As to price, the dealer's list is often lower than a specialty supplier, and a dealer's wholesale price is likely to be substantially lower.

Parts dealers specializing in older Chevrolet trucks are the next source of the rubber items on your list. Several of these suppliers are listed in the appendices. Two other sources of rubber items are Metro Moulded Parts, Inc., in Minneapolis, Minnesota, and Lynn Steele Inc., in Denver, North Carolina. These suppliers manufacture rubber parts for a wide range of vintage cars and trucks. If their catalogs don't list exact items for your truck, take measurements (or in the case of weatherstripping, examine the profile of the original) and compare these with the universal items shown in the catalog. The same rubber parts are often used on many vehicles.

Although universal rubber may work for door seal, don't fall into the trap of ordering a universal floor mat. Reproduction floor mats meeting OEM (original equipment manufacturer) standards are available for most year Chevrolet trucks at reasonable prices. While it's usually possible to trim a universal floor mat to match your truck (they're molded oversized to fit the widest possible range of vehicles), problems arise in trying to match any pre-cut holes with the actual location of the clutch and brake pedals, floorshift lever, accelerator and starter control on your truck. In addition, universal mats usually aren't contoured to your truck's transmission hump, so they won't lie flat.

If a reproduction floor mat isn't available, it's always possible to have a trim shop cut carpeting to fit the cab floor. If you want to dress up your older Chevrolet truck with carpeting, you'll also find floor covering kits available. Carpeting has two drawbacks, however. First, no one put carpet in a truck until the mid 1970s when trucks began to assume much the same general transportation role as cars, so carpeting in a pre 1970s truck is definitely not original. Second, if you intend to use your truck for hauling a boat to the lake and toting occasional supplies home from the lumber yard—not especially dirty work, but jobs where you will track some grit inside the cab—you'll find it easier to sweep a floor mat than vacuum a carpet.

Occasionally, it's possible to find original rubber parts at swap meets. To be sure you've found the right part, look up the part number in advance, or better yet, bring along a cross section or the complete original part. If you buy any new-old-stock (NOS) rubber parts, make sure they are still pliable, and don't listen to a vendor's story that a stiff rubber part can be softened with a couple of coatings of Armor All.

You should plan on replacing most, if not all, of the rubber parts on a light truck that's twenty or more years old—especially if the vehicle has spent most of its life in warm, sunny climates. Cost of the replacement rubber will typically run between $500 and $700. It's wise to assemble the complete rubber inventory early so you will be able to install new rubber items whenever they're called for in the rebuilding process.

The guideline is to purchase replacement rubber only from parts vendors who carry quality Chevrolet reproduction parts (such as Jim Carter) or from specialty rubber parts vendors (such as Lynn Steele and Metro Moulded). Avoid dealing with discount mail-order parts outlets that may carry parts for older cars and trucks as a sideline. Although these catalogs sometimes show a lower price for the few rubber parts they may list as fitting Chevy trucks, the discount parts are likely to be of inferior quality, and worse yet, may not fit.

Rubber Parts Installation

Rubber parts are typically installed as part of a larger process (like replacing the windshield) or as a detailing step after repainting the exterior or refinishing the interior. Usually the only difficulty in installing rubber parts is making sure they're not forgotten and in some cases recalling exactly where they go. If your truck is still intact (awaiting a mechanical and cosmetic upgrade, or thorough restoration), be sure to take photos and make notes on the locations of rubber parts before taking

After the patch material has dried, it is sanded smooth. This is an easy step because the material is soft and sands easily. To disguise the repair and give the rubber a fresh look, the part is given a coating of semi-gloss trim paint. The rubber repair process shown here may also be desirable for improving the appearance of aged rubber on an otherwise original truck.

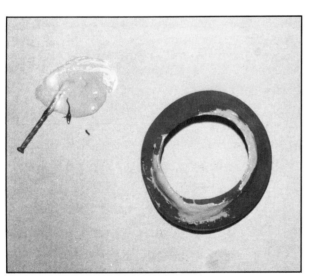

The filler is mixed with hardener in equal amounts just as you would with epoxy glue. You'll know when the material is thoroughly mixed because it will have a consistent gray color. A small nail or toothpick works well as an applicator. The patch material is dabbed into the cracks and over any age marks in the rubber. You'll find that the material has to be worked relatively quickly, as it dries in about fifteen minutes.

If the old glass is enclosed in a frame, you'll first have to open the frame. Here the windshield frame of a late 1930s Chevrolet truck is being pried apart using a hammer and screwdriver. Once the frame begins to open, you can pry out the glass quite easily.

the truck apart. If the truck is already apart, you can get this information by taking photos and noting the locations of rubber parts on other original or restored trucks you may find in scrap yards or see at club events. You can also clarify the proper location of many rubber items from a factory assembly manual, available in reprinted form for Advance Design and Task Force series trucks.

An example of where the original rubber part, or illustration in the factory assembly manual, is helpful is in showing where to glue the door weather seal. The question here is not only the correct placement of the rubber, but also the proper location of the seam. The seam location is important on a truck that will be entered in show

competition, but even if competition is not your aim, it makes sense to attach the door seal in the original, rather than a haphazard, location.

In almost every instance, rubber parts are installed after painting. Hood lacing should also be attached after painting, and the same applies to door window channel and sweepers. In some cases, as with fender welting, the rubber items will be replaced as part of an assembly step. This means that on the older models where welting is used to prevent squeaks and seal the seams between fenders and body or box against moisture, the fenders would be painted separately, then installed. You'll discover that this approach requires great care to avoid nicking or scratching the paint in the process of bolting the fenders in place. Later model trucks do not use welting on the rear fenders. However, where the welting is not used, a bead of suitable sealer (liquid anti-squeak or rubber caulk) should be applied to the fender lip

Spraying on a strip of material called channel liner with light oil. The channel liner fits between the glass and the frame and is what holds the glass in place. If you are replacing door window glass, you will also use this channel liner to hold the glass to the cranking mechanism.

In preparation for replacing the vent window glass in its frame, wipe the glass with painting prep solvent. Note that we've covered the work area with an old towel to prevent scratching the paint on the vent window frame.

188

where it contacts the box to prevent moisture from penetrating this seam.

Rubber parts that are installed as part of mechanical repair, such as shock absorber bushings, are fitted in place during the reassembly step. If you're replacing the steering column floor seal, it'll be necessary to remove the steering column from the truck and disassemble the tube from the steering box. This effort is warranted on a frame-up restoration where you may be overhauling the steering box and applying a high-gloss finish to the column, but if you're only doing needed mechanical and cosmetic work, removing the steering column to replace the post pad probably isn't worth the effort unless the original pad is completely deteriorated or missing—and then you may want to slit the replacement pad so as to fit it onto the post.

Many rubber items, both inside the cab and on the truck's exterior, are replaced as part of detailing after the truck is painted. Examples inside the cab would include the pedal pads, draft seals and glovebox bumpers; examples on the exterior would be the gas-tank filler-pipe grommet and tailgate chain rubbers. Most of these items just slip into place. If the fit is snug, as will most likely be the case with the filler-pipe grommet and tailgate chain rubbers, a light coating of liquid dish soap to the rubber surface will allow the items to slide easily into place.

Door weather seal attaches with special glue. This process is relatively simple, but does involve several steps. At some point, the old rubber has to be removed. Usually this is done in preparation for rust repair and repainting. Although the old weather seal can often be pulled loose by hand, usually some of the rubber and glue sticks to the metal and has to be scraped clean with a putty knife. If you just want to replace the rubber and aren't planning on repainting, you will need to scrape very cautiously to avoid scratching the paint. Prep solvent, used to remove wax and tar from a finish in preparation for painting, can be

Now wrap the oil-saturated channel liner around the edge of the glass that will be pressed into the vent window frame. Because the channel liner is oil-soaked it will slide easily off the glass. Hold the liner in place by pinching it against the glass at either end.

Here the glass is being fitted into the vent window frame. The glass should not slide easily all the way into the frame channel. If it does, a thicker strip of channel liner should be used or the channel should be narrowed slightly. A press-fit is needed to hold the glass in place.

used to soften the old glue and should be used to clean the surface before gluing new weather seal in place.

The metal around the old weather seal may look solid, but you're likely to find rust scale behind hardened or decayed rubber. If so, it's essential to clean away the rust before proceeding. When metal work isn't planned, you can clean surface rust with a wire brush or spot sandblaster, then prepare the metal with Naval Jelly, a phosphoric acid gel available in hardware stores. The white residue left by the gel should be wiped off with a damp cloth before painting. The metal can then be primed and touch-up painted. If refinishing is planned, the weather seal channel can be sandblasted and any rust damage repaired.

Weather seal cement is available at auto parts stores. This glue comes in two types. One is applied to the metal and the rubber is pressed in place before the glue sets. With the other, a bead of glue is applied to both the metal and rubber. With this type, you wait until the glue becomes tacky before pressing the weather seal in place. With either type, you should be careful not to dab the glue on painted areas outside the weather seal channel. Any extra glue can be cleaned up with prep solvent, but it doesn't come off easily. If necessary, the rubber can be held in place on curves and the bottom of the door openings while the glue sets with strips of masking tape. Normally the glue is sticky enough to hold the rubber snugly in place without the tape. Be sure to give the glue time to set before closing the doors. Cowl vent and foot vent seals are attached using the same method.

On most trucks, window channel simply press-fits into the U-shaped channel on the door frame. On some, however, it glues in place against blocks, or is held by screws. If you removed the old channel, then the attaching method should be clear. If you didn't, when you buy the replacement channel ask the vendor which attaching method applies to your truck. To install new window channel, first measure the channel distance (sides and upper window frame area), then cut and bend the channel to fit the contour of the window frame.

Installing door glass sweepers is somewhat trickier. On older trucks, the sweeper strips are held in place with clips. On newer models, the sweepers are secured with staples, but clips can be used if holes are drilled for them. When installing the sweeper, make sure the glass is rolled down as far as it will go. If you need even more glass clearance, you can detach the glass frame from the roll-up mechanism and let it rest against the bottom of the door. The sweeper has to be installed after the glass is in the door, and the problem here is the risk of breaking the glass while squeezing the clips to secure the sweeper. If the window is made of non-tempered automotive glass (as found on older trucks and commonly used as replacement

for side windows and flat windshields) it will crack very easily.

Window channel and glass sweeper material are commonly supplied in 8 ft. strips. These items can be purchased by mail order from vendors such as Restoration Specialties and Supply in Windber, Pennsylvania (see appendices for address), or directly from the vendor at large swap meets. It's advantageous to buy these longer items at swap meets because they have to be cut or folded to meet postal or UPS shipping regulations.

New rubber window seal is installed when the windshield and rear window glass are replaced after painting. Unless you have experience working with the large glass pieces that make up a windshield and side window, it's best to leave this job to professionals. Besides making glass installation look easy, the professionals will also make sure that the rubber is sealed to the window channel to prevent future seepage. Replacing ventilator pane weatherstrip (on trucks with vent pane windows) requires that the window glass and frame be removed. This procedure is described in the window glass section that follows.

Rubber Parts Preservation

Rubber deteriorates (dulls, hardens and cracks) when exposed to sunlight, so to keep rubber parts soft and pliable, and to preserve their freshly installed glossy look, it's a good idea to treat the rubber each time you wash your truck. The product to use is Armor All, a rubber moisturizer and protectorate, available at any discount mart's automotive department. Armor All can be sprayed directly onto the rubber, or applied to a rag and wiped on, where it freshens the rubber and leaves a glossy sheen.

New rubber and other weather seal items change a truck's appearance more than you'll realize until you see the new parts in place. They give a restored or upgraded truck that finished look while making the truck more comfortable to drive by sealing the cab against drafts and water leakage.

Rubber Parts Repair

While specialty parts suppliers are doing an excellent job providing reproduction rubber parts for Chevrolet trucks, on early models especially, there may still be a few rubber items for which replacements are not available. The repair methods described here can be used when enough of the original rubber part remains to serve as a basis for the repair, but the part is too badly deteriorated to use as is. This process does not apply to making new rubber parts.

If a cosmetic touch-up is all that's needed—to cover cracks or build up worn spots—the part can simply be dipped in Plastic Shield or a comparable product. Dipping rubber items to renew their finish only works when the original doesn't have large cracks or chips.

The procedure for repairing more badly damaged rubber starts with cleaning the part with a prep solution of the type used to clean metal in preparation for painting. This product is available at any auto parts store selling automotive refinishing products. When the prep solution has evaporated, a dam is built under the chipped or cracked areas using masking tape. If the rubber is torn, the sides of the tear should be pulled together for the repair. This can be done by clipping the edges of the tear together with a staple.

To fill the cracks and mend any tears, you'll use a two-part epoxy designed to repair chips in facia, fender flares or other soft plastic or rubber parts on modern cars and trucks. NAPA's Martin-Senour Flexible Bumper and Plastic Patch, product number 6352, is formulated specially for this purpose. Other refinishing suppliers have similar products.

The filler is mixed with hardener in equal amounts just as you would with epoxy glue. After squeezing out two equal dabs of the filler and hardener onto a small square of cardboard, the two are mixed together. Now the filler can be spread over cracks or chips using a nail, toothpick or similar small applicator. The patch sets up quickly (in about fifteen minutes), and any excess can be sanded smooth with the surrounding surface. The patch product makes a permanent bond and has the pliability of fresh rubber.

To give the entire rubber part a new look, and disguise the repair, use a semi-gloss paint designed for trim moldings on modern cars and trucks. Martin-Senour's semi-gloss black trim paint, product number 7812, works well for this purpose.

The procedures are a cosmetic repair and don't restore the softness and suppleness of new rubber. But where replacements are not available, these procedures make it possible to use an otherwise unusable part.

Window Glass Replacement

Breakage and cracks aren't the only reasons for replacing window glass in an older truck. Automotive safety glass turns cloudy along the edges with age and exposure to sunlight. In time, this cloudy band can extend several inches into the window, sometimes obscuring vision over nearly all the window area. If you've held off replacing cracked, clouded or even broken glass in your Chevrolet truck, thinking this was a job you'd have to take to a professional, there's no reason to live with the blemished glass any longer. Replacing side windows, including vent pane glass, calls only for basic mechanical skills and enough dexterity to avoid breaking the glass.

Start by deciding which glass needs replacing. Windshield and rear window glass, as well as rear corner windows on Advance Design five-window cabs, or on Suburbans, is held in place by rubber gaskets and requires a different technique than that presented here. Although it is possible for hobbyists to replace this gasket-retained glass, since windshields are expensive (particularly those that are one-piece or wraparound) and in some cases may be hard to find, it's better to have these pieces installed by professionals.

Before removing door window glass, you must remove the trim panels on the inside of the doors. This panel will be held in place by screws. The inside door handle and window crank also need to be removed and secured with clips or screws. To remove the clips, it is necessary to push in on the trim panel and slip the C-clips loose from the shank

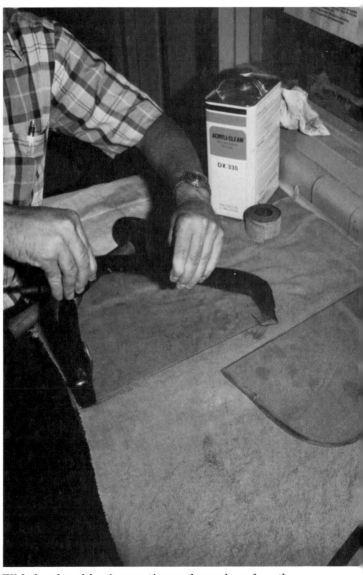

With the edge of the glass resting on the work surface, the glass can be pressed into the frame. It is important to use moderate, even force to avoid cracking the glass.

of the handle or window crank with a screwdriver or, preferably, an upholstery clip tool. When removing the last of the hardware, hold on to the trim panel so that it does not fall to the ground.

When the inside door-trim panels have been removed, you will be able to reach the window mechanism through the opening of the inner door panel. On trucks with vent panes, the vent pane frame needs to be removed in order to allow the door window glass to slide out of its channel at the rear of the vent pane assembly. The vent pane assembly is removed by loosening the molding screws around the vent window frame, plus the screws that attach the vent pane channel to the inner door panel. With these screws removed, the vent pane assembly should pull up and out of the door.

Before attempting to remove the door glass, you will need to detach the weather seal that lines the lower edge of the window opening. This strip (which has a whisker-like appearance on older trucks and is made of rubber on more recent models) is typically held in place with clips and can be carefully pried loose.

Glass Removal

Now you can begin the process of removing the door glass itself. To do this, fit the window crank back on its lever and roll the window up or down until you see the screws that attach the window frame to the arm that raises or lowers the window. Now position the window so that you can reach these screws with a wrench. Remove these screws, being careful not to drop them down in the bottom of the door (if this happens you may need a magnetic rod to fish them out). Be sure to hold on to the

window glass to keep it from falling down in the door. Once the window frame has been unbolted from the window slide, the window glass and frame can be pulled up through the window slot in the door.

If the door glass is enclosed in a frame, as is the case with early Advance Design and Task Force models, you will need to work the frame loose from the glass. The easiest way to do this is by squirting gasoline along the edge of the window frame on both sides. The gasoline will soften the seal that holds the glass into the frame. Now you can remove the bolts that hold the upper channel to the lower channel and pull these two pieces apart. As the gasoline softens the channel seal you will be able to work the glass out of the upper channel. In some cases, this seal will have dried enough for the glass to pull out easily. In other cases, the seal may have hardened and you will have to pry out the glass. You can do this by tapping on the frame. Be very careful not to bend or break the channel. It will be used with the new glass.

With the glass out of the frame, you will need to clean the channel. On early Advance Design trucks the frame is painted, whereas on Task Force series the door glass frame is brightmetal. If the painted frame has surface rust, you will want to sandblast and refinish it. If the frame has more severe rust damage, it should be repaired or replaced. To give a brightmetal frame a new look, the metal can be buffed following the instructions given in chapter 16.

The closest source of replacement glass is the local glass shop (not a hardware store, but a business that specializes in replacing commercial windows and auto glass). This shop will use the old glass as a pattern to cut new replacements, so if the glass is missing or broken, you may have to use another source. The major problem with glass from a local shop is that the new windows will lack the factory markings. These markings, which include the manufacturer's name and sometimes the production date, are etched into factory glass and vehicles entering rigorous AACA or other national competition can lose points if fitted with glass that lacks these markings. Specialty glass suppliers can etch the original factory markings into the replacement glass. As a third option, it is sometimes possible to find new-old-stock glass at swap meets. If you buy glass at a flea market, be sure to check the stock number (taken from either the original glass or a parts book) of the replacement glass and carefully inspect the edge of the glass to make sure the seal between the glass layers has not deteriorated and that the glass is free from clouding.

If you have the factory markings placed on the glass, you will want to note carefully their position on the original glass. There is no left or right to side door glass. This means that the marking will be on

---

Sealing the Cowl Vent

by Ronald Olsen

When I bought my truck, the cowl vent was sealed closed with silicone seal. Last summer I wanted the vent to open so I freed it up and of course it leaked when I washed the truck or it rained (not unheard of here in Oregon). The solution was to apply a bead of silicone seal under the cowl, between the cowl and the water track. Surprise! No more leak.

My truck's radio and speaker were out when I applied the silicone and made a great window to the underside of the cowl. Without the radio, this area is easy to work in. I am not sure of the reason for the leak, but I was delighted that the fix was so easy. The rubber or foam vent gasket is apparently a draft seal and not a water seal.

the inside of the glass on one side and on the outside on the other. Small detail points like this are important in the rigorous upper levels of AACA competition.

Glass Fitting

As you prepare to replace the glass, you will need to gather several items. These include channel liner (a thin, rubbery strip available from most bodyshops that do glass replacement), windshield sealer/glue and new window channel weather seal. To install the new door glass, a strip of channel liner is cut slightly longer than the glass and placed over the section of glass that is being fit into the channel. For most years, this will be the bottom edge, though on some models Chevrolet also enclosed the upper glass outline in a metal channel.

To be sure the glass doesn't work loose from the channel at some point in the future, you should spread a bead of glass adhesive in the channel before fitting the glass. Some adhesive will be squeezed out of the channel when the glass is inserted, but can be scraped off with a putty knife and the glass washed with prep solvent, a product used to prepare the surface for painting.

Now the glass can be pressed into the channel. If the fit is tight, you may have to tap the channel onto the glass. If you do this, place a hardwood board on the channel and rest the glass on another board. Tap gently only against the wood so as not to crack the glass. Fitting glass into a channel that covers only the bottom of the glass is usually not difficult. Fitting glass into a frame can be more difficult, however, and you may want to have this done at a shop that installs automotive glass. There the glass will be fitted into the frame using a clamping device. When the glass is seated in the frame or channel, you can cut off the excess channel liner and clean up the glue.

Fitting replacement glass into the vent frames follows the same process. If the vent frame is out of

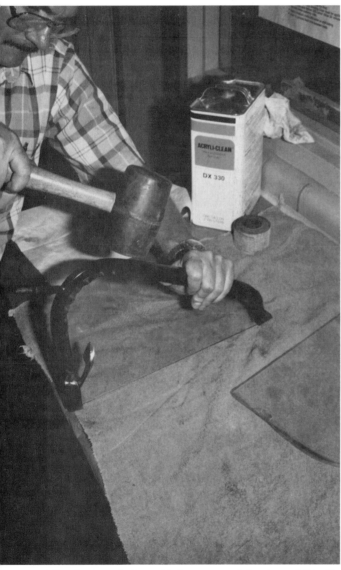

The glass needs just a little more nudging to seat it in the frame, so we tapped lightly with a rubber mallet.

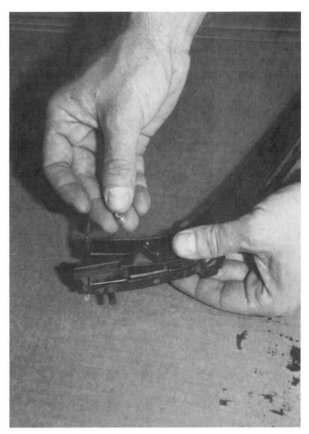

The last step before fitting the vent window back in the truck is installing a new hinge rivet. The original rivet was drilled out in order to remove the vent window from its frame assembly.

the truck, it is possible to force the glass in place by resting the frame on a block of wood, placing another block of wood (a short length of 2x4 works well) against the glass and tapping the wood gently with a hammer. Remember that glass is delicate; forceful tapping can easily crack or break the glass.

If the window channel liner is worn and needs replacing, this should be done before fitting the glass back in the doors.

Fitting the glass back in the doors is basically a matter of reversing the procedure you used to remove it. First, you will slip the glass and frame down into the window slot in the door. Next, you will bolt the frame to the window slide. What's important here is to align the frame so that the glass doesn't bind in the channel. Cranking the glass up and down will test the alignment. Be sure to oil all moving parts of the window mechanism while the door panel is off and the mechanism is accessible.

The vent pane frame also installs in reverse order of how it was removed. If the hinge rivet was cut to remove the vent frame, a new rivet will have to be installed. These are available from vintage Chevrolet parts suppliers. With both the vent pane and door glass in place, roll up the door glass and close the vent pane to make sure the glass is fitted properly. Now roll the door glass all the way down and replace the weatherstrip that seals the glass at the window opening. Chances are the tiny clips that hold this weatherstrip in place are still in their sockets on the door. When fitting the weatherstrip into the clips, be careful not to pry against the door glass. Localized stress of this type can crack the glass.

With the weatherstrip in place, the door panels and handles are replaced and the job is finished. New glass gives any vehicle a fresher look and improves visibility as well.

16

Pickup Box Restoration

Rust and dent damage to the pickup box on an old truck is common. Depending on the region where the truck has spent most of its working life, rust can vary from surface corrosion where the paint has worn thin to complete rust-out of the side panels, cross braces, stake supports and tailgate. Fortunately, replacement sheet metal and entire replacement beds are available for most Chevrolet and GMC trucks from 1937 to 1966. It should be noted that these replacements are for trucks with the narrow Stepside beds. Replacement sheet metal or the wide Fleetside boxes that first appeared in 1958 and quickly became the top-selling box style is more difficult to locate. Also, Fleetside boxes with their welded construction, particularly those with metal flooring, are more complicated to repair.

The metal-floored Fleetside boxes are not impossible to repair, however, as wood flooring kits for 1967–1972 trucks with the wide Fleetside boxes are available. Wood flooring was an option on these Fleetside models, even though most came from the factory with metal floors. To convert a later Fleetside box to a wooden floor you will need to replace the front panel and rear cross sill, and bed support cross sills. These parts are all available. The conversion makes it possible to restore a box that is otherwise unusable due to rusted metal flooring for which replacements are no longer available.

Pickup Box Restoration

Box restoration begins by removing the pickup box from the frame and determining the extent of the rust damage. This is done by jabbing a screwdriver into suspected rust areas. The bottoms of the stake supports are particularly susceptible areas for rust. If the fender welting rotted out or has been removed from the seam between the rear fenders and box sides, it is also possible that the sides are rusted in this area. If the box sides are sound and not badly dented, you may decide to replace only the stake supports. These can be removed by drilling out the spot welds, purchasing

Clean up the box and floor and take pictures of all the details and make notes for reference at assembly time. Make notes also on sequence and fit, and list all fasteners (by size, type and location). Remove the fenders, lights and wiring. Order new wood, skid strips and angle braces. If the box sides, front or tailgate are badly dented or rusted and need replacing, also order these parts. New metal is available for Chevrolet pickups from the 1930s through 1960s.

new stake supports from one of the vintage Chevrolet truck parts vendors and welding the new supports onto the side panel.

Removing Angle Strips

by Mark Sharp

On Stepside boxes from 1973 and up, the angle strip bolts which go through the wood are apparently welded to the angle strip. If the bolts are being replaced when installing new bed wood they must be drilled out. I recommend that you use care when removing the nuts so that these bolts can be reused. The old wood must be destroyed to get it out from under the angle strips, and the holes on the new outer boards will have to be slotted to the edge in order to be inserted under the angle strip. If the bolts are to be drilled out and replaced, I recommend using "ribbed neck" carriage bolts which can be pressed into the old bolt hole.

If the damage is more extensive, the decision you will face is what to replace and what to repair. If your truck has the narrow Stepside box, you can unbolt and replace whatever pieces are rusted or dented beyond repair as the box sides, cross sills, even tailgates are available in remanufactured form. If the box is beyond repair, you can purchase an entire new box which will be shipped in knocked-down form. You'll need to bolt the box together before painting and mounting it on the truck.

If you are restoring your truck for show competition, you'll probably face the temptation to fill the spot welds and other imperfections in the metal—with the aim of giving the box a mirror-smooth finish. However, it is important to leave the spot welds and other markings made by the manufacturing process, since that's the way these boxes came from the factory. After all, there are certain things that make a truck a truck, and spot welds joining the stake pockets on the box sides are among them.

For those who like a custom look, there are several modifications you can make to give the box

To make room for working underneath, remove the pickup box from the frame and set it up on sawhorses or stands. Remove the old bedwood, skid strips, bolts and cross-members.

196

a special look. Louvered tailgate covers can be welded over the old rusted or dented tailgate. Rear pans, louvered or plain, can replace the bulky step-and-tow bumper (or absence of a bumper on some trucks) to give the rear of the truck a sleek, finished look. These pans even have cutouts for the license plate.

Thanks to the availability of quality, replacement sheet metal and other parts, even the most derelict Chevrolet Stepside box can be rebuilt to look like new. If new box sides are used, no welding is required, making rebuilding our pickup's box a project that most of us will want to do ourselves.

Wooden Bed Restoration
By Bruce Horkey

One job that is nearly always required in restoring an old truck is replacing the wooden floor-ing in the pickup box. The wood may still be intact, but scarred and scraped—a condition that gives a truck a well-worked look. Whether you are restoring or rebuilding, you'll want to renew your truck's wooden pickup box flooring. This is a job you can do yourself; all the parts and pieces you'll need are available from a number of suppliers. When you're done you'll not only have the pride of your accomplishment, but you'll realize that nothing sets a vintage truck off like new wood in the pickup box.

Restoration of wooden bed floors in trucks from the 1930s to 1960s can be accomplished in several ways, but when it comes to winning show trophies, care and professional quality are all-important.

Strip or sandblast the box metal. Next, do any needed dent and metal repair work, refinish the box sides, front and tailgate. Varnish or paint the new wood.

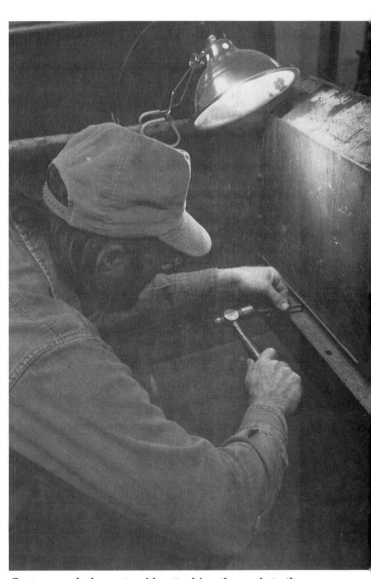

Center-punch the spot welds attaching the angle to the box. These welds will be drilled out with a spot weld cutter. Set the depth of the cutter to drill only through the angle. After drilling out the spot welds, remove the old angle.

Wooden Bed Varnishing

Although Chevy pickups didn't leave the factory with varnished flooring on the pickup box, most truck owners prefer a high-gloss finish on the pickup planking over the dull black or painted coatings that were applied to the wooden flooring as the box came down the assembly line. Actually, the varnish finish is important for more than just appearance. It also protects and in so doing extends the life of your truck's bed wood. Here are the steps to follow in applying a quality varnish finish.

To begin, you will need to gather the following tools and materials: file with safe edge (no teeth on one side), 120 or 280 grit sandpaper, tack cloth, Scotchbrite pad, two varnish brushes, two 2 lb. coffee cans or similar containers, two qt. Marine spar varnish, one qt. quality paint thinner, wipes and sawhorses.

The first step is to take the file and strike off the sharp edges of the boards. This will prevent the edges from snagging the brush and ensure better adhesion for the varnish. When filing the edge of the groove, lay the file on the groove at a 45 degree angle and allow the safe edge (no teeth) to ride on the bottom of the groove. Next, sand the faces and edges of the boards by hand with 120 grit sandpaper. When you are satisfied with the smoothness of the boards, you can prepare for varnishing.

Applying Varnish

The space you select to do the varnishing should have good ventilation (this is healthier for

Set edge boards in place and mark holes to attach angles to them. Remove boards and drill holes with ⅜ in. diameter bit.

Set new angles in place, following notes made earlier, and mark hole locations to box side. If you are working with angles that have no holes on the shorter side, note fender and stake pocket locations and decide where to drill holes to attach the angles to the box sides. Drill holes in the box side and attach angles. For originality, the angles should be spot welded in place instead of bolting.

you and gives faster drying). Clean the area thoroughly. Sweep the floor well, then wet it down to settle the dust. Now arrange the boards on sawhorses and get out the varnishing supplies.

To make sure there is no dust on the boards, vacuum all surfaces of the wood, then wipe the boards with a tack cloth. For the first varnish coat, mix a half quart of varnish with a half quart of thinner. The 2 lb. coffee can makes a good mixing container. Apply this thinned varnish to the wood completely and evenly, coating all surfaces. Let this first coating dry overnight (eight to twelve hours).

When the first coat is dry, move the wood away from the varnishing area and lightly sand with 280 grit sandpaper. Wipe the boards again with a tack cloth. Bring the wood back to the varnishing area and apply a second coat of 50:50 thinned varnish. This second coating will ensure that the varnish penetrates thoroughly into the wood. After curing, these first coatings provide a barrier that will let subsequent layers build up on the surface.

When the second varnish coat has dried thoroughly, again move the wood away from the varnishing area and lightly sand with 280 grit paper. Wipe the boards with a tack cloth to remove all dust. The third coating is thinned only twenty-five percent (seventy-five percent varnish to twenty-five percent thinner). This coat is also sanded with 280 grit sandpaper. Be careful not to cut through the varnish on the edges of the wood. Tack off the boards to remove all dust.

For the fourth coat, use a fresh can of varnish and a fresh, clean brush. Do not shake or stir the

Install edge boards and drop bolts through the angles. Loosely install the cross-members.

Install one board and skid strip at a time. Install bolts, nuts and washers loosely from the inside of the box by reaching over and under the boards. Install boards in an alternating pattern, first on one side of the box, then on the other.

Install the center board and last two skid strips and bolts. Measure the box diagonally to ensure squareness. Align the boards and adjust everything to fit.

From the underside, loosely install the remaining nuts and washers. Make one final check for alignment and squareness. Hand tighten all nuts. After you're satisfied with the fit, set the box on the truck frame. Place a blanket over the front box panel to protect it and the cab from bumping together and scratching the finish.

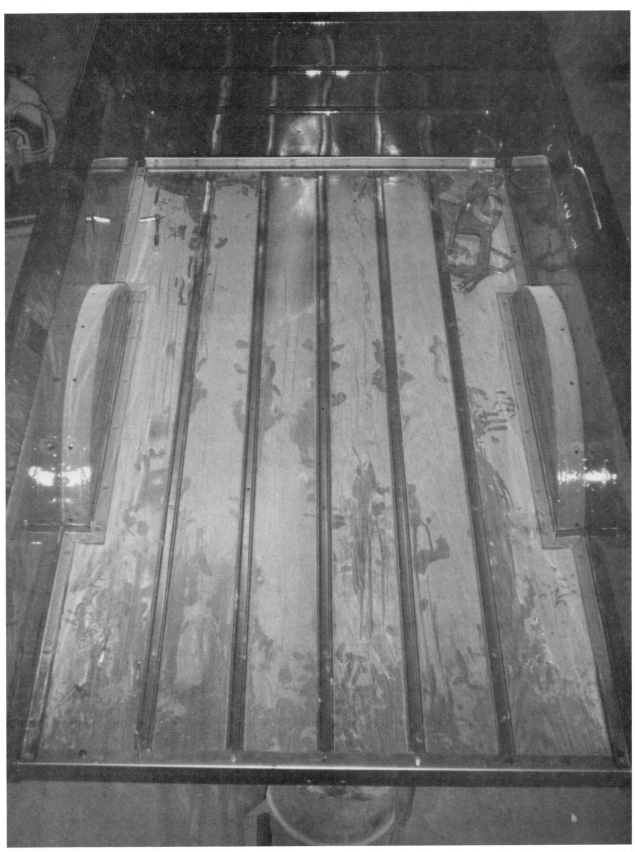

Drop in the hold-down bolts and washers. Square the box on the frame and make alignment adjustments, then bolt the box in place. Caution: Don't overtighten the skid strip bolts. Now stand back and admire your work.

Although not entirely original, a high-gloss varnish finish on the box's wooden flooring greatly increases the beauty of the truck. This example, a 1958 Cameo, deviates from original not only in the varnish finish but also in the use of oak flooring instead of pine, and stainless-steel skid strips in place of painted strips. If you are building a truck for the show circuit you will stick with authenticity, but if you want to make the pickup box floor one of the truck's highlights, you may want to make these special touches part of your truck. Trent Stephan

All replacement sheet metal is available for both short and long, narrow Stepside boxes from the late 1930s through the mid 1960s. A pickup box consists of a front panel, side panels, cross sills (to support the floor) and tailgate (not shown). With the exception of the angle braces which may be spot welded to the side panels, these boxes are bolted together. Mark Sharp

varnish. Bubbles can present a problem and are sometimes created by wiping off the brush on the edge of the can. To prevent bubbles, wipe off the brush as needed on the edge of an empty coffee can. This fourth coating is not thinned. Apply first to the backside, edges and ends—and allow the boards to dry. Then apply the varnish full strength to the face side. When the boards have dried thoroughly they can be assembled in the box. When you have expended this much care and labor to achieve a furniture-like finish on your truck's pickup box floor, you will want to treat the wood like fine furniture. Wipe off any dust that accumulates with a soft cloth. A tonneau cover is recommended to protect the box flooring from sun and weather.

Treating the Box Wood

The box flooring on Chevrolet trucks from 1947 to mid 1955 came from the factory for a dull black coating of a somewhat thin consistency. This means that if you are restoring your truck for national competition, you will need to avoid the more finished looking varnished or painted planking. Mike Cavey, who has restored an AACA national prize-winning truck of this vintage, says that he finds a mixture of linseed oil and lamp black creates the correct finish for the bed wood. The correct wood for the bed is yellow pine.

Later trucks had painted box wood. To achieve a quality-looking, durable painted finish on the box flooring, first prime the boards, then apply a semi-gloss alkyd (oil) base enamel paint. The prime coating should be thinned slightly with min-eral spirits and worked into all surfaces of the boards. When this coat has dried, the boards should be sanded lightly on the face with 280 grit sandpaper and wiped with tack cloth to remove all dust. Then a second prime coating should be applied, allowed to dry and again slightly sanded. This is followed with the enamel paint which is applied full strength to all surfaces of the boards.

Refinishing should be done after all machine work and hole drilling are completed. This will ensure that all exposed surfaces are protected by the finish coating.

The stake supports are spot welded to the box sides, as shown. If all the box sides are solid and only the stake supports need to be replaced, the spot welds can be drilled out and the old supports removed.

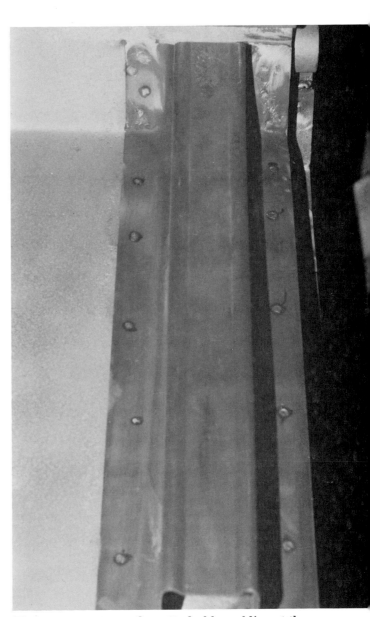

The new supports are then attached by welding at the locations of the old spot welds. Mark Sharp

The new replacement box sides have the stake supports already spot welded in place. This side with three stake supports is for a 1947–1953 long box. Mark Sharp

For many Chevrolet models, three styles of tailgate are available: an authentic replacement tailgate with the Chevrolet lettering stamped into the sheet metal, a plain tailgate without the Chevrolet lettering and the tailgate cover shown here. The cover fits over the existing tailgate giving a smooth, somewhat custom look. Mark Sharp

To ensure paint coverage of all surfaces, the best approach is to paint the box before assembly. Note the box wood and skid strips laid out separately in the rear of the photo. When this approach is used, care must be taken to avoid scratching the new finish when the box is assembled. Mike Cavey

Rear pans are also available to give a truck without a rear bumper a finished look. These were not factory items and would not be used on a show truck, but are a stylish addition to an everyday driver or custom truck. Mark Sharp

The rear pan gives a smart, finished look to 1973–1987 series and 1988 and newer models. The earlier model has been mildly customized by removing the taillights from the rear quarter panels and placing them in the pan below the tailgate. The smooth tailgate cover has been added to remove the Chevrolet lettering. Mark Sharp

17

Plating Trim

One advantage of restoring a truck, as opposed to a car, is that in most cases there's only a small amount of brightwork (chrome and stainless trim) to redo. Of course there are exceptions, most notably the later fifties deluxe cab models and the ultra-fancy Cameo with their chrome bumpers and grille and bright moldings around the windows. Cameo restorers also have to contend with plated diecast taillight housings, a chrome band at the front of the bed and for 1957 and 1958, plated trim bands on the sides of the box. On most trucks, however, chrome trim is limited to the headlight

In most years when a chrome grille wasn't standard equipment, it was available as an option. A gleaming chrome grille really dresses up a vintage and is a particularly desirable feature if you plan to enter your truck in show competition. The grille on this truck had to *be sent back to the plating shop three times to get the desired result. Having to send unsatisfactory parts back for rechroming is a frustrating, expensive and time-consuming process. Mike Cavey*

206

rims, possibly the grille and front bumper, name-plates, door handles and miscellaneous small knobs and control handles inside the cab. In the 60s and 70s, stainless and aluminum replaced chrome on the grille, again simplifying this phase of the restoration process.

Nothing brightens up a restored or upgraded truck like gleaming chrome and shining brightmetal trim. In contrast, neglecting the trim will leave a truck looking shabby regardless of the quality of the finish. In the restoration timetable, parts can be sent away for rechroming at any time. In fact, it is wise to send parts out for rechroming well before final assembly is anticipated because two months or more can elapse between the time that you deliver the parts to the plater (or ship them out) and when they are ready to be picked up or arrive back at your door. When the approach is rebuilding, sending parts out for rechroming is best done during refinishing.

The big question with chrome plating is how to get the best quality at an affordable price. Facing the rechroming stage also brings fears as to whether one will receive his parts back looking like new or whether the parts will come back looking like expensively plated junk. The other fear is whether or not the replating cost will be exorbitant. The advice that follows should help you avoid the traps that can occur in the replating process.

Professional Plating

Think of chrome plating as being like a coating of clear lacquer. Chrome plating doesn't cover any surface imperfections. Any pits or damage on the surface will still be visible through the brightmetal coating and indeed will be enhanced by the shiny chrome finish. If you take parts that are dented, rusted and pitted in for plating, you will receive poor-quality results unless the plater goes through a time-consuming (and expensive) process of straightening, buffing and filling the metal prior to plating. Platers will tell you, and their advice is to be heeded, to give them good parts and they will give you good-quality plating at the most reasonable cost.

Let's say that you own an Advance Design truck with a plated grille. Not only has the chrome on the grille bars lost its shine, but the bars are coated with orange rust that has eaten into the metal. Either the grille will have to be taken through an expensive restorative plating process (explained later), or you will receive back-plated bars still flecked with pits. A better approach in this case would be to locate a painted grille without rust (make sure the paint is original and not a new coating hiding metal work as well as pits) and have these grille bars plated. Of course, better parts are not always available.

Mike Cavey found this to be the case in trying to replate the grille on his 1951 Chevrolet pickup.

Since this was a standard truck, the grille was originally painted. (A plated grille was available as an accessory on standard trucks in the Advance Design series and included on deluxe models.) The grille bars on Cavey's truck were straight, essentially free from pits, but two of the bars had rust damage at the ends. Although he looked extensively for a rust-free, undamaged grille, Cavey couldn't find a set of grille bars that were better than what he had, so he had no option but to repair the rust, finish the surface as smooth as possible (no body putty or lead can be used under plating) and take the bars to the plater. Cavey recalls asking the plater if the repair would show in the final finish. He was told it wouldn't. However, three chroming attempts were needed before the parts

Plating shops fall into two categories: commercial platers and restoration plating shops. Most commercial platers will not attempt to replate diecast trim pieces. Also commercial plating shops typically produce one level of quality. Restoration plating shops will work with diecast (though the process may be expensive) and typically offer show chrome, which has a deep, lustrous look, or more economical, somewhat less brilliant plating for collectors who are primarily fixing up their vintage vehicles for recreational driving. Several samples of show-quality plating are shown here.

The first step in the chrome-plating process is to remove old plating layers through reverse electrolysis. This step also removes any rust. Once the bare metal is exposed, the parts will proceed to the buffing department. This process, which is much like sanding, removes any pits and other surface blemishes.

were perfect. Having to send unsatisfactory parts back for rechroming is frustrating, expensive and time consuming. The way to avoid this, when possible, is to deliver straight, undamaged parts.

Types of Plating

As you look for a plater, you need to be aware that there are two types of plating services. The first are commercial platers which can be found through the Yellow Pages of larger-city telephone books. The other are restoration plating shops which advertise in old car and truck hobby magazines. Chances are, if you call a commercial plater about redoing the trim parts on your truck, the first question you'll be asked is whether or not any of these parts are diecast. Diecast is a man-made metal that melts at low temperatures and is therefore ideal for making molded trim parts. It was used for years to make taillight housings, trim plates, hood ornaments, control knobs and other decorative items on cars and trucks. More recently, manufacturers have replaced diecast with plastic.

Commercial platers are reluctant (most will refuse) to replate diecast for some very good reasons. First, the metal is porous. This means that during the electrolysis process which is used to strip off the old plating and apply the new copper, nickel and chrome layers, chemicals from the plating solution may seep into the metal. When this happens, the chemicals will eventually work their way back out to the metal's surface where they will be trapped by the plating layer. Unable to escape,

the chemicals will separate the plating from the metal surface and raise bubbles in the finish. Second, rust pits in diecast cannot simply be ground or buffed smooth. Rust enters diecast like a cancer, eating deeply into the metal. To restore rusted diecast, the rust pits are often drilled out and replaced with brass or other noncorrosive metal. A commercial plater does not have the time to work a restoration process with diecast and knows that anything less will not result in customer satisfaction. So typically, the shop will simply say no.

Commercial platers will replate steel parts like bumpers and non-diecast grille parts. For a truck that you plan to use as a driver, commercial plating will give very acceptable quality—if you bring in good parts. The best parts for commercial plating are bumpers or other trim that was painted originally and is not dented or rusted. The plater will remove the paint and any surface rust in a chemical dip and then can plate over fresh metal that has been protected by the paint finish. Here truck restorers have an advantage over car rebuilders in that chrome bumpers and grilles were the exception on trucks in most years, so painted parts are relatively plentiful. As cautioned earlier, avoid buying parts for plating that have been repainted. You don't know the condition of the metal underneath the new paint. What you're looking for are bumpers and grille items with a sound, original finish.

In most cases, you'll need to contact a restoration plater for replating diecast trim plates, hood ornaments, control knobs and grilles on earlier (1930s) trucks. Fortunately, there's not a great deal of diecast metal on a truck because replating these parts can get expensive fast. Unless you deliver your parts to a restoration plating shop's vendor space at a major swap meet, you will probably make contact by phone or mail. Typically you will be asked to send the parts for an estimate, then wait several weeks (possibly two to four months) for the work to be completed. Often you will have a choice of quality, with show chrome being the most expensive, but also giving the brightest shine and most perfect finish.

As you think of quality, you should consider more than just the cost. The primary factor is your intended purpose for the truck. If your plans include entering the truck in show competition, quality is important at every step of the restoration process. If the truck will be driven and enjoyed, then show-quality plating may not be desirable for two reasons. First, chances are you won't maintain the finish and chrome at its peak brilliance and so the show plating's glistening shine will soon be hidden under a coating of dust. Second, if you have other parts (the bumper for example) redone by a commercial plating service, the difference in quality between show chrome on the trim and commercial plating on the bumper will be noticeable. It's better that all brightwork be of a uniform grade.

The Plating Process

To understand the differences in plating quality, let's look at what happens when parts arrive at the plating shop. Typically, the parts are first dipped in a chemical bath to remove dirt, grease, paint and other coatings. This completed, they move through a series of baths where existing plating layers are stripped off by reverse electrolysis. Chrome plating is removed in one tank, nickel in another and so on, until only bare metal remains. Now the parts go to a buffing room where the metal is ground down on a buffing wheel to smooth any pits or other surface imperfections. It's at this step that the quality of the parts becomes important. Buffing is a manual operation and is labor inten-

sive. If parts need only minimal buffing to smooth the surface, the cost for this step will be low. Badly pitted parts will need extensive buffing which not only adds to the bill, but also can result in the shape of the parts being distorted as the buffer attempts to remove pits by cutting away at the metal.

In restoration plating (which is the only alternative if better quality parts are impossible to find), rather than remove pits by buffing away the metal, a soft copper plating layer is applied, then the parts are buffed so that the copper coating becomes a filler thereby preserving the part's shape. Commercial platers do not perform the copper buildup step prior to buffing.

After buffing, the parts go into the copper plating tank for the base copper layer. Depending on the desired final quality, parts may stay in the copper tank anywhere from twenty minutes to

Attention given to the parts during the buffing stage is a major factor in determining the ultimate quality of the plating process. In restoration plating, parts that are badly pitted may go through the buffing stage more than once. Between buffing steps, the parts will be given a copper coating which will be used to fill surface blemishes.

The penetrating bluish luster that seems to lie deep in the finish of show chrome plating results from thick underlying nickel and copper layers. Between plating steps, parts are thoroughly rinsed to prevent chemicals in one tank from contaminating the next. Chrome plating is the final step and takes only a few minutes. When parts emerge from the chrome tank they are covered with a butter-colored film.

four hours. The penetrating bluish luster that seems to lie deep in the finish of show chrome plating results from thick underlying nickel and copper layers. With restorative plating, the parts may be buffed again and go back through the copper plating step yet another time. Nickel plating ensures a good chrome bond and helps give the chrome its deep, rich finish. The parts will spend about twenty minutes in the nickel plating tanks. Between each plating step, the parts are rinsed thoroughly to keep chemicals in one tank from contaminating the next. Chrome plating is the final step and takes only a few minutes. When parts emerge from the chrome tank they are covered with a butter-colored film. The shiny chrome finish appears after the final rinse. As can be seen, a part's quality results almost entirely from the steps preceding the actual chrome plating.

Along with sending out the best-quality parts possible for replating, another step restorers can take to stretch their plating dollar is to disassemble the parts, rather than have the plater do this. An example of a small assembly that should be taken apart for plating would be a ventipane latch. An example of a larger assembly would be a grille. Unless you want the plater to replate the grille intact (as could be the case with the grille of a mid-30s Chevrolet truck), you should remove the grille bars and send just the parts needing to be plated.

Replating Plastic

On 1960s and later trucks, some of the interior trim (most notably the dash on 1966 and later

Brightmetal trim can be restored to its original luster by a polishing and buffing process that you can do yourself. All that's needed is an electric motor, a buffing wheel and a set of aggressive to mild buffing compounds.

trucks, as well as steering wheel hubs, knobs and air conditioning controls) have a chrome-plated look, but the base material is plastic. In almost all cases, the bright finish on these parts will have dulled or disappeared and need to be replaced to return the truck's interior to its original appearance. The deterioration of the bright finish on these chrome-plated plastic parts isn't caused by wear or corrosion, but results from the natural exposure to ultraviolet rays and atmospheric ozone. Although these parts look like chrome, they are not actually chrome plated (at least not in the restoration process). Rather, a thin layer of vaporized aluminum is applied over the plastic in a process called vacuum metalizing. Several specialty companies now offer this vacuum metalizing service.

As in the normal chrome-plating process, any surface imperfections will show up in the bright finish applied over plastic parts. For this reason, it is important to be alert to scratches, gouges, cracks and breaks in the plastic. When scouting for better parts in a scrap yard, watch for a white, powdery substance that may have collected on the plastic where the finish has worn off. Areas where this white powder has collected are difficult to plate and parts showing this residue should be avoided.

The guidelines for having plastic parts replated (actually vacuum metalized) are the same as for chrome plating. Send the best parts possible. Disassemble components (such as the dash) so that you send only the plastic unit. Contact the plater for a price estimate on the parts. With plastic plating you should also ask if the service applies a lacquer clear coat over the bright finish. The clear coat will protect the metalized finish from evaporating, as occurred on the original part. Finally, be prepared to wait four to six weeks for the plater to return the parts.

Restoring Brightmetal

Most of the brightmetal trim on Chevrolet trucks back to the 1940s is stainless steel or aluminum. This trim doesn't need to be replated, but it probably needs to be restored to its original luster and may need some straightening as well. While there are services that restore brightmetal trim, you can do this work yourself at considerable savings. All you'll need is a set of polishing and buffing wheels, an electric motor and an array of polishing grits and buffing compounds. The expense to set up a buffing stand can be minimal if you have an electric motor on hand. Even if you buy a commercial buffing stand, you'll still be money ahead doing your own brightmetal straightening and buffing. Polishing and buffing supplies are available from mail-order restoration suppliers such as The Eastwood Company.

Before describing the brightmetal restoration process, let's understand two key terms. In this setting, polishing doesn't mean applying the final sheen as it would if you were polishing the truck's finish. Instead, the polishing step is like sanding in that it removes the deeper scratches or repair marks. Buffing is the series of steps that produce the shiny luster that is our goal on these brightmetal trim parts. Polishing could be done by hand using a series of progressively less coarse sandpapers. But this process would be slow and very time consuming. A much faster approach is to use an expander wheel (a flexible wheel that will conform to the contours of the part) mounted on an electric motor. Working a repaired area of a brightmetal part with descending-grit sandpaper belts fitted over the expander wheel will quickly smooth the surface to the stage where it can be brought back to a shiny finish.

The steps in restoring a damaged piece of brightmetal trim, such as a dented aluminum grille surround on a 1969-1972 Chevrolet truck, or the stainless-steel window trim on a deluxe cab 1955-1957 pickup, begin by removing the trim piece. The next step is to straighten any kinks or dents. This is done using a drift, a flat-headed bolt, a hardwood dowel or special small-headed hammer (available from the polishing and buffing supplier) to flatten the dent. You will work out the dent by tapping around the dented area in a spiral motion, starting at the outer edge of the dent and working in.

When the surface feels and looks flat, polish the repair area with the expander wheel to smooth the marks made by the straightening process. The first sanding pass may reveal depressions and raised spots that still need to be straightened. For rough polishing, you would start with a 120 grit belt, then use descending grits of 220, 320 and 400 to smooth the repaired area to the point where it can be restored to a shiny finish by buffing. Each time you change sanding belts you should work the part at a right angle to the previous passes. Remember to wear gloves to protect your hands from heat buildup on the parts and possible contact with the sanding wheel. Also wear a face shield to protect your eyes and face from flying debris.

Buffing and Polishing

The buffing process will remove the anodizing film on aluminum and minor scratches on aluminum or stainless trim, and restore the metal to its original brightness. Buffing is done with various grit compounds applied with cloth buffing wheels. (Although the buffing wheels are made of cloth, they are available in varying coarseness.) A combination of a rough cloth wheel and harsher grit provides more aggressive cutting for harder metals such as stainless steel. A smoother cloth and finer grit are used for finish buffing and for softer metals or plastic.

With hard metals like stainless, the buffing sequence begins by coating a buffing wheel designed for fast, aggressive cutting with a coarse emery grit. Buffing is done in small sections until the whole part has been worked. At this stage it is important to watch out for rapid cutting that could distort the part's contours or cut holes in the metal. After coarse buffing, the part is worked again with a softer wheel and milder grit. The typical buffing setup is a double arbor motor with a coarse wheel

A professional buffing setup and supplies can be purchased from a specialty tool company. The double arbor motor enables you to mount a coarser and milder wheel so that you can take parts through several stages of the buffing process without changing wheels. The Eastwood Company

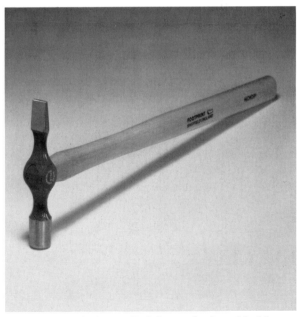

Dents are worked out of brightmetal trim with this special small-headed trim hammer. To work out the dent, tap in a spiral motion starting at the outer edge of the dent and working inward. The Eastwood Company

An expander wheel is used to remove rough pits from plated diecast or deep scratches on brightmetal trim parts that have been taken through the dent removal process. The expander wheel is made of soft rubber so it conforms to the shape of the part. The buffing process begins by coating the wheel with compound. The bright-metal part is then worked across the wheel in small strokes, rejuvenating one section at a time. After the initial coarse buffing, the part is brought to a gleaming finish with progressively milder compounds. Not only stainless-steel, but aluminum and plastic parts can also be restored through careful buffing. The Eastwood Company

on one end of the shaft and a softer wheel on the other. This way it is not necessary to change wheels between buffing steps. The intermediate buff is followed by finish buffing using a soft wheel and a coloring compound to bring the metal to high luster.

Plastic parts can also be returned to a glossy finish by buffing. A soft wheel and special plastic buffing compound are used to avoid cutting into the plastic. Along with brightening the finish, plastic is also buffed to remove scratches. Plastic taillight and parking light lenses are ideal candidates for the buffing process because if these are the original parts, they most typically have dulled from scratches caused by dust and road debris. When buffing plastic, be careful not to remove part numbers or other detail features.

The typical problems encountered by first-time buffers are applying too much grit to the wheel and failing to clean the wheel before going to a milder grit. Putting too much compound on the wheel is not only wasteful, but clogs the wheel and prevents effective cutting. One sign of too much grit is black streaks on the work piece. These can be cleaned off with a soft cloth soaked in solvent. The easiest way to make sure that none of the harsher compound remains on the wheel as you move to a milder grit is to use a separate wheel for each buffing step. Lacking this, you can remove leftover compound from the buffing wheel with a tool called a rake. One other caution: Never take your eyes off the part while buffing.

Besides brightening and restoring trim and plastic items, polishing and buffing can also be used to produce a chrome-like finish on alternator housings, intake manifolds and any other aluminum parts. These components did not have a shiny finish from the factory, so polishing and buffing the castings to a high-gloss finish would not be done as part of restoration. However, giving engine components a shiny appearance appeals to street rodders and others who just want to enjoy their truck and perhaps display it in local shows. To give these cast-aluminum parts a uniform glossy finish, hand-held grinders can be used to polish small recesses that can't be reached by the expander wheel.

Although trucks don't use a lot of chrome and brightmetal, upgrading these trim pieces will make an enormous difference in your truck's appearance. Indeed, you may find that if your truck is a standard model with mostly painted trim, you may want to add some of the brightmetal found on the deluxe models.

18

Storage and Care

Collector trucks spend more time sitting than driving. Seeing a truck resting in storage may give us a good feeling, a sense that our truck is enjoying a well-earned retirement in which it will last forever. But in reality, storage can do more damage to a truck (or any collector vehicle) than regular driving. Deterioration resulting from storage can take many forms. The 1969 Chevrolet Longhorn pickup shown in numerous places in this book leaked automatic transmission fluid during the months it spent in the auto bodyshop. The cause: torque converters will drain during long periods of idleness. If storage is in a barn or shed that is accessible to rodents, all kinds of mayhem can result—from chewed wiring to nests in the upholstery (if the mice or squirrels can get into the cab). Where the truck's underside is exposed to moisture from a dirt or concrete floor, rust damage can be extensive. Here is what you can do to make sure your truck comes out of storage in as good a condition as it went in.

Storage can be thought of in two categories: long term and short term. Long term can mean the winter months (November through March, let's say) or an even longer period—perhaps years. Most show trucks exist in a perennial state of long-term storage with the truck only being started and driven out of its enclosed trailer onto the show area, then back into the trailer at the end of the show. Short-term storage is the time your truck spends sitting in the garage between occasions when you take it out on the road. For trucks that see frequent use, short-term storage extends only a few days or weeks. Requirements for short-term storage are little more than keeping the truck out of the weather. The requirements for long-term storage are much more critical if the truck's mechanical condition and appearance are to be preserved.

No vehicle should be stored outside for long periods of time. Moisture from the ground will rot the underside while sunlight will fade the paint and harden the rubber. Rain and dew will seep past the window seals into the doors and penetrate into joints in the metal such as the seam between the rear fenders and box. Moisture will also be trapped under the hood, corroding wiring connections, and enter the engine via the carburetor and open intake valves as well as through the exhaust system and open intake valves. A truck that is stored outdoors can deteriorate quite substantially in a short period of time.

Indoor storage is not a guaranteed panacea, however. With a roof overhead and dirt floor underneath, a truck may actually experience more moisture damage than if left outside. This is particularly true of metal buildings. The optimum storage is warm, dry and dark with relatively little temperature fluctuation year round. Unfortunately, not many of us have a storage facility that meets

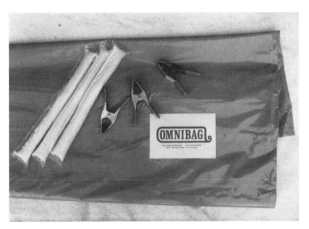

The product to use to protect your truck during long-term storage is called the Omnibag. Basically a gigantic bread bag, the Omnibag seals your truck against moisture. The Omnibag isn't a car cover; it's a car enclosure. The kit consists of a vinyl bag large enough to hold the entire truck, a set of instructions, packets of desiccate material, and clamps. After the truck is "in the bag" the desiccate will be removed from its plastic wrapper and placed inside the bag with the truck to absorb all moisture.

all these requirements. But don't give up; there's a way to achieve all the conditions of optimal storage, even if the only storage you have for your truck is a tin-roofed, dirt-floored shed.

Long-Term Storage

The way to obtain optimal long-term indoor storage conditions is to put your truck inside a product called the Omnibag. Looking like a gigantic bread bag, the Omnibag is a large plastic bag that you roll the truck into. Once the truck is inside, you will also insert several packets of desiccate (moisture remover), then roll up the bag and seal the opening. The truck will now stay desert dry for the duration of its storage. Moisture cannot creep up from underneath, because the truck is sealed from the floor by the bag. Changes in temperature or outside humidity cannot soak the truck in beads of sweat because the desiccate has removed the moisture from the bag. Sunlight cannot harden the rubber or dull the paint because the bag keeps your truck in the dark. Rodents will not attack your truck's wiring because they are not attracted to what they cannot smell and the bag seals in the aroma of fresh vinyl and whatever else causes squirrels and mice to chew wiring insulation and nest in upholstery. Moisture will not enter the engine because, as already noted, the bag seals your truck to a no-humidity environment.

The only precaution for placing your truck in an Omnibag is that the storage be inside. The bag is not recommended for out-of-doors use because wind will whip the plastic, causing tears which will let in moisture that will then be trapped inside the bag. In this condition, what was formerly the best storage situation becomes the worst. With indoor storage, if a tear occurs in the bag through carelessness, it can be mended with duct tape and the ideal storage conditions will be restored. With care, the Omnibag can be reused year after year. An Omnibag supplier, Pine Ridge Enterprises, of Bath, Michigan, is listed in the appendices.

Preparation

Before placing your truck in an Omnibag, or any long-term storage setting, certain preparation steps need to be taken. The tires should be pumped to slightly over road pressure and the truck should

For short-term storage a soft flannel cover should be used to protect the paint from dust and to shield rubber parts from sunlight. The Eastwood Company

214

be washed underneath and on top and allowed to dry thoroughly. It's also a good idea to wax the finish; then when the truck comes out of storage it will be shiny and ready to go or show. Some collectors will apply wax to the chrome, but do not buff off the dried coating. This will protect the chrome from oxidation (a step that is not necessary if the truck is stored in an Omnibag). Along with the exterior, the interior should also be cleaned thoroughly.

The last time the truck is run before storage, you can give extra protection against rust inside the engine by slowly pouring about a half cup of clean engine oil down the carburetor throat. You will need to advance the carburetor above idle to keep the engine from stalling and once the oil is in the cylinders (detected by smoke rolling out the exhaust), you should shut off the ignition. This oil coating will prevent rust from forming on the cylinder walls and guard against ring seizure. You

should also add gasoline stabilizer to the fuel tank. This will help avoid the problem of varnish settling out of the gasoline and clogging the fuel lines and filters. The radiator coolant should be checked to make sure it is protected adequately against freezing. Draining the coolant and storing the truck dry is not advised since antifreeze with rust inhibitor is the best insurance against corrosion inside the radiator and engine coolant passages. If the truck is not stored in an Omnibag, it's a good idea to place bread bags over the exhaust and carburetor to seal out moisture which will otherwise enter through these openings. Also, if an Omnibag is not used, the truck should be covered to protect the finish from dust and keep out sunlight.

The last step before rolling the truck into an Omnibag or covering it for its winter slumber is to remove the battery. Although the battery in a vehicle that is driven regularly requires very little care, a battery will deteriorate rapidly in storage. Battery care has its own set of conditions which are described at the end of this chapter.

Short-Term Storage

Short-term storage should also be inside, if possible, with the vehicle covered. It is not advisable to cover vehicles stored outside for the same reasons that the Omnibag manufacturer does not recommend that its product be used with outside storage. A cloth truck cover will whip in the wind and the action of the cover rubbing against dust that has collected on the truck's finish will do serious damage to the paint in a short time. For

On Advance Design series Chevrolet trucks, the battery is located under the cab floor on the right side and is reached by rolling back the floor mat and pulling up the cover. This is not a very convenient location and encourages poor battery maintenance.

The best cleaning regimen for your truck is a yard hose with cold water. High pressure sprays from a car wash can drive debris into seams and crevices and can abrade the finish. It's important to wash the truck on an overcast day or in the shade to avoid marring the finish with water spots.

short-term storage, it is advisable to install a battery disconnect switch, supplied by Bathurst, Inc., Tyrone, Pennsylvania, to prevent the battery from discharging due to a possible short in the electrical system. It's also a good idea to tricke-charge the battery during the storage interval. An easy, effective way to do this is with the solar charger described earlier.

Coming Out of Storage

Even though an Omnibag will deliver a truck from storage in virtually the same condition that it went in (the chrome will still be bright and shiny and there will be no trace of mildew or other humidity damage), there will still be items that need checking. Gaskets and seals can shrink during storage, especially in a low-humidity environment, so always check fluid levels (engine, transmission, brake reservoir, coolant) before operating the truck. You'll need to replace the battery and you'll find that pouring a small amount of gasoline down the carburetor intake plus spraying a couple of shots of carburetor cleaner into the carburetor intake as the engine first cranks over will save grinding on the starter while the fuel pump replenishes the gasoline supply. Once the truck is running, let it idle for several minutes to reestablish good lubrication throughout the engine before applying power to move the truck from its resting spot. If you've stored the truck in an Omnibag, you can fold up the bag and put it away for the next storage season.

Trucks with bias-ply tires will ride a little bumpy for the first few miles after storage until the tires warm up and round themselves out again. Also, after the first outing it's a good idea to check fluid levels and top up where necessary. If any leaks are detected they should be monitored to see if the gaskets seal as the truck is driven.

Care

In comparison with a daily driver that may roll up several thousand miles on the odometer in just a few months, a collector truck that is driven far fewer miles may seem to need infrequent maintenance. Actually, this is not the case. Caustic chemicals that collect in the crankcase as the engine oil breaks down are actually more damaging in a vehicle that is driven infrequently than in one which goes out on the road every day. As a result, you should change the oil and give the truck a complete lubrication at least once a year. The best time for this is right before putting the truck in storage. Trucks that see more than occasional use should receive a complete lube and oil change every 2,500 to 3,000 miles.

If you use the owners manual for your truck as a guide, you're likely to discover that your truck has several dozen grease fittings which are located not just on the steering linkage and front suspension, but also on the spring shackles, universal joints, clutch and brake pedal shafts and numerous other places. Take the time to service all these fittings; your truck will drive and ride smoother as a result. While servicing the engine and chassis, remember to squirt a couple of drops of oil on the manifold heat valve and generator bushing cup and check the fluid levels in the steering box, transmission, rear end and brake master cylinder.

On engines built prior to PCV (positive crankcase ventilation) systems, this annual maintenance check is also the time to wash the oil filler cap in solvent and a few drops of oil added to the wire mesh. The filler cap and screen ventilate the engine crankcase. The carburetor air cleaner (whether oil bath, wire mesh or paper filter type) should also be serviced at this time. An oil bath filter is serviced by dumping out the old oil (pour the oil into a plastic milk jug or other suitable container and take it to a recycling center; don't pour the oil onto the ground) cleaning the oil reservoir and filter in solvent, then refilling the reservoir with fresh oil. A wire mesh cleaner is also washed with solvent and dried. A few drops of oil are squirted into the mesh before replacing this air cleaner on the carburetor.

On engines using a paper filter air cleaner, the filter housing should be removed from the engine and washed in solvent. The filtering sponge at the PCV valve hose inlet should also be washed in solvent or replaced with a fresh filter. A new paper filter cartridge will be installed after the air cleaner housing is replaced on the carburetor. On newer engines don't forget to check and change the PCV valve if the valve is clogged.

Like engine oil, antifreeze solutions contain additives that break down in time. This means that if the cooling system is not flushed periodically (annually is the recommended interval) and refilled with fresh antifreeze, internal corrosion could result. Many collectors are also unaware that manufacturers recommend flushing and refilling the hydraulic brake system on an annual basis. The reason for this is that polyglycol brake fluid soaks up moisture like a sponge and you'll recall that the master cylinders on older trucks are vented (to prevent a vacuum from forming in the system) so moisture is easily absorbed into the brake fluid. The way to avoid this moisture problem—and to save the time flushing and refilling the brake fluid—is to use DOT 5 silicone fluid instead of the DOT 3 polyglycol product.

The annual truck-care session concludes with putting a few drops of oil on the hood latch mechanism, hood hinges, rotary door latches, door hinges, seat track (on trucks with adjustable seats) and wiper linkage. The door latch striker should be lubricated with special stick wax.

Cleanup Tips

You may look at this heading and say, "Hold it, I don't need to be told how to wash my truck!" While that's probably true, you may discover a few techniques and tricks to caring for a collector vehicle that you haven't used in cleaning up that daily driver. The first is a warning that low-pressure water from the yard hose works better for cleaning your truck than a high-pressure spray at the car wash which can force dirt and debris into seams and crevices. Also, with a collector vehicle washing is done underneath as well as on the visible surfaces. Glass Wax works better than commercial chrome cleaners for keeping chrome plating and brightwork shiny. To make the windshield and cab windows sparkle, add a dash of kerosene to a bucket of clean water, wipe the mixture on the glass and buff dry with a wad of newspaper. The combination of the kerosene film and newsprint will give the glass a mirror sheen. Rubber, including the tires, can be restored to a bright, black coloring with coating of Armor All—which also serves to protect the rubber against cracking.

After washing, the finish can be protected and given a glossy lustre with a quality liquid polish. A product called Ultra Finish is being used here.

On the inside of the cab, a damp cloth or sponge works well to clean vinyl seat coverings and to remove the dust from door panels and the headliner. The rubber floor mat can be vacuumed, wiped down with a damp cloth and renewed to its factory-freshness with Armor All. Other interior rubber (the gearshift boot on trucks with a floorshift), pedal pads and other items should also be given the rubber renewal treatment.

Under the hood, the engine compartment should be wiped down to clean off road dust and whatever oil film has developed. If the engine has gotten too grimy to be cleaned with a light wipe-down, you can spray on a coating of Gunk, let the degreaser stand for ten to fifteen minutes and wash off the grease film with the lawn hose. Be careful not to spray water on the distributor or other electrical parts. Used according to the directions on the can, Gunk will not harm paint.

Periodic Care

If your truck's engine predates the mid-sixties and has not been fitted with hardened valves and seats, it's prudent to add a valve lubrication additive during fill-ups. Burning unleaded gasoline in an engine that was designed for fuel containing tetraethyl lead can cause severe valve seat recession (wear) in a relatively short period of time if the engine is worked hard (as would be the case in a several-hundred-mile trip across hilly terrain, for example).

Beyond this, it is wise to establish a cycle for checking wheel bearings, cleaning and gapping

Rubber parts such as door weatherseal should be kept resiliant protected against cracking by applying a coating of Armor All. This product can be sprayed directly onto the rubber (any overspray can be wiped off the surrounding finish without harm). The milky liquid is then spread uniformly over the rubber with a soft rag.

217

spark plugs, filing and resetting ignition points—routine maintenance of this sort. Be sure to do a maintenance run-through on these and other mechanical checkpoints before a major trip if your truck is driven only occasionally. Remember, just because a truck spends much of its time not being driven doesn't mean that idleness ensures that it stays in road-ready condition. Spending a couple hours giving the truck a good checkover before heading out of town is a better time investment than being stranded on the highway with fried ignition points or a dry wheel bearing.

Battery Care

The secret to long battery life is contained in three simple steps: (1) keep the case clean and dry, (2) keep the electrolyte level above the plates and (3) keep the battery fully charged. Dirt and grease on the case form a path that electrical current can follow to discharge the battery. After removing the battery from the truck, wash the case with a cloth soaked in ammonia or a baking soda and water solution. When washing the case with baking soda, be careful that none of the solution gets into the cells as it will neutralize the electrolyte. Wipe the case dry and put the battery in a location where it won't pick up condensation. (Don't store the battery on a cement floor for the reason that condensation will form under the case, creating a path for electrical discharge.)

Before charging, check the level of the electrolyte in the cells. Some electrolyte is lost each time the battery charges and discharges. If the liquid falls below the top of the plates, permanent damage to the battery will result. Distilled water should be used to raise the electrolyte level. On most batteries, the correct electrolyte level (¼ to ½ in. above the plates) is indicated by a ring in the cell port. Because a battery will discharge on its own, periodic charging is required to keep the battery in peak condition. In vehicles that are driven regularly, recharging is handled by the generator or alternator. In storage, recharging is done with a battery charger.

The ideal charging rate is 4-6 amps, the output of most home/shop battery chargers. The reason many old-truck owners experience premature battery failure is that they hook up the charger for a few hours thinking they've brought the battery back to peak energy. Actually this brief charging period only lifts the battery slightly from its discharged state. To bring a battery up to full charge may take a day or more.

There are two ways to tell when a battery is fully charged. The simplest and most accurate is to take a reading with a hydrometer. The other, when using a slow charger, is to watch the amp reading on the battery charger's scale cut back to 1 or 2 amps and stay there. As the battery nears full capacity, its internal voltage rises, causing the charging rate to decrease.

During recharging, it's important that the battery be able to "breathe" (release the hydrogen gas that is created during the charging process). The vent caps contain small holes through which this highly volatile gas can escape. If the vent holes are plugged, pressure will build up inside the battery that can cause an explosion. A simple trick to prevent any risk of fire or explosion during recharging is to remove the cell caps and place a damp cloth over the top of the cells. As the hydrogen gas is released, it will be absorbed into the cloth where it will harmlessly combine with the water molecules. After recharging, the top of the battery case should be wiped dry and the cell caps replaced.

A battery should not stand for more than a couple weeks without recharging. As a battery discharges (and this will occur even in storage), large crystals form on the plates that prevent the electrolyte from making contact with the active plate material. These crystals are harmful only when the battery remains discharged for several weeks (or if the electrolyte drops below the tops of the plates). When the battery is recharged, these crystals recombine with water in the electrolyte to form sulfuric acid. However, if these crystals are allowed to harden (which will happen if the battery remains in a discharged state), they form a crust that does not fully dissolve during recharging. If this neglect continues, the plate surfaces eventually become coated and the battery must be replaced. Frequent recharging is the secret to long battery life.

Before replacing the battery after storage, coat the posts and cable clamps, battery hold-down frame and bolts, even the battery case with Plasti Dip—a rubberized coating that is applied with a brush. This coating will seal out moisture and corrosive vapors to ensure good contact between the cable clamp and post. Whenever the battery has been removed, always remember to replace and tighten the case support and hold-down clamps.

Tips for maintaining batteries in stored vehicles
• Charge battery every two weeks.
• Store battery in as cool a place as possible to minimize self-discharge.
• Keep case clean and dry.
• Don't allow electrolyte level to fall below the tops of the plates.
• Install a shut-off switch or remove battery cables while vehicle is in storage to prevent possible shorts in the electrical system from discharging the battery or starting a fire.

Showing Your Truck

Extra-special care is called for if you plan to enter your truck in show competition. Cleaning and waxing need to be done with care and thoroughness that includes wiping wax residue out of cracks with a toothbrush and making sure that the chassis is as sanitary as the exterior. Beyond cleaning, show competition also requires close attention to the many small details that make your truck authentic for its period. These include such seemingly picayune items as the correct valve-stem caps (plastic valve-stem caps didn't appear until the early 1950s; trucks from the 1940s should have metal caps) and spark plugs with plated bases on trucks from an era when the spark plug base was painted black.

In their enthusiasm for having an unusual show vehicle, some collectors dress up their trucks with accessories. While these add-ons can be great conversation pieces, they can also cost a truck points in show competition if the judges dispute their authenticity. In questions like this, the judge is supposed to ask the owner to produce documentation verifying that the accessory was a bone fide Chevrolet part. But if the judge thinks that add-on is an aftermarket item, you may not be given the chance to prove otherwise. One way to avoid this problem, and keep the accessory, is to make the documentation part of your display. This can be done by mounting pictures from dealer catalogs showing unusual accessory items in a display stand. The pictures will highlight the accessories for those viewing your truck while also alerting the judges to their authenticity.

A nicely displayed truck helps win the judges' confidence. Serious competitors will go to seemingly ridiculous lengths in setting up their truck, including even rotating the wheels so that the Chevrolet script on all four hubcaps aligns horizon-

A coating of Armor All also keeps the tires looking show-room fresh. Besides heightening the rubber's black color, Armor All helps prevent the rubber from stiffening and cracking. Armor All can also be applied to vinyl door panels to renew the color. This product can also be used to brighten vinyl dash coverings.

tally. Subtleties like this can have an effect, even if they're not consciously noticed.

A last tip for those entering prestigious AACA (Antique Automobile Club of America) competition. You are entitled to request a judging evaluation after each competition round. You will not see the actual judging sheet, but you will be guided to those areas with which the judges found fault. Correcting these oversights before the next competition will greatly improve your chances for continued competition success.

Appendices

If you have recently acquired a vintage Chevrolet truck, you may have all kinds of questions about sources or parts, or may want to make contact with others who enjoy preserving and driving an older truck as much as you do. The listings that follow provide answers to those questions. First, you'll find the addresses and brief descriptions of clubs for owners of Chevrolet light trucks and their GMC cousins. Of possible interest, too, are special-model registries. A registry is not a club in the sense that information is shared by frequent newsletters and other activities. It is simply a listing of all known vehicles of this type. This listing may be published periodically, or you may have to request a listing from the keeper of the registry. Since registries are maintained only for very low production vehicles, their primary benefit is in providing a way to get in touch with the owners of similar trucks. Otherwise, if you own a Chevrolet truck with a rare NAPCO 4x4 conversion, for example, you might wait a long time to meet another owner at a show, or see another listed in an ad. Listings of helpful literature are included as well.

In this section you'll also find addresses of well-stocked suppliers of Chevy truck parts, including such replacement parts as wood and other items needed to rebuild your pickup's bed, quality wiring harness manufacturers and other specialty items. These are followed by service listings, and a discussion of other Chevy truck collectibles.

Clubs
Chevy-NAPCO Registry
P.O. Box 1162
Big Rapids, MI 49307

Owners of Chevy trucks with the NAPCO 4x4 conversion can send a description of their truck, along with the serial number and a photo if desired, for inclusion in the NAPCO registry which is printed periodically in the Light Commercial Vehicle Association's newsletter *Plugs 'n Points*.

Classic Chevy Cameo & GMC Suburban Pickup Club
4505 S. County Road 7

Midland, TX 79073

The Cameo and Suburban club is a regional organization headquartered in the South. This group publishes a small newsletter and encourages restoration and preservation of 1955–1957 Cameo and Suburban pickups.

Corvair Society of America (CORSA)
P.O. Box 550
Midlothian, IL 60445

Formed by and for those who appreciate the Corvair automobile, this national club publishes a monthly magazine called the CORSA *Communique*. The publication includes feature articles, news and events, technical articles and classified ads. CORSA has an Eastern, Central and Western Division, and local chapters. The club sponsors an annual convention and sanctions various regional events. It also sponsors a museum fund to protect and preserve Corvair memorabilia. The group welcomes owners of Corvair 95 commercial vehicles.

Inliners International
RD 3, Box 83, Rt. 44
Pleasant Valley, NY 12569

This national club is devoted to early Chevrolet and GMC racing engines and other inliners. The organization publishes a semi-monthly newsletter, *The 12 Port News*, which contains technical articles, features and racing news, and offers free ad privileges to members. Inliners has technical advisors covering Chevrolet, turbocharged GMCs, GMC engines, Ford, International BD and BG series, Australian Ford Six (cross flow), Model A and B Ford four-cylinder, Hudson Six, Ford Falcon, Dodge-Plymouth-Chrysler Flathead Six, and supercharged sixes. The group sponsors an annual Inliners picnic.

Kamino World
P.O. Box K5288
Chatsworth, CA 91313

This owners association includes all El Camino and Chevelle vehicles. The group is dedicated to preserving Chevrolet A-bodied cars and car pickups of the 1964–1987 period.

Light Commercial Vehicle Association (LCVA)
Rt. 14, Box 468
Jonesboro, TN 37659

The LCVA is national in scope, with members in Canada, western Europe, the Near East and Australia. This group's charter embraces all makes of light trucks, but the club gives particular attention to Chevrolets, with a regular Chevy column in its semi-monthly newsletter, and frequent Chevy technical and feature articles. The LCVA also keeps a registry of rare NAPCO 4x4 conversions and lists technical advisors for this desirable conversion. In 1986, and again in 1988 and 1989, the LCVA's newsletter, *Plugs 'n Points*, received *Old Cars Weekly's* Golden Quill award.

Vintage Chevrolet Club (VCCA)
P.O. Box 5387
Orange, CA 92613

The Vintage Chevrolet Club of America has over 7,000 members spread throughout the world. Local regions in the United States sponsor a variety of activities and get-togethers. The club has technical advisors and provides free member ads in the quality monthly publication which presents articles on Chevrolets from 1912 to 1975. The VCCA sponsors judging meets in various locations with an anniversary meet every four years.

Literature
Classic Motorbooks (Motorbooks International)
P.O. Box 1
Osceola, WI 54020

World's largest source for automotive literature.

Walter Miller
6710 Brooklawn Parkway
Syracuse, NY 13211

Huge assortment of original 1910–1980 sales literature, repair and owners manuals for Chevy trucks and other vehicles.

Parts Sources
Ar-Jay Sales Co.
P.O. Box 9520
Grand Rapids, MI 49509

Parts for Advance Design panel truck (bank) and COE semi-tractor.

B&T Truck Parts
P.O. Box 799
Siloam Springs, AR 72761

Chevrolet 1960–1966 parts.

Bathurst, Inc.
Box 27

Tyrone, PA 16686

Battery disconnect switches.

Bruce Horkey Cabinetry
RR 4, Box 188
Windom, MN 56101

Stock or custom pickup bed floors and complete boxes.

Chevy Duty Parts, Inc.
4319 NW Gateway
Kansas City, MO 64150

Large selection of 1947-72 Chevrolet and GMC pickup parts

Ciadella Enterprises
3757 E. Broadway, Suite #4
Phoenix, AZ 85040

Chevrolet truck seat and interior kits.

Custom Autosound
808 W. Vermont Avenue
Anaheim, CA 92805

AM-FM radio with stereo cassette conversion for Chevrolet and GMC trucks 1947–present.

Custom Mold Dynamics Inc.
5161 Wolfpen Pleasant Hill Road
Milford, OH 45150

Reproduction Chevrolet truck emblems.

The Eastwood Company
580 Lancaster Avenue
Malvern, PA 19355

Extensive line of specialty tools and literature for automotive and light truck restorers.

Eugene Gardner
10510 Rico Tatum Road
Palmetto, GA 30268

Large selection of good-quality license plates.

Fiberglass & Wood Co.
Rt. 3, Box 891
Nashville, GA 31639

Body and mechanical parts for Chevy trucks 1931-72.

Fifth Avenue Antique Auto Parts
502 Arthur Avenue
Clay Center, KS 67432

Chevrolet and GMC truck parts 1937-1962; six-volt alternators.

GLASCO
85 James Street
East Hartford, CT 06108

Replacement flat windshield and door glass.

Golden State Pickup Parts
P.O. Box 1019
Santa Ynez, CA 93460
    Large selection of Chevrolet truck parts.

Jim Carter's Vintage Chevrolet Parts
1508 E. Alton
Independence, MO 64055
    Mid-thirties to mid-sixties Chevrolet and GMC parts: new, reproduction and used.

Lynn Steele Inc.
1601 E. Highway 150
Denver, NC 28037
    Large inventory of reproduction rubber parts.

Mar-K Specialized Mfg. Co.
8022 N. Wilshire Court
Oklahoma City, OK 73132
    Reproduction pickup bed parts for 1940–1987 Chevrolet and GMC trucks.

Metro Moulded Parts, Inc.
P.O. Box 33130
11610 Jay Street
Minneapolis, MN 55433
    Large inventory of reproduction rubber parts.

MikeCo.
c/o Michael Anthony Varosky
1901 Colonia Place, Suite B
Camarillo, CA 93010
    Pre 1975 auto and truck lens replacement specialists.

Mr. G's Rechromed Plastics
5613 Elliott Reeder Road
Fort Worth, TX 76117
    Screws and fasteners for 1955 and later Chevrolet trucks.

NAPA auto parts stores
(See your local telephone directory for listing.)
    Large parts inventory for modern and vintage vehicles, available overnight from regional warehouses.

OverDrive Inc.
P.O. Box 173
Portage, OH 43451
    Manual solenoid for overdrive conversion.

Pacific Antique Mfg. Inc.
14208 S. Western Avenue
Gardena, CA 90249
    Reproduction 1954 stepped rear bumper.

Pine Ridge Enterprises
13165 Center Road
Bath, MI 48808
    The Omnibag; dry-storage device that protects the entire truck during long-term storage.

Restoration Specialties and Supply
P.O. Box 328, RD 2
Windber, PA 15963
    Weatherstrip, fasteners, hardware.

Rhode Island Wiring Service
P.O. Box 3737
Peace Dale, RI 02883
    Wiring harnesses.

Roberts Motor Parts
17 Prospect Street
West Newbury, MA 01985
    Large line of reproduction parts for Chevrolet.

Solar Electric Engineering, Inc.
175 Cascade Court
Rohnert Park, California 94928
    The Maintainer solar battery charger.

Stovebolt Engine Co.
P.O. Box 166
Corbett, OR 97019-0166
    Water pump for Stovebolt six; automatic transmission adapter kits for Chevrolet or GMC Stovebolt six.

T.N. Cowan Enterprises
P.O. Box 900
Alvarado, TX 76009
    Wet/Dry paint stripper, Zintex rust neutralizer and other chemical restoration products.

Vern Sell
P.O. Box 650
Siloam Springs, AR 72761
    Chevrolet and GMC 1947–1959 truck parts.

Y n Z's Yesterday Parts
333 E. Stuart Avenue, Unit A
Redlands, CA 92374
    High-quality replacement wiring harnesses.

NAPCO Parts
Don Butler's Vintage Power-Wagons
302 S. 7th
Fairfield, IA 52556
    Some Dodge/NAPCO interchange parts.

Jim Carter's Vintage Chevrolet Parts
1508 E. Alton
Independence, MO 64055
    Limited supply of NOS NAPCO parts; reproduction NAPCO manuals and decals.

Performance Parts
Charlie Baker Vintage Development and Design
512 5th Street
Nevada, IA 50201
    Wayne, Edmunds and Fenton heads for 235 and 261 ci Chevrolet sixes.

Fifth Avenue Antique Auto Parts
502 Arthur Avenue
Clay Center, KS 67432
    Vintage speed equipment for Chevrolet and GMC sixes.

Patrick's
Box 648
Casa Grande, AZ 85222
    Chevrolet and GMC six-speed equipment, including new Mallory dual-point distributors.

Services
Bill's Speedometer Shop
3353 Tawny Leaf
Sidney, OH 45365
    Quality gauge repair.

David F. Lodge
RD 1, Box 290B
Saylorsburg, PA 18353
    Reproduces data plates.

Darren DeSantis
67 Lou Ann Drive
Depew, NY 14043
    Reupholsters sun visors.

Gas Tank Renu-USA
12727 Greenfield
Detroit, MI 48227

    Repairs and restores gas tanks to better-than-new condition. Franchises in the East and Midwest; expanding nationwide.

Mr. G's Rechromed Plastics
5613 Elliott Reeder Road
Fort Worth, TX 76117
    Rechromes plastic dash panels for 1966 and later Chevrolet trucks. Also sells rechromed dash knobs and accessories.

OverDrive Inc.
P.O. Box 173
Portage, OH 43451
    Retrofits overdrive transmission to any vehicle, including light trucks.

The Horn Shop
7129 Rome-Oriskany Road
Rome, NY 13440
    Repairs horns for most models.

The Key Shop
144 Crescent Drive
Akron, OH 44301
    Repairs and re-keys all locks.

Index